PROJECT MUSTANG

The Step-by-Step Restoration of a Popular Vintage Car

From AUTO RESTORER® Magazine

By Larry Lyles

BOWTIE PRESS®

A Division of BowTie, Inc.®
Irvine, California

Karla Austin, *Director of Operations and Product Development*
Nick Clemente, *Special Consultant*
Barbara Kimmel, *Managing Editor*
Ted Kade, *Consulting Editor*
Jessica Knott, *Production Supervisor*
Indexed by Melody Englund

Library of Congress Cataloging-in-Publication Data

Lyles, Larry.
  Project Mustang : the step-by-step restoration of a popular vintage car : from Auto restorer magazine / by Larry Lyles.
       p. cm.
  Includes index.
  ISBN 978-1-933958-03-3
  1. Mustang automobile—Conservation and restoration. I. Auto restorer. II. Title.

TL215.M8L95 2007
629.28'722—dc22

                              2007002951

BowTie Press®
A Division of BowTie, Inc.
3 Burroughs
Irvine, California 92618

Printed and bound in Singapore
16 15 14 13 12 11 10 09 08 07   1 2 3 4 5 6 7 8 9 10

Contents

Acknowledgments

I would like to thank the people who spent a lot of time and put in a lot of hard work helping transform this tired old Mustang into a very nice California Special.

John Sauer, AAPD; Pat Sikorski, The Antioch Mustang Stable; John Kenemer, American Designers; *Auto Restorer* magazine; BowTie Press; Troy Willford, California Mustang; John Sloane and Jim Richardson, the Eastwood Company; Perry York, First Paint & Supply; Legendary Auto Interiors; Kevin Marti, Marti Auto Works; Rick Schmidt, National Parts Depot; Norton Abrasives; Tom Eddy, Paddock Parts; Gary Wright, Painless Performance; PPG Automotive Refinishing; R-Blox Sound Control.

A special thanks to Dwayne Roark, the owner of one very nice California Special Mustang, and Ted Kade, editor of *Auto Restorer* magazine, who helped transform the articles first published in *Auto Restorer* magazine into such a great book. And finally, thanks to Pat, Bryan, and The Biscuit for their patience and understanding.

Introduction

For more than thirty years, I have been repairing, restoring, and rebuilding cars of all types. For the past ten years, I have shared much of that hard-won knowledge with the readers of *Auto Restorer* magazine and through the publication of two books, *Project Charger* and *Revive Your Ride*. If you have read any of my published articles or purchased either of my two books, you already know I use a detailed, hands-on approach to explaining the methods I use to repair and restore old cars. I don't just grab a handful of tools and dive in expecting you to follow along. I try to keep you, the reader, right there with me as I work.

I feel it isn't enough to tell you what I did. Anyone can do that. I want you to understand how I did what I did and why I did it that way. But don't think I am about to bore you with technical jargon or mundane details about the restoration process. Even I can't stay focused for very long under those conditions. I try to be light but informative, so in the end I believe you not only will have enjoyed what you have read but also will have learned a little more about the fascinating world of automotive restoration.

This book, *Project Mustang*, follows that same light-but-informative format. I don't claim to know everything there is to know about restoring a vintage Mustang. For that you will need a whole library of books on the Ford Mustang and perhaps the unlisted phone number for Lee Iacocca. But what I will give you is a solid, systematic course to lead you through the perils and busted knuckles of a total ground-up restoration of one of the world's most popular muscle cars.

If I could offer one useful piece of advice to anyone beginning the restoration of a vehicle, it would have to be *organization*. Of course, organization begins by determining where you are going with the project and how you're going to get there. That means doing a little research, seeking out a few good suppliers, and analyzing the vehicle itself. It also means spending a little time making a list or two and taking a lot of photographs as the project progresses.

If it is part of the car, it gets photographed. If it gets photographed, it gets listed. Over the course of a restoration, I take hundreds of photographs and make several lists. If I somehow become lost in the process or can't recall how or where a particular part should mount, I then have plenty of reference material to put me back on track. This is why lists are made and why photographs are taken.

I do try to keep the lists simple. Computers make this task even easier. Spreadsheets can be built that list every part of the car, the estimated cost for replacing the parts, and the actual amount of time and money spent purchasing and installing the part.

To that end, I start with a master list that documents the condition of every part removed from the vehicle in the order the parts are removed. If nothing else, this list will serve as a reconstruction blueprint to make sure every part is put back on the vehicle in the reverse order the parts were removed. From the master list, I compile two other lists: a new parts list denoting every part that must be replaced, and a repair and overhaul list that contains the parts that I can repair, refinish, overhaul, and return to the vehicle. The final list, which is nothing more than two columns added to the master list, is a ledger of time and money spent. For example, I spent 1,051 hours restoring Project Charger. I know this fact because I made a list.

For photographic purposes, I use a 35mm film camera. Film is cheap, and I take as many shots as possible. Digital is fine, but you just can't beat having an actual photograph to keep in the toolbox as reference when needed. Besides, laptops don't like dust, and restoration shops are full of the stuff.

CHAPTER 1

PROJECT MUSTANG

The car I'm about to restore is a 1968 California Special Mustang. This was Ford's take on the popular Shelby Mustangs of the sixties and as the name implies was manufactured for the California market. As project cars go, this one is in pretty good condition. It has a little rust and a few dents and shows a little wear and tear, but all in all, this car has the makings of a great project.

I'll offer you a few tips on where to find parts, how to determine what options came with your car, and, most important of all, how to inspect a car to determine its overall condition.

FIND MUSTANG PARTS

Luckily, new replacement parts for Mustangs are plentiful, and prices for these parts are reasonable. Pick up any Mustang parts catalog, and you will see that almost any part ever made for a Mustang can be purchased without breaking the bank. Some of the better Mustang parts suppliers include the Paddock Parts, National Parts Depot, Marti Auto Works, California Mustang, and Aftermarket Automotive Parts Distributing (AAPD). All of these companies offer free catalogs and list parts online; they carry a parts inventory that has to be considered vast, to say the least. Contact information for all of these companies can be found in the appendix at the end of this book. Of course, when the time comes to place an order with any of these great companies, the first question you'll be asked is, "What do you have?" If you reply, "It's a coupe, I think, and I'm pretty sure it's a '67, or maybe a '68, and the engine is blue," you may have enough information to get the oil changed, but it isn't going to help much when placing a parts order.

DETERMINE WHAT YOU HAVE

The VIN, or Vehicle Identification Number, is the place to start to determine the exact model of your car. The two most important pieces of information identified on the VIN are the year model and engine size. The VIN plate on the '68 California Special is located on the right side of the dash panel and is best viewed by looking through the windshield. The VIN may also be found on the left fender apron, on the left side of the dash, or on the left door, depending upon the year model of Mustang being restored. To find information specific to your year model, try your favorite search engine on the Internet; far more VIN information than I could ever hope to list here is only a click away.

Here is an example of a typical Ford Mustang VIN: 8R01C123456. The letters and numbers of a VIN contain a great deal of information about a car.

- **8:** designates this Mustang as a 1968 model
- **R:** indicates the car was built at the San Jose, California, plant, which helps verify the California Special aspect of this car
- **01:** indicates it is a coupe
- **C:** specifies the engine size to be 289 CID
- **123456:** the last six digits indicate the vehicle production number for the particular year

Knowing my car is a 1968 Mustang, as verified by the VIN, is actually a very small part of determining exactly what this Mustang really is. Verifying that this car is a California Special makes the vehicle more valuable than a standard run-of-the-mill Mustang, but how do I know this car wasn't simply badged as a California Special to improve its resale value?

To compound the problem of correctly identifying this car, the data plate (or patent plate) normally found on the left door is missing. The data plate could have told me a lot more about the car. The car is painted Augusta green and has a black interior, but without that data plate from the door I can't be certain Augusta green is the correct color for this car.

One phone call to Marti Auto Works set me on the right path. I gave Marti Auto Works the VIN, they did a quick check of their vast Ford reference file, and presto—the car is indeed a California Special, and Augusta green is the correct color.

While I had Marti Auto Works on the phone, I also placed an order for a duplicate data plate to replace the one missing from the left door. On the 1968 Mustang, this metal tag displays the car's serial number, which can also be found on the right side of the dash, as well as encoded data about the different equipment options that came on the car.

Other tags available from Marti Auto Works include engine tags, axle tags, body buck tags, carburetor tags, and even owner cards for the glove box. Most of these tags are self-explanatory, but what's a body buck tag? This is a small metal tag found in the engine compartment, usually on the firewall, that contains the manufacturing data for the body as it moves down the assembly line. For example, the buck tag tells the technician if holes need to be punched in the firewall for air conditioning or lets the painter know which paint combination will go on the car. This tag goes on before the car is painted and usually ends up bent and wrinkled as the different technicians handle the tag.

TIME FOR AN IN-DEPTH INSPECTION

Now that I'm armed with enough good information to let me know this car is indeed a rare pony, I can get to the task of determining the overall condition of the car. This is also the ugly part of any car inspection, but it has to be done.

This is a forty-year-old vehicle, give or take a few years, and a lot can happen to a vehicle over such a long span of time. For example, has the car ever been wrecked? If so, did the repair shop do a good job making the necessary repairs? Body shop repair methods have changed dramatically over the years. The common solution to repairing major collision damage when this car

was new was to hit it with a big hammer. Today, if this car was in an accident and repaired correctly, it might be impossible to tell the car had even been wrecked. This just wasn't the case thirty to forty years ago.

Initial car inspections are often made from twenty feet away. But at that distance, I can't tell much about a car. To do that, I need to get up close and personal and inspect the exterior and interior of the car.

INSPECTING THE EXTERIOR

I start with the exterior and walk around the car to look for telltale signs that might give a little dent-and-ding history on this pony. I start at the left front wheel. With the front wheels aimed straight ahead, I measure the distance between the rear of the tire and the leading edge of the fender, as shown in photo 1. In this case, the distance is 3½ inches. I'll compare this measurement to the right side and look for any difference.

This is a crude driveway measurement, but a very telling one. A difference of less than ½ inch between the two sides is acceptable on an unrestored forty-year-old Mustang, but a greater difference could indicate the car has been in trouble at some point and will need to be closely examined by a competent body shop or front-end alignment professional to determine what, if any, problems exist. The difference between the left and right sides of this Mustang measured less than ¼ inch; an acceptable measurement.

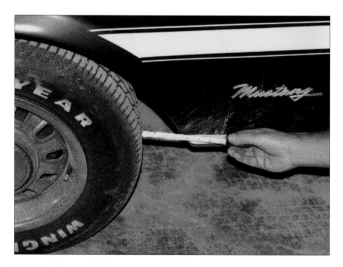

PHOTO 1: A rough measurement of the wheel base is taken by measuring the distance between the rear of the front wheel and the leading edge of the fender. This measurement, which is about 3½ inches, is compared with the right front wheel. A difference of more than ½ inch could indicate a structural problem with the car requiring professional help. Both sides measured almost the same, 3½ inches.

Next, I look at the overall condition of the body, starting with the front structure. With the hood closed, I examine the fit of all the panels. In particular, I want to examine the way the hood aligns with both fenders. Notice that I've already marked many of the problem areas where the gaps are too narrow with a colored water pencil. A water pencil is a marker that uses water-based color instead of a permanent ink or dye. It washes off easily and won't harm the finish. Unfortunately, this poor fit was common in its day and is acceptable in some circles even today.

The real test is demonstrated in photo 3. The rear edge of the hood should be parallel to the cowl with no deviation whatsoever. On this car, the right rear corner is tight against the cowl panel, whereas the left rear corner has a wide gap. This indicates that at some point someone made adjustments to the fit of the hood to get it to open and close without binding. This could indicate structural damage to the front of the car, so that's where I need to look next.

I start by opening the hood to look for obvious signs of structural damage. This usually is found in the form of hammer tracks, slotted fender mounting holes, or damage to the fender aprons or core support that has not been repaired. In the hood, I find evidence that someone had hammered and banged around on the right apron (highlighted by the colored water pencil).

Aside from the hood not fitting and the hammer tracks on the fender apron, another sure sign this car had been in trouble in the past is the left fender marked Taiwan. Ford made its own fenders in 1968, and its factory wasn't in Taiwan.

Because of all of the above-mentioned problems, I'll need to take some structural measurements before making the car undrivable. Why? If the engine compartment cross measurements I take are not equal, the car may need to visit a body shop to receive some structural alignment repairs, and I'd rather not have to push it. But that's for later. For now, I continue my inspection.

The fit of the left door is terrible. This is far worse than what would be expected from a factory fit or even from many years of wear and tear on the door. It doesn't follow the contour of the quarter at the top and sticks out more than an inch at the bottom. Ideally, I'd like to see this door sitting flush with the quarter panel and exhibiting no more than a ¼-inch gap between the two panels. But even the factory wasn't that precise. Ford liked to see the panels flush but would tolerate up to a ½-inch gap between the two panels.

PHOTO 2: A visual check of the hood to fender alignment is made. The damaged areas are marked, as are the areas where the fit between the three panels is not acceptable.

PHOTO 3: This gap is critical. Here the left hood to cowl gap is wide, and the right gap is narrow, indicating that the hood as been shifted at some point. This could mean the car has been in a crash and needs to be examined by a competent body repair professional.

PHOTO 4: Another sign this car has been wrecked. Hammer tracks were found along the top of the right fender apron.

PHOTO 5: The fit of this door is far worse than would be expected from forty years of wear and tear.

PHOTO 6: Inside the door, I found the cause of the problem. The outer skin has been replaced, as evidenced by the poor welding job. Also notice that the data plate is missing. Marti Auto Works will make us a new one.

PHOTO 7: This large circular break in the fiberglass deck lid will require some attention later on.

PHOTO 8: Where does the jack instruction decal belong? This photo will tell the tale.

PHOTO 9: A quick way to measure the square condition of an engine compartment is to measure from the rearmost fender mount bolt to the forwardmost fender mount bolt on the opposite side, then repeat this measurement from the opposite side. This Mustang is square to within ¼ inch.

PHOTO 10: Problems, problems. This marker lamp isn't falling off the fender. The mounting hole was stamped wrong, and this was some body man's idea of a good fit.

There are more telltale signs of this door having been in trouble before. At some point in this car's life, the outer panel on the left door had been replaced. This is seen in the poor welding job along the edges of the panel and confirmed by the poor fit of the door.

Moving to the back of the car, I need to inspect the fiberglass deck lid, where I find cracked paint. How do I know the panel is made of fiberglass? The edges are thick and appear molded, not rolled as they would be if the outer skin were made of steel. Also, as evidenced in photo 7, damage to steel doesn't result in a large ring of cracked paint such as the one found here. Steel bends and dents; fiberglass panels crack in this circular pattern when they've been in an impact.

Inside the deck lid are the jacking instructions. A picture is better than all the guesswork in the world when it comes to deciding where to place the new instructional decals once the car has been refinished.

So far, I haven't found any problem with the car that can't be overcome. But then, I haven't finished the inspection of the front unibody structure. Remember the poor-fitting hood? I need to take a closer look at this problem.

Most vehicles have symmetrical engine compartments. This makes taking alignment measurements very easy. I've stretched a tape measure across the engine bay from the right rear corner of the fender apron to the front left corner of the core support and noted the measurement. In this case, it's 56 ¼ inches. This same measurement is taken from the left rear to the right front; in this case, the measurement is 56 inches. When compared with the first measurement, I have a difference of ¼ inch. Dividing that number in half tells me the front structure of this car is ⅛ inch out of square. Not much, considering how far the hood sits out of alignment.

Remember the Taiwan fender found on the initial inspection of the car? I already know it fits like a '53 Cadillac fender on a '99 Toyota; this poor fit is more than likely the cause of the hood on the Mustang not fitting properly. However, being reasonably sure the front structure is in good alignment, I'm going to forgo aligning the hood until I have all the chrome, glass, moldings, and other hardware removed from the car. I'll start that in chapter 2. Also, check out photo 10. No, this marker lamp isn't about to fall out of the hole. The mounting hole was actually stamped that crooked. This fender has other alignment issues that will require some heavy-duty realignment procedures, but that's for chapter 4.

PHOTO 11: It's a little difficult to tell what portion of the car this photo shows, but this is the floor pan under the rear seat, a common area to find rust on early model Mustangs. The arrow points to a series of rust holes.

PHOTO 12: The radio surround trim panel will need rebuilding. We'll send it to Just Dashes for a professional restoration.

INSPECTING THE INTERIOR

Inside the car, I find the typical Mustang problem of rust in the floor pan. The rust is slightly more extensive than most in that it has migrated under the rear seat. However, the rust isn't bad enough to create any major problems. Aftermarket floor pans are readily available for this vehicle, and installing them won't be that difficult.

The interior components are in very good condition considering the age of the car, but problems do stick out, and the padded radio surround will require some extensive repair.

Now that I have completed a walk around the car and have determined its overall condition, the next step is to mark all the problem areas found on the body. Every dent, misaligned panel, rust hole, crack, and broken part needs to be marked with a colored water pencil.

CHAPTER 2

BEGINNING
THE TEARDOWN:
THE EXTERIOR

Now that I have completed inspecting the Mustang's exterior and interior, I have a much clearer picture of the work that will be involved in restoring the car. Before I can begin working on the car, however, I need to gather a few tools, have the air conditioning system tested, establish a good working height, and drain the fluids. Once this is done, I can begin the exterior teardown.

TOOLS

Putting this Mustang back on the road is going to require a little more than just the desire to get the job done. I will also need a few tools, starting with an assortment of common hand tools found in almost everybody's toolbox: end wrenches; sockets; screwdrivers, both flat-blade and Phillips-type; pliers; and hammers.

The tools not found in most toolboxes are those more specifically designed for auto body repair work. Most of these are one-of-a-kind tools and serve a specific function to aide either in tearing down a vehicle or in making needed repairs to a vehicle. These are the types of tools that may not be readily available at the local automotive parts store but are nevertheless necessary for restoration work.

The Eastwood Company supplies many of these hard-to-find tools. Along with each tool that I list, I'm going to include its part number so you can find it easily in the catalog. As I move deeper into this project, I'll show you where and how these tools are to be used.

Eastwood auto body repair tools include:

- **Body Hammer #31219:** removes dents and other imperfections in the metal
- **Panel Gap Gauge #31129:** aligns doors, fenders, hood, and deck lid to achieve a uniform gap between adjacent panels
- **Planishing Hammer #28116 PH:** shapes replacement patch panels when repairing rust damage
- **Reversed Door Trim Tool #52297:** safely removes door trim panels attached with metal spring clips
- **Shrinking Hammer #31034:** removes small areas of stretched metal

PHOTO 1: Specialty tools from Eastwood. From left to right: body hammer, shrinking hammer, reversed door trim tool, wide blade trim tool, door handle clip tool, windshield reveal molding tool, tubing bender, and panel gap gauge.

- **Trim Removal Set #52021:** includes a wide blade trim tool primarily used to remove plastic door panel clips, a door handle tool, and a windshield clip tool
- **Tubing Bender #49041:** fabricates brake and fuel lines

Eastwood metalworking dollies include:

- **General Purpose Dolly #31032:** the work horse of metal-repairing dollies with a unique saddle shape that makes it comfortable to use, and it is almost unlimited in its applications

PHOTO 2: Metal working dollies. From left to right: general-purpose dolly, heel dolly, and metal shrinking dolly.

PHOTO 3: Pneumatic tools. From left to right, top to bottom: ½-inch impact wrench, air chisel, ⅜-inch drill, die grinder, and metal nibbler.

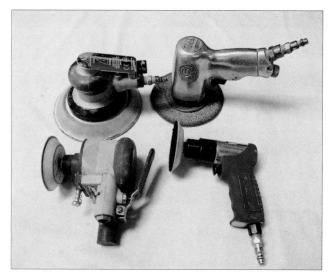

PHOTO 4: Pneumatic tools. Left to right, top to bottom: DA sander, mini grinder, mini DA sander, and right angle mini grinder.

PHOTO 5: Sanding blocks. Left to right: 16-inch plastic body filler block, (top) 16-inch wooden handled primer block, 8-inch primer block, and round finish sanding pad; (bottom) 8-inch block, 5-inch block, and soft foam block.

- **Heel Dolly #31225:** shaped like the heel of a shoe, this dolly is used primarily on curved panels
- **Shrinking Dolly #31083:** used in conjunction with Shrinking Hammer #31034 to remove small areas of stretched metal

Tools you will find at the local automotive parts store include the following commonly used pneumatic tools:

- **Air chisel:** makes short work of removing rusted-out panels
- **⅜-inch drill:** covers tasks from drilling needed holes to drilling out old spot welds
- **½-inch-drive impact wrench:** removes those "stuck in place for 20 years" bolts and nuts
- **Die grinder:** cuts metal, removes excess metal after welding, and does a number of other operations that come up only during the heat of panel replacement
- **Metal nibbler:** valuable when trimming or fabricating new sheet metal replacement panels

Pneumatic tools that are specific to body repair work include:

- **Dual action (DA) sander:** used to sand or remove old paint
- **Mini dual action sander:** allows access to difficult-to-reach areas as well as allows finite smoothing of paint nibs once the finish has been applied
- **Mini grinder:** takes the place of a larger, more cumbersome, full-size grinder
- **Right angle polisher/grinder:** allows access to difficult-to-reach areas requiring grinding or polishing

Body repair tools that operate only under manual labor include an assortment of sanding blocks. Common sizes include:

- **16-inch block:** used on huge flat panels to sand plastic body filler
- **8-inch block:** used for sanding plastic body filler and to sand smaller flat panels and lightly curved surfaces
- **5-inch block:** used for sanding plastic body filler and to sand small areas on flat panels and deeply contoured panels
- **16-inch primer block:** used to sand primer and surfacer and to sand large flat surfaces; has a padded sanding surface
- **8-inch primer block:** used to sand primer and sur-

facer on smaller flat panels and to sand lightly curved surfaces; has a padded sanding surface

- **Soft foam block:** used to sand primer and surfacer; can be used to sand small areas but works best when used on highly curved or contoured surfaces
- **Round finish sanding block:** the round design allows this soft foam block to accept most 1000-, 1500-, and 2000-grit finish sanding discs when sanding clear coats

Once the right tools are in hand, the next consideration is supplies. Here is a list of body repair supplies taken from the Norton line of sanding and prepping products (part numbers are included):

- **Norton 40-grit File Paper #23615 and Norton 80-grit File Paper #23614:** the 3½ x 18-inch sandpapers are used for block sanding plastic body filler; start with the 40 grit and finish with the 80 grit
- **Norton 180-grit roll #31687 and 320-grit roll #31683:** 3½-inch-wide rolls of sandpaper that are used primarily for block sanding. The 180 grit allows you to quickly cut and level large primed panels and prep them for repriming, whereas the 320 grit is used as a finishing sandpaper prior to applying the final seal coat.
- **Norton 80-grit DA sandpaper #31480, 80-grit sanding disc #31481, 180-grit DA sandpaper #31477, and 320-grit sandpaper #31473:** 6-inch-round discs that can be used for many tasks, including removing old paint (80 grit), feathering back old paint around repair areas (180 grit), and final sanding areas not requiring primer (320 grit)
- **Speed-Lok grinding disc #38675 and Speed-Lok disc #9185:** grind and clean difficult to reach areas
- **Bear-Tex Scuff Pads #58000:** use anywhere light sanding is needed
- **PSA 1000- and 1500-grit discs #31552, #31550:** for final sanding clear coats
- **¾-inch-wide masking tape #2492:** masks off panels or areas of the car not being painted

The result of using the above-mentioned supplies is the need for a top-quality line of refinishing products. For those, I've turned to PPG Automotive Refinishing. I'll explain the necessary additives and mixing ratios once I am ready to use the products. Here is a list of the primary products I'll be using on this project:

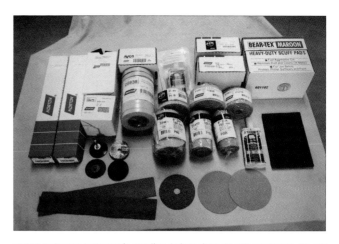

PHOTO 6: **Norton body repair supplies. Left to right: 40-grit sandpaper; 80-grit sandpaper; 3-inch, 24-grit sanding disk and arbor; 3-inch cutoff wheels (for use with a die grinder); 24-grit, 5-inch grinder disk; ¾-inch-wide masking tape; structural adhesive; assorted DA sandpaper including 80, 180, and 320 grits; assorted rolled sandpaper including 80, 180, and 320 grits; and a box of scuff pads.**

PHOTO 7: **PPG professional grade refinishing products. Left to right, top to bottom: DCU 2002 clear, D8072 sealer, D8005 primer/surfacer, DP74LF epoxy primer, DBI black, and BC base coat.**

- **PPG DCU 2002 Concept Polyurethane Clear:** a high quality clear coat used for overall spray applications chosen simply on the merit of my experience with the product
- **PPG 2K Chromatic Sealer D8085:** a dark gray sealer designed for use over D8005 chromatic 2K A-Chromatic Surfacer, which is also part of the PPG Global refinishing system
- **D8005 2K A-Chromatic Surfacer:** a light gray primer/surfacer taken from the PPG Global Refinishing System and used to cover the epoxy coated surfaces as well as all areas of the vehicle that have been filled or repaired

PHOTO 8: DeVilbiss GFG 670 Plus gravity feed spray gun and the DeVilbiss Sri 630 mini-spray gun.

- **PPG DP74LF Epoxy Primer:** an epoxy primer that is red oxide in color to match the base primer coat color Ford applied to the vehicle during manufacturing
- **Base color coats:** colors selected for this car are PPG Global BC #43644 Augusta green poly, and PPG Deltron 2000 DBI 9600 black

For applying the above listed paint products, I've selected the following spray guns:

- **DeVilbiss GFG 670 Plus spray gun:** comes with three different spray tips, 1.2, 1.3, and 1.4 mm and requires 9 cfm at 30 psi when spraying clear coats
- **DeVilbiss Sri 630 mini–spray gun:** ideal gun for getting into all those tight areas
- **Binks M1-G HVLP spray gun:** primarily used to spray primer coats and base color coats

SOME GROUND RULES

Total restorations begin from the ground up, and normally that means finding a good working height for the car itself. But in this case, the car is air conditioned, and that means before the car can be disabled and placed on jack stands, the system must be checked by a qualified air conditioning service center to determine if it still holds a charge (many old systems are not charged because of their age). If charged, the service center will drain the system using the appropriate capture equipment. This is not a do-it-yourself operation. Air conditioning system repair requires specific equipment used by certified technicians. Most important, these systems must never be drained into the atmosphere. It is illegal and extremely harmful to the planet.

The good news is that this air conditioning system contains R-12 Freon worth between $30.00 and $90.00 per pound once collected and cleaned. I'll use that as a bartering chip, I hope, to make a trade with the repair station.

With the car back at the shop, my first step will be to disconnect the battery. My next step will be to place this car at a comfortable working height. I stand about six feet tall, so 18 inches off the floor is about right for me. Depending upon your height, you may want the car positioned either higher or lower. To achieve that height, I'll set the car on jack stands. To ensure a degree of safety, I'll also add a 12 x 12 x 1-inch thick wooden platform under each jack stand to prevent the steel jack stands from slipping on the hard concrete floor. Normally, jack stands are placed under the suspension components just inboard of each wheel to properly support the vehicle. But since I will be removing the suspension from this car in the near future, that placement won't work.

A Mustang is a unibody vehicle, meaning this car doesn't have a bolt-on frame assembly supporting the drivetrain and suspension components, so placing the jack stands under the frame assembly is out. What I can do is place the jack stands under the unibody frame rails to give the car sufficient support without having the jack stands in the way once I'm ready to remove the suspension components.

The next step in jacking up a car is to compensate for overhang once the car is on the jack stands. *Overhang* is a body shop term used to describe a condition caused when a vehicle is supported by means other than the suspension, which leaves the engine to basically overhang the front of the unibody structure. This overhang causes undue stress on the body and can result in twisting the body out

PHOTO 9: Project Mustang positioned in the shop and placed on jack stands. Notice the wooden platforms under the jack stands to prevent the stands from slipping on the hard concrete. The height measures approximately 18 inches from the floor to the rocker panel.

of alignment. A telltale sign of this overhang effect is to mount the car on the jack stands and open the doors. With the engine still in the car, the doors may not shut. They are suddenly out of alignment due to the weight of the engine straining against the unibody structure.

To compensate for this strain, I place a hydraulic jack under the front cross member and apply just enough upward pressure with the jack to relieve the stress on the unibody structure. The stress has been compensated for when the doors once again open and close without binding. At this point, all four wheels can be removed from the car to allow for better access under the car.

DRAIN THE FLUIDS

The next step is to drain all the fluids from the vehicle. In this case, that means draining the radiator of antifreeze, the engine of oil, and the transmission of fluid. The Freon has already been drained from the air conditioner.

Radiators are drained via a petcock found near the bottom radiator hose. Be sure to remove the radiator cap to prevent a vacuum within the system. Engines are drained of oil via a drain plug found at the lowest point on the oil pan. Don't forget to remove the oil filter while under the car. The automatic transmission is drained by carefully removing the square pan on the bottom of the unit. Begin by loosening all 13 of the pan bolts by at least two full turns. Gently pry the pan loose from the case housing. Fluid should begin to flow from around the edges of the pan. Slowly remove the pan bolts one at a time, allowing the pan to tip and begin to drain. Once drained of fluid, the pan must be reinstalled on the transmission to prevent contamination. Properly dispose of all of the old fluids at a local recycling center. Check the Yellow Pages for the center nearest you.

THE TEARDOWN BEGINS

If it is bright and shiny, soft and spongy, or clear and hard, it needs to come off. I want this car stripped of everything but the drivetrain and sheet metal. The drivetrain

PHOTO 10: To compensate for overhang caused by stress on the unibody structure from the weight of the engine, a hydraulic jack is placed under the front cross member with just enough upward bias to support the weight of the engine.

stays for now because it is easier to remove its items once everything else has been removed. The sheet metal stays because there are too many body lines on this car that don't line up. Once everything else has been removed from the car, I'll spend a little quality time with a body hammer and pry bar getting the panels aligned. I'll concentrate first on tearing down the front of the car then move to the back of the car. I'll save the interior and glass removal for chapter 3.

As I disassemble this unit, I note the condition of each molding on the master list for use later when I'm ready to start placing orders for new parts. I also take the time to lay out each part in the order it was removed from the car in an exploded view (much like the illustrations in parts catalogs) and take photographs. These photographs will become extremely valuable a year from now when I'll be trying to determine what goes where. Don't forget to number and date all of the photographs once they are developed. This not only gives you an exploded view but also gives you a chronological sequence of events that can be reversed once assembly begins.

TEARING DOWN THE FRONT

I'm working from the front of the car to the rear. I start with the shiny parts on the front of the car. With the exception of the valance panel, everything up here mounts behind the bumper. That means the valance panel has to be removed before the bumper can be removed, and the bumper has to be removed before most of the bolts holding the grille assembly can be accessed for removal.

PHOTO 11: The front bumper is bolted directly to the unibody frame rails and can be removed only after the valance panel has been removed.

PHOTO 12: An exploded view of the grille parts removed from the front of the car. Everything is laid out as it would be found on the car to make assembly easier later on.

To remove the valance, I need to remove several bolts that hold it in place: two on each end, four across the width. I also need to unplug two parking lamps.

To remove the bumper, I remove the two mounting bolts on either side of the front frame rails plus an additional bolt behind each fender near the outermost corners of the bumper. I'm removing the bumper as a unit and will disassemble it later.

Before removing the grille, I had a question about the authenticity of the fog lamps that were mounted on the grille. Ford used several different fog lamps, most of which were round, whereas Shelby had a tendency to use rectangular Lucas brand fog lamps. At first, these Lucas brand lamps appear to be too large for this car, but upon closer inspection, I found the appropriate Ford number, C8WZ-15L 203 A, taken from a 1968 Ford parts book to verify that these are indeed the correct fog lamps for this vehicle.

The grille assembly goes next. This includes all of the moldings surrounding the grille as well as the front molding on the hood. This molding is considered part of the grille and should be stored along with those parts.

Although the headlamp housings could be considered part of the grille assembly, I'm going to leave both of them on the car for now because they will be used to align the front sheet metal panels. Since they bolt directly to the front of the fenders, they will affect the way the fenders align with the hood. They not only have a direct bearing on the gaps between the hood and the fenders but also help determine how far forward the hood can be adjusted, as the leading edge of the hood must align with the leading edge of each headlamp housing once everything has been properly adjusted.

TEARING DOWN THE REAR

After disassembling the front of the car, I move to the rear. The rear bumper mounts with four bolts found inside the trunk compartment above the floor pan on the right and left sides. Once removed, the rear bumper is stored with the front bumper.

The taillamps are mounted in a rear body finish panel with the entire unit being mounted to the rear body panel. I unbolt this unit from the inside of the trunk and remove it as one piece.

Behind the taillamps are the original lamp openings for the Mustang-style taillamps, and these openings have been filled with specially made enclosures. I remove these enclosures and store them with other parts that will require refinishing.

Under the bumper is the rear valance panel. I leave the backup lamp assemblies in the panel for now and remove the valence panel as a complete assembly.

The first model year for factory installed side marker lamps was 1968. Ford's better idea was to opt for reflectors instead of lamps. I remove these along with the name plates and store them with the taillamp assemblies.

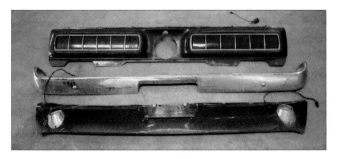

PHOTO 13: An exploded view of the rear body panel components.

NOTES

CHAPTER 3

CONTINUING
THE TEARDOWN:
THE INTERIOR

Now that both ends of the car have been disassembled, the next step is to tackle the middle of the car. The parts that need to be removed here are the door components, the seats, the seatbelts, the windshield, the glass pieces, the headliner, the top cover, and the console.

DISASSEMBLE THE DOOR

Back in 1968, making the doors uncomplicated and easy to disassemble wasn't exactly "job one" with Ford. Although the doors aren't seriously technical to take apart, each mechanism within the doors must be removed in the correct order, or this task can quickly become frustrating, and the urge to pick up a big hammer to help the situation will become extremely great. But resist the urge to smash something, take your time, and you will find that although these doors aren't the easiest in the world to take apart, they aren't the most difficult either.

It's time to bring out the camera. As I said, tearing down the doors on this car isn't that technical, but they do contain a lot of parts, and it is important to know where and how these parts are removed from the doors.

REMOVING THE DOOR TRIM

One of Ford's better ideas in 1968 was to keep the interior door trim pieces as basic as possible. It even went so far as to texture a portion of the inner door frame to simulate the interior trim. My guess is this was done because Mustang drivers sit so low in the seat they have a tendency to push against the door with their foot when they open it, and that would scuff any soft trim near the bottom of the door.

I begin the trim removal process by removing the arm rests and the window crank handles. Both of these pieces are screwed on, with the screw to the crank handle hidden behind a garnish tab on the handle. I use a sharp, small flat-bladed screwdriver to gently lift a corner of the tab and remove it. It is held in place with rubber cement so it comes off fairly easy. If it hadn't come off easily, I would have tried warming it with a hair dryer to soften the cement. The tabs are easily destroyed during

PHOTO 1: The attachment screw for the window crank handles is hidden behind this small chrome cover. The cover is glued in place, so care must be taken when removing it.

PHOTO 2: The metal clips holding the trim panel on the door are carefully removed using the Eastwood panel remover tool.

removal, but that isn't a problem, as the suppliers listed in chapter 1 all carry new ones. Any that I do ruin will be added to the new parts list.

Next, I gently pry the metal clips attaching the trim panel free of the door and remove the panel using the Eastwood Door Panel Remover Tool #52035. While I have this tool in hand, I can also remove both the inner and outer door glass belt weather strip pieces. This makes removing the door glass and vent glass assembly easier.

PHOTO 3: An exploded view of the mechanisms inside the door. All of the parts are laid out in the position they would be found in the door to make assembly a little easier.

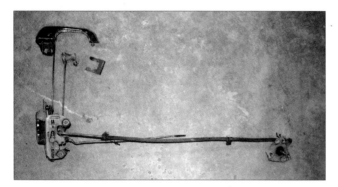

PHOTO 4: The latch assembly is also removed and photographed.

In photo 3, I've laid out the working components of the left door to get a better idea of what's actually in the door. It can sometimes be difficult to remove a part if all you know about the part is that it fell to the bottom of the door when unbolted. All of the parts are placed as they would be located inside the door.

REMOVING THE WINDOWS

With the door glass rolled three-quarters of the way up, I hold the glass in place and remove the window regulator (bottom center, photo 3). The regulator has four bolts, and once unbolted it will slide off the lower glass channel and out of the door.

Removing the regulator frees the glass to slide up and down the front and rear run channels. To remove the rear run channel, look for the bolt hidden behind the rear door

<table>
<tr><td>TIP</td></tr>
</table>

The wife, the next door neighbor, or—if you are lucky enough to own one—a teenager can be used to help hold the glass in place while removing the regulator.

glass seal that holds the top of the rear run channel in place. With all the bolts removed, I can slide the glass full up and remove the rear run channel (far left, photo 3).

With the rear run channel out of the door, I allow the glass to slide to the bottom of the door and remove the vent glass assembly attachment bolts and then the vent glass assembly from the door (far right, photo 3). I will take this unit apart and replace the weather strip later, but for now I store the piece.

Finally, I can lift the door glass, slide it back into the opening created by removing the rear glass seal, and lift it out of the door. With all the glass parts laid out, as shown in photo 3, I can inspect each piece for wear, note any parts requiring replacement (particularly the rollers) on the new parts list, and store everything together in a box marked Left (or Right) Door Glass.

REMOVING THE HANDLES, THE LOCK CYLINDERS, AND THE MIRRORS

The outer door handle, lock cylinder, and mirror can also be unbolted, removed, and stored, but I'll leave the door latch on the door for now. Being able to latch the door will be important once I'm ready to bang and twist on this door to gain a better fit at a later time.

You might want to consider removing the latch with all its linkages intact and photographing the complete assembly while the tools and the camera are handy. Figuring out where all of the linkages go after they have been stored for a year can be tough. Reinstall the latch after photographing, and continue with the teardown.

REMOVE THE SEATS AND THE SEAT BELTS

The quarter windows go next, but the need to comfortably climb in and out of the car takes precedence. That means removing the seats and seat belts from the car.

The back seat pops right out by pressing down and back on the cushion to free it from the retainer hooks. Removing the front seats requires going under the car and looking for the eight rubber plugs capping the access holes to the front seat mounting bolts.

Is there anything else that might be found under the seats? Out in the fantasy world of automotive restoration, the original build sheet for the car would have been left under the rear seat. Although a company like Marti Auto Works can tell me virtually anything I could ever want to know about the car, having the original build sheet makes a great addition to the written history of this pony. I didn't get that lucky. All I found under the rear seat was rust.

What else might be found after removing the seats? How about the seat belts? I can't think of anything worse than sorting through a pile of seat belts trying to decide which belt goes to which seat. To prevent that dilemma, I remove the belts and lay them out according to placement and photograph them. I label each belt as to location before storing.

REMOVE THE INNER QUARTER PANEL TRIM AND THE QUARTER GLASS

I start by removing the quarter window crank handle and trim panel. That gives me access to the quarter glass regulator. Lubricate the regulator and guide channels with WD-40 before reinstalling the crank handle to roll the glass up and down to see if it works. Quarter windows are rarely operated, and they tend to collect grit and grime around the rollers. Operating the regulator before lubricating the unit can cause the rollers to seize and break. If they do, don't fret. New rollers are available from most of the suppliers listed in chapter 1.

Next, I remove the bolts located behind the two round openings near the top of the inner quarter structure. One bolt is just visible in the upper left opening. The bolts are attached to small L-shaped window stops that will drop to the bottom of the quarter once the bolts are removed. I collect these stops and bag them along with everything else removed from inside the quarter. After that, I can slide the quarter glass up and out of the run channels to remove it.

Next, I remove the four bolts holding the window regulator plus two additional bolts holding the short regulator run channel (photo 5, arrow). With the regulator loose, I can remove any remaining bolts, including two at the bottom (photo 6, lower arrow) and one located near the round opening near the top of the quarter assembly

PHOTO 5: The quarter glass is removed by removing the attachment bolts found inside the round holes located near the top of the inner quarter panel structure.

PHOTO 6: The remaining bolts, located near the arrows, are removed. This allows the window regulator support assembly to lift up and out of the quarter structure.

(photo 6, upper arrow) that hold the regulator support assembly in place. Then, I carefully shift the loosened support assembly back and remove the regulator through the large opening near the bottom of the inner quarter structure. Finally, I lift the regulator support assembly (visible through the wide opening at the bottom of photo 6) up and out through the glass opening.

REMOVE THE WINDSHIELD AND THE BACK GLASS

Both of these glasses are set in rubber gaskets so removal will be fairly easy. I start by removing the reveal moldings. The Eastwood Molding Removal Tool #52021 C is used to free the moldings from the retainer clips by carefully sliding the tool between the glass and the reveal molding and using the point of the tool to hook and lift the retainer clip, as shown in photo 7. The reveal molding will then pop free of the clip and lift out of the glass channel. I repeat this procedure around the windshield and the

PHOTO 7: The Eastwood glass trim removal tool #52021C is used to hook and lift the reveal molding clips to free the windshield reveal moldings.

PHOTO 8: A plastic windshield knife is used too gently pry the glass from the rubber weather strip. Gentle outward pressure will also help remove the glass.

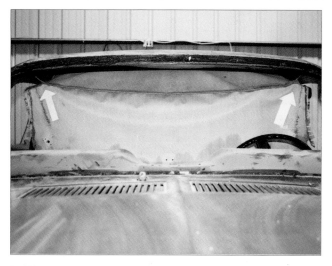

PHOTO 9: The headliner bows are pulled down to release the tension and allow the headliner to be removed.

back glass until all of the reveal moldings have been removed. I label and note the condition of each molding on the master list before storing, and I add any damaged moldings to the new parts list.

To remove the windshield and back window glass, I use a plastic windshield knife and carefully pry the rubber gasket free of the glass opening. I apply gentle pressure against the back of the glass with the palm of my hand to help dislodge the glass and push it out. Be careful because too much outward pressure can crack the glass. Use the plastic windshield knife to complete the removal, and never use a metal object of any kind to pry against the gasket or glass; otherwise, breakage could occur.

I don't know if it is a shop curse, but I rarely manage to salvage a windshield. Removing one usually means breaking one. But that's OK because a new windshield is a standard replacement item for any restoration. The back glass, however, is a different story. I just take a bit more time getting this glass out knowing it has seen little abuse and that saving it is important. Once the glass is out of the car, it must be safely stored. But how do you store a large piece of glass?

Never store a piece of glass flat; always stand the glass on its edge. Just the weight of a curved windshield can cause it to crack if stored flat. I use a discarded windshield shipping box to store glass. These boxes can be found almost anywhere windshields are sold. Usually, windshield guys are happy to get rid of a box or two, and one box will hold all the glass removed from a project.

REMOVE THE HEADLINER

Next on the list for removal is the headliner. This is a bow-hung fabric piece—*bow-hung* meaning Ford used spring steel rods stretched across the inner roof to hold the headliner in place. The ends of the rods, or bows, are notched into holes in the roof structure and can be removed only by pulling down the center of each bow to release the tension before sliding the bow out of the notches.

But before the bows can be removed, the edges of the headliner must be freed. The headliner is glued across the front and rear as well as along both sides of the roof. That should explain why the windshield and back glass were removed first: to gain access to the front and rear edges of the headliner.

The sides of the headliner can be accessed only after the upper door and the quarter glass weather strips located along the roofline of the car are removed. Ford preferred to glue these weather strips in place, so a flat-blade screwdriver can be helpful in removing these pieces. I don't like breaking the old rubber weather strips, which can easily occur, so I take all the time needed to gently remove them from the metal tracks. Having the old weather strips to compare with the new weather strips can prevent a lot of headaches later.

Once the headliner is out of the car, I lay it on the floor and mark each bow. Notice in photo 10 that I marked the front of the headliner and numbered each bow. Each bow is a different length and must be put back in the same order it was removed. Also notice the two wires at the rear of the headliner. The new headliner will be installed in a reverse order, starting with the rear bow. The wires are attached near the rear of the roof and are there to hold the headliner in place as the bows are repositioned.

REMOVE THE TOP COVER

Next to be removed from the car is the vinyl top cover. This one has aged considerably and has already begun to crack and break apart. That makes me leery of the condition of the roof panel. I could have quite a bit of surface rust under there, so getting rid of the old cover is very important.

Before removing the cover, however, I need to ensure the new cover matches the old cover. I need to measure the distance between the seams. On this car, that measurement is 40¾ inches. I also need to check the placement of the seams on the new cover to be sure they are straight and parallel to each other. Finally, I need to check the grain pattern. I just want to be sure the grain and texture of the new cover matches that of the old cover.

All car manufacturers have a mean streak when it comes to certain moldings. The two nuts shown in photo 11 hold the quarter to roof molding in place, and unless at least part of the headliner is removed, there is no way to access these nuts. That should explain why the headliner has already been removed.

Speaking of mean streaks, photo 13 demonstrates the easy way to remove the extremely fragile drip rail moldings. I use a wide-blade trim removal tool, Eastwood #52298 to catch the inner lip of the molding and gently unroll the molding from the drip rail. But that isn't all. As seen in photo 14, behind the drip rail molding is yet another molding. This one is hooked under the edge of

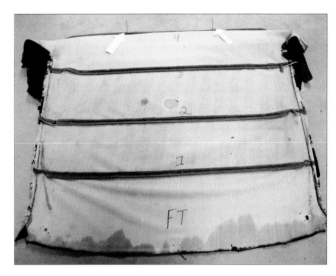

PHOTO 10: The old headliner is laid out on the floor and the front marked. Each bow is then numbered for ease of installation into the new headliner.

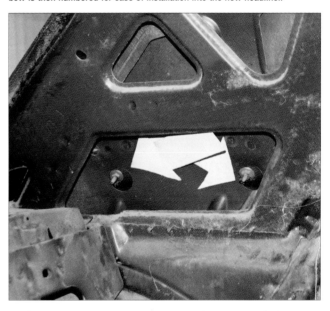

PHOTO 11: The arrows point to the roof belt molding retainer nuts. This molding must come off before the vinyl top can be removed.

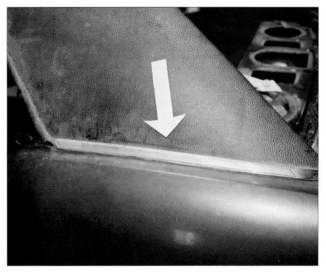

PHOTO 12: The roof belt molding.

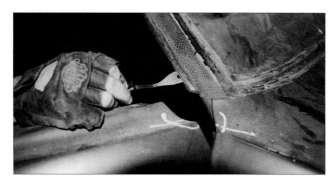

PHOTO 13: This roof drip rail molding is gently pried off using a wide-blade trim tool to lift the inside edge of the molding and release it from the drip rail.

PHOTO 14: Behind the drip rail molding lies yet another molding. This one hooks under the drip rail and must be carefully pried off.

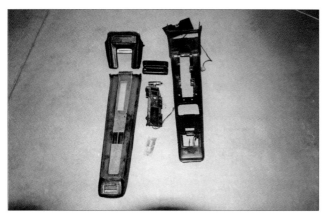

PHOTO 15: The console goes next. The components are laid out and photographed before storing.

the drip rail and serves as a close-out molding for the vinyl top cover. It really cleans up the look of the top by covering the cut edge of the vinyl, but it can be difficult to remove. A small flat-blade screwdriver works great to gently lift and roll the molding from under the drip rail. Finally, the vinyl top is ready to come off. Unfortunately, in this project it comes off in pieces.

What is the condition of the roof panel mentioned earlier? Surprisingly enough, Ford was careful to apply a solid coat of green paint to the roof and about double the

amount of adhesive required to hold the top cover in place. Any rust worm looking for an easy meal was out of luck with this car.

REMOVE THE CONSOLE

Next on the teardown list is the console. This one consists of three major components: the lower base, the top cover, and a radio surround piece. The bad news here is that once I unbolt and remove these pieces from the car, I find that the radio surround piece and the radio housing had been hacked apart by someone determined to install an oversize CD player in the dash. Salvaging this part of the car may prove to be my undoing. But in keeping with the rule of body repair of always putting off until tomorrow what was promised yesterday, I move on.

PROJECT SUMMARY

Before continuing with the restoration, I want to pause and take stock of what has been accomplished so far. I've taken over one hundred photographs detailing the parts removed from the car and their approximate mounting locations, paying particular attention to the intricate inner workings of both doors and quarter panels. I want to be sure that months from now, when I start assembling this car, I can easily tell where and how each part should be installed. I've also noted the condition of all these parts on the master list, making a note beside each entry that will require additional parts or a complete overhaul later on. Parts that need to be replaced are then transferred from the master list to a new parts list, and once I have a substantial list compiled, I'll place an order.

To that end, it is time to pick up a few catalogs and spend a little quality time making a wish list of needed parts. Over the years, I've learned that the more parts ordered at the same time, the better the discount and the more savings on freight cost. It also helps to consider time and distance. The farther away the parts supplier is located from your front door, the higher the shipping cost (generally) and the longer it takes to get the parts (sometimes). But I don't let either of these factors stop me from using a company that has treated me like a real customer in the past. At one time or another, I have either ordered from or sought information from all of the companies listed in chapter 1 of this book. That's why they're here: they all treated me like I was the only customer they had that day.

NOTES

CHAPTER 4

REPAIRING THE
SHEET METAL

After stripping the exterior and the interior, the Mustang is a shell with the engine, drivetrain, and dash assembly still in it. I have an engine stand just waiting for the engine, but something I learned a long time ago is that engines and drivetrains are a lot easier to remove with the front sheet metal already off the car. But because panel-to-panel alignment back in the days of "build it faster because everything looks good at 80 mph" was not a priority, I still have a lot of sheet metal work to do to this car. So for now, the engine stays put and the body hammer comes out.

The next step in the restoration project is to work on the sheet metal. This includes aligning both fenders to the hood and making a serious lead repair on the right fender.

ALIGN THE FRONT PANELS

Body Shop 101 teaches body repair technicians that every panel on the front of the car aligns to the hood. That is to say if the hood isn't in perfect alignment with the body structure of the car, nothing else, including the doors, will line up.

What do the doors have to do with the front sheet metal alignment? Photo 1 is a good example of what I'm talking about. Think of this fender as if it were hinged near the front of the door. Swinging the front of the fender outboard will cause the rear of the fender to shift inboard, particularly at the point marked by the *X*. That, in turn, closes the gap between the fender and the door just below the stripe (lower arrow). This also causes the gap at the top of the fender to widen (top arrow). A closer look shows this is exactly what is wrong with this fender. It has been shifted outboard at the front, causing the gap at the top to widen and the gap near the bottom to narrow.

Note: When I shifted the right fender, shown in photo 1, inboard at the front, the top rear of the fender moved back and outboard slightly. This slight shift closed the wide gap at that point and caused the gap along the area near the *X* in photo 1 to widen slightly. The result was a

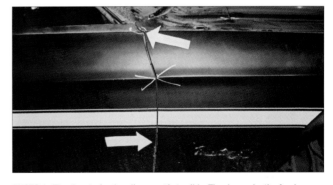

PHOTO 1: The door to fender alignment is terrible. The door rubs the fender near the lower arrow, and the gap is much too wide near the upper arrow. All of this is because the fender has been shifted outboard at the front.

better gap line between the door and the fender, which was what I needed to happen in the first place. That's why alignment always starts with the hood. The alignment of everything else keys off this single panel.

Photo 2 shows where I'll start the alignment process. The hood must be aligned with the cowl, which means the gap between the cowl and the rear edge of the hood must be even and parallel. I make the necessary adjustments by loosening the hinge bolts and shifting the hood either forward or backward as needed. I use the Eastwood Panel Gap Gauge shown in chapter 2 to help make this gap perfect.

PHOTO 2: Fender alignment actually starts here, with the hood. The hood must be aligned with the cowl first, then the fenders aligned with the hood.

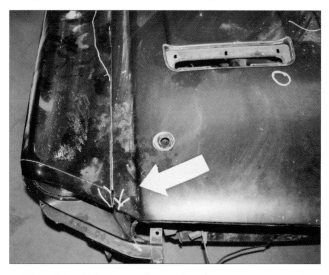

PHOTO 3: Although the hood and cowl alignment is critical, the alignment between the hood and the tip of the headlamp housing is critical as well.

PHOTO 4: This is the result of our alignment work. All gaps are even, about ¼ inch wide, and the tips of the headlamp housings align with the leading edge of the hood.

At the same time the rear gap in the hood is being established, attention must be paid to the alignment between the leading edge of the headlamp housing and the leading edge of the hood. Recall I had left the head-lamp housings in place? I did this because they play an important role in getting the hood into perfect alignment with all the other front sheet metal pieces, such as the fenders.

Note: The fit between this headlamp housing and the fender is far from acceptable, but it isn't something to worry about at this time. Whoever installed this housing failed to attach all of the mounting bolts, so the housing moves at will. I've already had the headlamp housing off once, and I know I can easily shift it into the correct position when needed.

When both fenders are in perfect alignment with the hood, you should have the result you see in photo 4. All gaps are even and not too wide, about ¼-inch width is normal, and the hood is in alignment with the leading edge of both headlamp housings. What are all the marks on the panels? When the initial inspection of this car was made, I marked every problem area I could find, including dents and align-ment problems, so that nothing would be overlooked once I began the sheet metal repair work on the car.

Did I have to do anything special to reach this point in getting all the front panels aligned? Other than adjust-ing the hood and loosening the fender bolts shown in photo 5 (arrows) to shift the right fender inboard, not really. Whoever worked on this car previously simply did a poor job of aligning the panels. Speaking of fender bolts, look closely at photo 5, and note the two addition-al fender bolts at the front of the radiator support. These bolts must be loosened any time fender alignment adjust-ments are made.

But then, everything isn't dipped in chocolate sauce here in Mustang land. The left fender, the Taiwan refugee, still fits like a saddle on a hog because the top rear of the fender stands a full ¼-inch taller than the cowl panel in that area.

> **TIP**
>
> *If a perfect alignment between the leading edge of the headlamp housing and the hood cannot be made, the problem lies with the fender. It will need to be shifted either forward or backward until alignment is achieved.*

I mentioned in chapter 3 that this fender would need some major rebuilding to make it fit. My thought was that the fender had been stamped incorrectly and the only solution would be to turn to the Eastwood Planishing Hammer #28116 PH and reform this portion of the fender. But I got lucky. Once the fender was removed from the car, I noticed the edge of the fender (photo 6) had been left too tall. This was a manufacturing flaw, but one with an easy fix. The cure was to grind away the excess metal in that area. That allowed the fender to sit lower on the cowl, and—presto—my fender troubles were over.

REPAIR THE RIGHT FENDER

I spent a couple of hours getting the front sheet metal on this car aligned and looking good. But after all that work, I still had one major problem to overcome. The body line where the right fender meets the hood is crushed about midway along the length of the fender, shown in the marked area about mid-fender in photo 4. I can hammer and dolly-work this area to bring it to a point where only a small amount of filler will be required to finish the job, but this is an area I don't like to apply plastic body filler to. Old cars need maintenance, and that means people leaning over the fenders to access the engine. The last thing I want is to risk having a tiny bit of filler chipped away from the edge of the fender by someone's belt buckle.

So instead of using plastic body filler to complete this repair, I'm using lead. I've selected Eastwood's Deluxe Body Solder Kit #31126, which contains everything I need to make this repair. Items found in the kit include lead bars, body file, tinning butter, tallow for protecting the wooden paddles, wooden paddles, and tinning brushes. Items not found in the kit but still needed include 3M P100 respirator #7183, eye protection, #00 steel wool, baking soda, and heavy gloves and a torch (not shown). I prefer a plumber's propane torch for lead-working because it supplies plenty of heat and is easy to handle.

Lead-working any panel begins by cleaning the repair area of all the old paint. I elect to grind away the old paint using a Norton 40-grit disc #23606 on a grinder. It quickly removes the old paint and leaves the metal extremely smooth with no deep grinder marks. I grind at least 6 inches past the repair area to give myself plenty of room to apply the lead.

Once the paint has been removed, the next step is to apply a coat of tin to the metal. Because lead does not

PHOTO 5: The arrows point to the row of fender attachment bolts. These, plus the two vertically mounted bolts at the front of the core support, must be loosened before the fender can be adjusted.

PHOTO 6: Once the left fender was removed, the problem became apparent: too much metal on this lip. I marked the area of metal to be removed and ground it away. This will let the fender sit lower on the cowl and correct the fit.

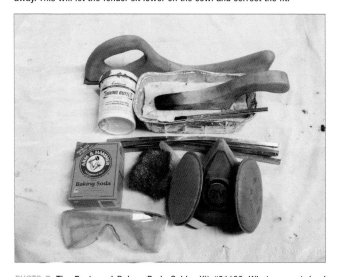

PHOTO 7: The Eastwood Deluxe Body Solder Kit #31126. What you get: lead bars, tinning butter, tallow, lead-working paddles, body file, tinning brushes, and an instructional video. You add the rest.

PHOTO 8: A layer of tinning butter is applied to the bare metal. Lead won't stick to an untinned surface.

PHOTO 9: The tinning butter is heated. A caramel colored film will develop over the surface as it is heated. Use the #00 steel wool to wipe away the film and expose the bright tin beneath.

PHOTO 10: The lead bar is heated to a point at which it is almost melted. At that point, the bar is pushed into the warmed tin.

TIP

If the panel you're working on has small bits of old paint trapped in the dents where the sanding disc can't reach, try heating the trapped paint with a propane torch; once they char, use a wire brush to remove the specks.

stick to bare metal, the tin acts as a flux to get the lead to adhere. I start by generously painting the repair area with the tinning butter and applying it using the tinning brushes provided in the kit.

After coating the repair area, I heat the tinning butter with the propane torch to form a layer of tin over the steel. Tinning butter is gray in color when applied, but after heating it begins to melt, and as it does a caramel-colored film develops over the surface. This film must be removed, and to do so I use #00 steel wool to wipe away the film and expose the bright tinned surface beneath.

Once the tin has been applied, the next step is to apply the lead. Applying the lead is a simple matter of warming the repair area with the torch while concentrating most of the heat on the lead bar. Hot lead, like everything else liquid, reacts quickly to the forces of gravity; I want to apply the warm lead above the dent so it can work its way down into the dent. I heat the bar until it just begins to melt, then push the heated end into the warmed tin, much like snuffing out a cigarette. I allow the bar to melt and separate, leaving a clump of lead on the repair. This process is repeated several times as I work to form a very lumpy buildup of lead.

Once the lead has been applied, it must be smoothed using a wooden paddle. Notice that in photo 11, my wooden paddle has become charred on the working end. The tallow provided in the kit should be applied to the paddle to prevent it from burning when it comes in contact with the hot lead, but it won't prevent the paddle from charring under the heat of the torch. A little extra tallow on the top of the paddle will reduce this charring as well as lengthen the life of the paddle.

The process of leveling hot lead with the wooden paddle is not unlike spreading warm butter over a slice of

TIP

It may be necessary to file the repair smooth, then apply additional lead to fill any low areas.

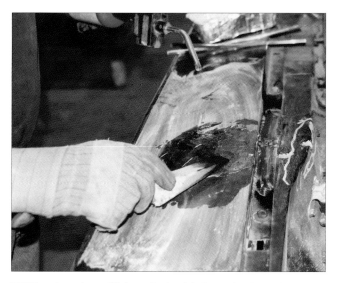

PHOTO 11: A wooden paddle is used to level the hot lead and smooth the repair area. Before use, the paddle was dipped into the melted tallow to form a protective heat barrier to prevent the paddle from burning.

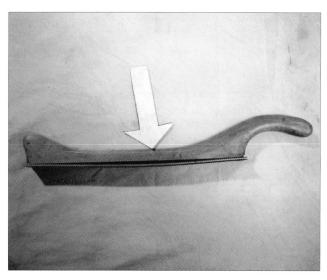

PHOTO 12: This is an old body-man's trick. A small ¼-inch nut was slipped between the blade and the handle to form a gentle curve. This curve ensures that most of the cutting is done near the center of the blade and not at the ends, where the blade would have a tendency to gouge the repair.

bread. Too much heat, and the butter (lead) just melts and runs off. Not enough heat, and the butter (lead) tends to clump and become lumpy. But apply just enough heat, and the lead moves to where you want it and immediately skims over to hold itself in place once the heat is removed. The tallow also helps in this cooling process, so don't be afraid to use it generously on the paddle.

Once leveled using heat and a paddle, the lead repair can be refined using the body file provided in the kit. How about an old body-man's trick? In photo 12, notice that the center of the file blade has been raised off the base of the file. I loosened one end of the blade and slipped a ¼-inch nut between the blade and the base. This acts to curve the blade to prevent its sharp ends from digging into the soft lead. Don't worry, curving the blade won't affect the way the blade cuts the lead, nor will it have much effect on how level the repair becomes as it is filed smooth.

I prefer to file the soft lead until the edges feather into the metal surrounding the repair, as shown in photo 13, then change to a block with 40-grit sandpaper to do the final smoothing.

Once the repair is complete, the acid in the lead must be neutralized. This is one of the most important steps when making a lead repair because neutralizing the acid

PHOTO 13: The repair is filed flat using the modified body file.

allows any subsequent coats of primer or body filler to permanently adhere to the lead. To neutralize the acid in the lead, I mix a portion of baking soda and water into a thick paste, about the consistency of toothpaste, apply the paste with a clean shop towel, and scrub the repair area thoroughly. I repeat this step at least twice, then do a final rinse with clean water.

NOTES

NOTES

CHAPTER 5

REPAIRING THE DOOR AND THE DECK LID

In the world of automotive restoration, plans are drawn up, but it's kept in mind that changes may have to be made. The plan at this point is to begin removal of the engine and drivetrain, but as I've already pointed out, panel-to-panel alignment wasn't a top priority at Ford back in 1968. It didn't help matters when a less-than-expert body technician mauled the left door on this Mustang and left it bent and twisted in an effort to replace the outer skin. So the problem now is the same problem I had previously: getting all the body lines on this car to match up and getting all the panel-to-panel alignment gaps to be uniform in size. So rather than remove the engine and drivetrain, I need to continue to work on the sheet metal. I decide to make repairs to the doors and the deck lid.

REPAIR THE DOORS

I started the alignment process in the last chapter with the front end sheet metal pieces. I continue now with the left door. Previously, I showed how the door frame on the left door was twisted so much that the lower rear corner of the door stuck out past the quarter panel almost ½ inch. You're probably thinking, "Oh my gosh, how do I fix that?" Believe it or not, it's not that difficult.

But before I start, I want to explain why this door ended up twisted in the first place. At some point, the left door was hit hard enough to require a new outer panel. Possibly, whoever replaced the panel simply cut off the old one and installed the new one without checking the fit of the door. Of course, once the door was painted and installed back on the car, improving the fit was out of the question without ruining the paint job. The result is what you see now, a lousy repair and a poor fit.

ALIGNING THE LEFT DOOR

So how do I improve the fit? Fortunately, I don't care about the paint at this point. My concern is panel-to-panel alignment. So leaving hammer tracks and pry bar marks on the paint is not a problem.

I already know the front of the door is in alignment with the fender and cowl because I had spent a lot of time aligning that area of the car previously. So that leaves the rear of the door as the problem child. Door frames are extremely tough at the bottom and weak at the top. Why are they strong down below and so weak up top? The door has a steel box–type of construction with a welded-on lid (door skin) that makes the bottom of the door rigid. The top is weak because most of the strength of the box has been taken away to allow the window to move in and out of the door. This weakness allows the door to bend and twist near the top and still remain rigid at the bottom.

The door on this car has been twisted inboard at the top. The telltale clue is that the striker plate has been moved outboard ⅛ inch in an attempt to align the top of the door with the quarter panel. That accounts for the ½ inch that sticks out past the quarter panel at the bottom of the door. People will notice an out-of-alignment condition at the top of the door long before they notice the same problem at the bottom of the door, which explains why an attempt was made to align the top of the door.

To correct the alignment problem on the bottom of the door, I need to shift the striker position inboard until the bottom of the door once again aligns with the bottom

PHOTO 1: A clue that the door frame is twisted is here. This striker plate has been adjusted outboard ⅜ of an inch to get the top of the door to align with the quarter panel.

PHOTO 2: With the striker plate readjusted to align the bottom of the door, the top of the door now sits inboard of the quarter panel almost ½ inch.

PHOTO 3: A long pry bar is used to take the twist out of the door frame.

of the quarter panel. Photo 2 shows just how far inboard the top of the door now sits in relation to the quarter panel (at least ½ inch) after the bottom of the door has been realigned with the quarter panel.

Remember that I said the bottom of the door is the strength and the top of the door is the weakness? Realigning this door to fit the quarter panel is now a simple matter of prying out the top of the door using a long pry bar to remove the twist in the door, as shown in photo 3.

While working on door alignment, keep in mind that shifting the door inboard at the lower hinge causes the top rear of the door to shift outboard. Shifting the door inboard at the upper hinge causes the bottom rear of the door to shift outboard. The opposite is true if the door is shifted outboard at either hinge.

Once the door is tweaked and twisted back into alignment, the rear edge of the door is subjected to the scrutiny of the metal straight edge. Any deviations along this edge line can be easily dealt with simply by using a body hammer and dolly.

The alignment of the right door on this Mustang is acceptable, so at this point both doors can be removed from the car. These doors are heavy, so I use a floor jack for support as I remove the bolts securing the hinges to the doors. While I'm at it, I remove the latch assemblies, the weather strips, and any clips that might remain on the doors and store those pieces with the parts previously removed from the doors. The right door goes into storage for now, but the troublesome left door is placed on a fold-out workbench for even more repairs.

REPAIRING THE LEFT DOOR

To repair the left door, I need to improve the poor welding job that is holding the outer panel on the door. I start by removing the paint around the inside perimeter of the door using a 3-inch Norton Speed-Lok disc #09186 with attachment arbor #55105. This is basically a round Scotch-Brite pad that can be chucked into a drill, and it will make short work of removing the paint around the welds.

After the paint has been removed, the bubble-gum welds are apparent and need to be ground down. Fortunately, not many of these welds were used to attach the outer panel, and smoothing them with a Norton Medallion Cut-Off Blade #89034 won't be that difficult. The blade is a 3-inch diameter by 1/16-inch thick grinding disc for use on a die grinder. The 1/16-inch thickness allows for more control over the disc, which results in a smoother appearance of the spot welds after grinding. I need to add more welds to better secure this door skin to the frame, but that can wait until I'm ready to weld in the new floor pans, which will be installed later.

For this project, I was able to repair the panel, but what if you need to replace a door skin? Before removing the old door skin, make any necessary repairs to the old skin to make sure the door is in alignment with the body. This ensures that no undue stress remains on the door frame and reduces the chances of the frame being twisted, something the previous body technician failed to do. Once the replacement skin is installed on the door frame, mount the door back on the car, and make any necessary additional adjustments. As long as the new door skin has not been welded to the frame, the door can be twisted, tweaked, and aligned without a problem. Once satisfied with the fit of the new skin, clamp and tack weld the panel in place before removing the door to complete the welding process.

Before I leave this part of the car, the door hinges need to be removed from the body. Prior to removing the hinges, I need to remove the torsion springs. I use a long, flat-blade screwdriver to pry the spring out of its locking position, then tap the top of the spring downward to release it from the hinge, as shown in photo 7. I repeat this procedure on the other side of the car, then remove all four hinges. Note: The hinge backing plates located inside the door posts will be loose and may even fall out once the hinges are removed. If the upper hinge backing plates don't fall out, it's OK. Once the dash is out of the car, I will have access to those plates at that time.

Photo 8 shows an exploded view of the lower hinge and spring. I normally don't disassemble the hinges at this point; I wait until I've had a chance to order new bushing and pins, then take the hinges apart. At that point, I will sandblast, rebuild, and refinish all four hinges.

REPAIR THE DECK LID

As with every other aspect of this restoration, the first step in repairing this deck lid is to bring it back into alignment with the body of the car. I start at the rear of the deck lid and can see that the spoiler molded into the lid is touching the left quarter panel extension. I can also see that the gap between the quarter panel extension and the deck lid is extremely wide at the peak of the spoiler. The areas indicated by the marks on the quarter panel and the

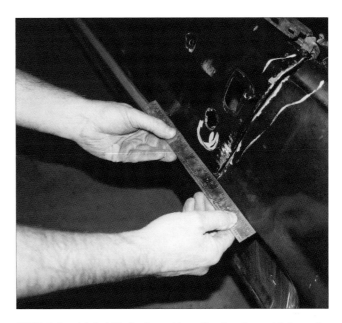

PHOTO 4: A metal straight edge is used to confirm the alignment between the door and quarter panel.

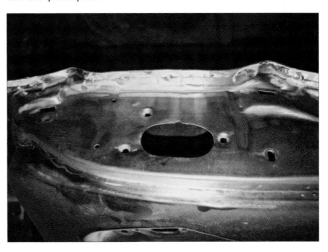

PHOTO 5: The paint is removed from around the sloppy welds holding the door skin on the frame, and then each weld is circled to ensure that no weld is missed when I grind them smooth.

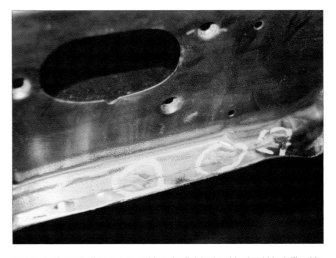

PHOTO 6: After grinding and smoothing, the finished welds should look like this, almost undetectable.

PHOTO 7: Before the door hinges are removed, the torsion springs on the lower hinge need to come off. Use a flat-blade screwdriver to pry the spring from its locking notch, and tap it out of the hinge with a hammer.

PHOTO 8: The torsion spring after removal from the hinge.

PHOTO 9: A closer look at the fit between the deck lid, quarter panel, and quarter panel extension shows that the actual fit leaves a lot to be desired.

quarter panel extension in photo 9 point to even more problem areas where these two panels do not align.

Once the alignment problems are corrected, I'll use structural adhesive to repair a crack in the deck lid, improve the fit between the deck lid and the quarter panel extensions, then finish by smoothing the deck lid by coating it with plastic body filler.

ALIGNING THE DECK LID

Looking at the right front edge of the deck lid, I can see an area where it rubs against the back glass filler panel every time the lid is opened. My first adjustment is to shift the position of the deck lid rearward on the right side to open this gap and stop the deck lid from rubbing the filler panel. This adjustment also results in the gap between the deck lid and the right quarter panel near the quarter panel extension opening and the gap between the deck lid and the left quarter panel extension closing.

Considering that the deck lid is already touching the left quarter panel, having it shifted even more to the left sounds like a bad thing. But considering that the gap between the top of the deck lid spoiler and the quarter panel extension spoiler is extremely wide on the left side, the shift will eventually help. Sound confusing? To help you picture this, find a square box with a removable lid. Invert the lid and place it on top of the box. Nudge it back just a little on one side and the other. When you see how much a small shift can affect every point of fit on the box, you will better understand how such a tiny shift in the position of the deck lid can change things.

What can be done to improve the gap between the deck lid and the left quarter panel in the area shown in photo 10? The left quarter panel where it touches the deck lid is actually lower than the deck lid. I can't be sure if this is a problem from the factory or if it's associated with some long-ago impact near the left rear, but this area of the quarter panel needs to be lifted straight up. Doing so forces the deck lid opening on the quarter panel to roll outward, thereby widening the gap between the deck lid and the quarter panel extension spoiler.

To lift the quarter panel, I place a hydraulic ram between the floor pan and the inner edge of the left quarter panel deck lid opening, and jack the quarter panel up slightly. Much care is needed here. Applying too much pressure can cause the quarter panel to buckle. Too little pressure and the quarter panel won't move. But just enough will cause the inside edge of the quarter panel to move up slightly and roll outboard, widening the gap between the quarter panel and the deck lid, exactly what is needed.

The deck lid and the quarter panels have been aligned. Yet despite all of my efforts, the fit between both quarter panel extensions and the deck lid failed to improve significantly. Because all three panels are made of fiberglass, I determined an acceptable fit between the three panels could be achieved only through rebuilding all three parts.

REPAIRING THE DECK LID AND REBUILDING THE DECK LID AND THE QUARTER PANEL EXTENSIONS

Along with rebuilding the deck lid and the quarter panel extensions, I need to repair a crack in the deck lid that I found when I first inspected the car. At some point, a significant impact on the right side of the deck lid cracked the gel coat and left a ring of broken paint behind. This is not something that can be ground and filled using plastic body filler. If I tried that, at some point in the future the filler would crack because the problem would have only been skimmed over and not repaired correctly.

The correct repair is to first grind away the old paint and gel coat to expose the fiberglass layers beneath, then reinforce the fiberglass using Norton Structural Bonding Adhesive #4618. I will repair the cracked deck lid at the same time I am rebuilding the deck lid and the quarter panel extensions.

To rebuild the deck lid and the quarter panel extensions and to fix the cracked deck lid, I first grind away the layers of old paint and gel coat at both corners of the deck lid and on the tops of both quarter panel extensions. Why remove the gel coat? This exposes the fiberglass layers and gives me a strong foundation from which to make the repair.

The next step is to build up the deck lid and quarter panel extensions using Norton Structural Bonding Adhesive #4618 as a filler to get the three pieces to align. This is a two-part adhesive product designed for use over clean and sanded bare metal or fiberglass. It has a 40-minute working time, which is enough time to mix and apply as much adhesive as will be needed to make this repair. This adhesive will also be applied over the crack.

I need to add roughly a ⅛-inch-thick layer of bonding adhesive to both sides of the deck lid where the panel curves upward to form the spoiler. I also need to add filler to make both quarter panel extensions thicker, and therefore taller, to properly align them with the deck lid.

Before mixing and adding the adhesive, the area needs to be prepared. Look closely at photo 13, and you can see

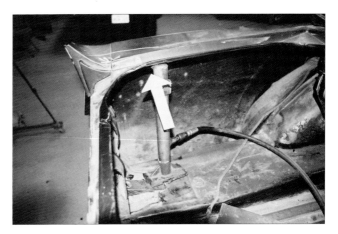

PHOTO 10: A hydraulic ram is used to push the inside edge of the left quarter panel up. This causes the quarter panel to move up and roll outward, exactly what is needed.

PHOTO 11: The fiberglass deck lid has a very large, circular crack in need of repair.

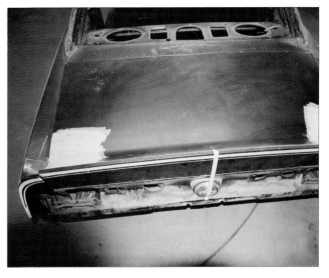

PHOTO 12: Both sides of the deck lid and quarter extensions are ground clean of the paint and old gel coat. I'll rebuild both sides using Norton Structural Bonding Adhesive #4618.

PHOTO 13: Looking from the left side of the car, you can see the masking tape dam along the seam where the extension meets the quarter panel and in the opening where the extension meets the deck lid. This well created by the masking tape is filled with adhesive.

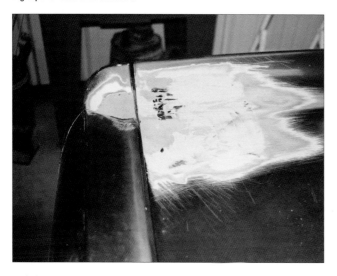

PHOTO 14: The crack in the gel coat has been repaired and the extension filled and brought level with the deck lid.

PHOTO 15: To finish the repairs to the deck lid, a thin coat of plastic body filler is applied.

the masking tape laid along the seam line separating the quarter panel from the quarter panel extension. The masking tape acts as a dam for the area where the quarter panel extension meets the deck lid. This little detail allows me to fill the low area of the quarter panel extension and bring it up level with the quarter panel without getting adhesive into the deck lid opening or into the seam and bonding the quarter panel extension to the quarter panel. Once the bonding adhesive begins to cure, I remove the tape by using a pocketknife to slice open the seam between the quarter panel and the quarter panel extension and lifting the tape. I'm left with a clean line of separation between the two panels as well as a thick buildup of adhesive where the quarter panel extension meets the deck lid.

A desirable characteristic of panel bonding adhesive is that it can be easily sanded smooth using 40-grit sandpaper on a 5-inch sanding block. I put on a dust mask and spend a few minutes sanding the adhesive smooth.

With both panels built up and sanded smooth, the fit between all three panels has improved dramatically.

FINISHING THE DECK LID REPAIRS

All that remains to finish the deck lid is to remove the remainder of old paint and to cover it with plastic body filler. This deck lid has no less than five coats of paint on it. Sandblasting and chemical stripping is out because the panel is made of fiberglass. Using a grinder is out because grinding tends to eat into the fiberglass. The solution is to convert the grinder to a sander by installing a Norton backup pad #43165 to the grinder and using a Norton 8-inch 40-grit sanding disc #23606 to quickly cut through the layers of old paint.

The last step is to cover the entire deck lid with plastic body filler. Why am I doing this? Even after using a grinder, the surface is still rough and pitted, so the best solution is to apply a thin coat of plastic body filler to the entire panel. Once the filler is block sanded smooth using 40-grit and then 80-grit sandpaper on an 8-inch block to progressively smooth the surface, the panel will be ready for primer.

REMOVE THE SHEET METAL

Now that I have finished repairing and aligning the sheet metal, I can remove the hood, fenders, deck lid, and quarter panel extensions. All are bolt-on parts, and I remove them one at a time, bagging and labeling the bolts as to which part they came from as I go.

NOTES

CHAPTER 6

REMOVING THE
MAJOR PARTS

At long last, the bolted-on sheet metal parts have come off the Mustang, and all I have left to do to make this ride an empty hull is to remove the driveshaft, the engine, the transmission, the suspension components, the steering system, the firewall, the dash, the fuel tank, and the differential.

REMOVE THE DRIVESHAFT, THE ENGINE, AND THE TRANSMISSION

Removing the engine and transmission is a relatively simple process, particularly when removing them as a unit. Of course, this means I also need to remove the driveshaft. All that is required is a couple of hours and following the correct procedures.

Although it's easy, engine and transmission removal can be messy because the remaining fluids may leak out. To help ease that problem, I have a 2 x 3-foot flat metal tray with a ½-inch lip that I slide under the car to catch the spills. I still employ the discount auto parts store plastic oil change tub to catch residual transmission fluid, oil, and antifreeze, but the real floor saver is the 2 x 3-foot catch tray.

Before removing any of the major parts, remember to take photographs to assist you when reassembling the car. For example, photo 1 may look like a useless picture

PHOTO 1: Some pictures tell a lot. For instance, how are the heater hoses and AC lines routed? Where are the engine compartment decals located? I could spend hours looking through shop manuals for this type of information or just a few seconds glancing at this photo.

of a very cluttered engine compartment, but actually this photo will become a key part of putting this car back together. Where does the engine information decal belong? How are the heater hoses and air conditioner lines routed? By referring to the photo, you can tell the decal is on the left fender apron, the heater hoses pass along the right side of the engine, and the air conditioner lines are routed along the left side (driver's side). Anything else that might be important later? How about the warning decal on the fan shroud? Both the engine information decal and the fan warning decal should be noted for replacement on the new parts list to be sure they get ordered at some point.

REMOVING THE DRIVESHAFT

I start the process of removing the engine and transmission by removing the driveshaft. First, I need to remove the two U-bolts connecting the rear universal joint to the rear axle pinion yoke. I slide the driveshaft forward just enough to free the universal joint from the yoke, then lower the driveshaft and pull it back, sliding it out of the transmission tail housing. I wrap the rear U-joint with masking tape to hold the caps in place. I will be replacing both the front and the rear U-joints with new ones from National Parts Depot later on, but just the same, I don't want the old caps lost or the needle bearings inside the caps to spill out over the floor.

REMOVING THE ENGINE AND THE TRANSMISSION

Once the driveshaft is removed, I can begin removing the engine. After taking a few good photographs, I start disassembly at the front of the engine and work toward the rear. The first parts to be removed from the car are the radiator and the air conditioner condenser. These are the

PHOTO 2: **A trick to keeping the U-joints intact is to wrap the unit with masking tape to secure the caps and prevent them from falling off.**

PHOTO 3: **How are the pulleys and belt brackets mounted? One picture tells it all.**

PHOTO 4: **The primary vacuum line tees to the Y connection that branches to the distributor that connects to the diaphragm that Y connects to the carburetor that tees to the . . . You get the picture.**

TIP

Label each belt as it is removed. One operates the alternator, another the air conditioner compressor, and the last works the power steering pump.

most fragile components in the engine compartment, and they must be protected at all cost. One wrong move can easily punch a hundred-dollar hole in the radiator or render the condenser useless. To remove the radiator, I remove the upper and lower radiator hoses first, and in this case I also remove the automatic transmission fluid-cooler lines attached to the bottom tank of the radiator. I then unbolt the radiator and lift it straight up and out.

The air conditioner condenser is mounted to the core support just forward of the radiator. Because I've already drained the air conditioning system, I remove the hose and unbolt the unit. Because of their fragile natures, I store both units in the same box with the glass.

With the radiator and condenser out of the car, the fan, fan shroud, pulleys, and belts can be removed.

For now, I unbolt the power steering pump from the engine and lay it aside. I do not remove the hoses at this time. Once the engine is out of the car, I'll have better access to the hose fittings where they connect to the steering control valve, and at that time the pump can be removed. Leaving the pump connected for now also helps reduce the mess under the car. Ever have someone accidentally turn the steering wheel with the steering pump hoses removed? It's like squirting oil from a can—everything gets oiled.

Next, I remove the pulleys and brackets. When putting the engine back in, you may ask yourself, "How were all those pulleys and brackets mounted to the front of the engine?" Without a picture, you may be in big trouble. Photo 3 could be traded to a Mustang restorer for a cold six pack any day.

Does anyone know why Ford likes vacuum hoses? I've yet to work on a Ford that wasn't covered with vacuum hoses. I counted no fewer than five vacuum hoses snaking around and through the front of this engine. The last thing I want is to try to guess where each one goes when I'm ready to replace them. Having a good picture of the hose routing is a must before removing the hoses. You may even want to draw a diagram of the engine compartment noting the origin and destination of each hose to help identify where it goes.

After the vacuum lines are removed, it is time to move on to the distributor and carburetor. I remove the distributor as a complete unit, wires and all, by removing the retainer bolt at the base of the unit and lifting it straight up and out of the engine. Next is the carburetor. I remove the four bolts attaching it to the intake manifold and to the throttle spring and linkage, and the carburetor comes right off. I store it in a plastic Ziploc bag to keep it clean.

I leave the fuel pump and the water pump on the engine for now, but I remove the rubber fuel line. Finally, the heater hoses, air conditioner lines, and compressor unit are removed.

The exhaust system on this car is a single pipe. I remove the old system in two separate pieces, hangers and all. The hangers are bolted on and, once unbolted, will allow the pipe to sag. The pipe can then be cut in half using a die grinder and the pieces removed from under the car. The only use this system will have later will be to give me an idea of where the hangers were mounted underneath the car. Who cares about that? I'm restoring the car as close to original as possible, so knowing where the hangers were mounted will come in handy.

The engine and transmission sit on rubber mounts. The engine mount incorporates a single bolt-through mount to attach the engine to the unibody. The transmission sits on a rubber mount on a cross brace located just forward of the tail shaft end. I use a floor jack to support the transmission and remove both engine-mount bolts, the four bolts holding the cross brace under the transmission, and the single bolt holding the transmission rubber mount to the cross brace. With all the bolts gone, the engine and transmission are ready to be removed from the car as a unit. The engine is ready for an engine stand, and the transmission can be stood on end in the corner of the shop.

REMOVE THE FRONT SUSPENSION

With the engine out of the car, this is a good time to take stock of all the components left behind. Everything shown in photo 6 must be removed, but not in a slipshod, wrench-happy way. Notice the cross brace extending from the left shock tower to the cowl and back to the right shock tower. This brace is in the way and needs to be removed but only after the other components are taken out. However, removing this brace isn't as simple as removing a few bolts and tossing it into the corner.

The cross brace is mounted to the top of each shock tower, and those are home to the front coil springs and the upper control arms. I could remove a few bolts, take out the shocks, and remove the cross brace, but that would leave the coil springs free to do whatever they wanted once I begin to disassemble the front suspension. Because coil springs are known to be extremely strong—

PHOTO 5: The engine and transmission are removed as a complete unit.

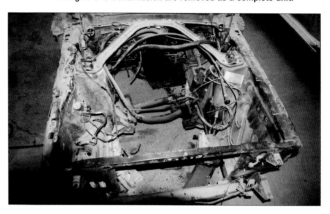

PHOTO 6: An empty engine bay will speak to you if you let it. What components need to be installed ahead of the engine once we are ready to rebuild this car? You can make a long list from this picture.

PHOTO 7: Coil spring compressing bolts are available at most automotive parts stores. Place one on either side of the spring, and tighten until the spring compresses and becomes loose in the mount.

after all, they are holding up the weight of the car—I'd rather have them under control at all times and not subject to popping out should I remove a wrong bolt.

The coil springs need to be removed before the cross brace is taken out. Step one is to corral the coil springs using a pair of coil spring compressing bolts. These bolts are hooked to the springs, one on either side, and tightened until the spring compresses enough to be wiggled within its perch. I use Eastwood's External Coil Spring Compressor #49016.

PHOTO 8: Right side suspension components. Each one of these parts must be removed in the correct sequence.

PHOTO 9: Break the steering column connection to the steering gear box here.

But compressing the coil springs doesn't mean it is time to grab the impact wrench. There is a method to the madness of removing all the parts making up a Mustang front suspension. Photo 8 is an exploded view of the right side (passenger side) suspension components; the right side suspension components are disassembled first. Upper center in the photo is the stabilizer bar that extends from the forwardmost cross member of the unibody out to the lower control arm. This bar is removed first, followed by the front sway bar (upper left in the photo), which extends from side to side of the car and is bolted to the unibody as well as to both lower control arms.

The drum brake assembly, hub, and brake backing plate go next (far right in the photo). Removing these items exposes the spindle (lower right in the photo). The spindle is bolted to an upper ball joint and a lower ball joint that attaches the spindle to the upper and lower control arms. A ball joint fork, a tool attachment used with an air hammer, may be required to separate the ball joints from the spindle. In most cases, a solid whack with a 2 ½-pound hammer against the spindle will jar the joints enough to cause them to separate.

Next to go is the outer tie-rod end, also attached to the spindle. A tie-rod separator or a stiff whack with the 2½-pound hammer should do the trick. The spindle can now be removed.

Repeat these steps to remove the suspension components on the left side of the car.

REMOVE THE STEERING SYSTEM

Once the engine, the transmission, and the suspension have been removed, the next to go are the steering system components. Looking from the driver's seat and moving from right to left across the car, the steering system comprises the right tie-rod, the idler arm, the steering gearbox's steering-control valve unit, the steering linkages, the inner tie-rod ends, the left tie-rod, and finally the steering column itself. I prefer to remove everything but the steering column as a unit because it simplifies the assembly process later when I start replacing individual steering components. That means I need to break the steering column connection to the steering gearbox at the bolt shown in photo 9. I leave the steering column in the car for now and will remove it once I'm ready to disassemble the dash. The remaining steering components are removed by unbolting the idler arm from the right frame rail and the power steering control valve from the left frame rail.

That brings me full circle to the cross brace in the suspension mentioned earlier and shown in photo 6. It can be removed now. The three bolts shown in photo 10 hold the cross brace to the shock towers. Notice the elongated holes next to the bolt studs. Once the brace is removed, the studs will slide free of the tower. I remove these studs and store them with the other small suspension pieces.

With the cross brace removed, I can now also remove the shocks, the upper control arms, and the coil springs, in that order. After those parts are all taken out, the lower control arms and the lower cross brace can be removed.

REMOVE THE FIREWALL AND THE DASH

The last components that need to be removed are the firewall and the dash. Let me begin by clarifying some terminology used to describe this area of the car. The area to which the doors are bolted and the windshield is mounted is known as the cowl. The portions of the cowl that the doors actually bolt to are known as the door posts. The area just in front of the windshield, where the fresh air vents are located, is known as the cowl vent panel. When you open the hood and observe the panel where the brake master cylinder is mounted, you are seeing the firewall. When you sit in the driver's seat and look straight ahead, you are seeing the dash panel; behind the dash, you will find the inner cowl structure.

REMOVING THE FIREWALL

Mounted to the firewall are the brake master cylinder, the brake lines, the brake metering valve, the air conditioner hoses, the heater hoses, the vacuum hoses, and the front body wiring harness. Whatever unbolts from the firewall gets removed, including any nuts I find on the firewall. The nuts hold the heater box in place under the dash, but removing them won't allow the unit to fall out from under the dash. The vacuum lines passing through the firewall are routed to the heater control switch, so I won't worry about removing them until later. The front body wiring harness also passes through the firewall, where it can be separated from the main wiring harness via several plugs.

REMOVING THE DASH

Now let's take a deep breath and step off into what has often been called the most dreaded aspect of auto restoration: removing the dash.

The steering column goes first. Six bolts attach the column to the dash panel, and six more secure the column to the inner cowl structure where it exits through to the firewall side of the cowl. I unplug the wiring harness before removing the bolts, then remove the entire column in one piece. Steering columns are always stored steering wheel down so the turn signal switch and horn ring are safe from damage.

The instrument cluster goes next. The speedometer cable restricts how far out from the dash the instrument cluster can be pulled unless the cable retainer clip on the firewall side of the cowl has been removed. With the retainer clip removed, the cable is free to move, and the cluster comes right out, bringing the speedometer cable along with it. I store this unit until I have a chance to improve upon the looks of the gauges with goodies from California Mustang.

PHOTO 10: After removing the cross brace, remove these stud bolts and store them with the other suspension components.

PHOTO 11: Vacuum lines connect the AC control panel (left arrow) to the AC control box (right arrow). Disconnect the vacuum lines at the control box, and label each one before removal.

At this point, the dash has that "I left my car parked at the mall, away from the lights for three days with expensive stereo equipment inside" look. Notice the arrows in photo 11. The arrow on the left points to the heater/AC control panel; on the right, the arrow points to the heater/AC control box. Both units are connected by vacuum lines. Ford didn't bother to add a quick disconnect plug to separate the units, so each hose needs to be traced from the control panel to the control box and disconnected one at a time from the various vacuum canisters controlling the door positions. I label each hose as to its position on the box as it is removed.

Once all the vacuum lines have been labeled, they can be pulled through the dash to the driver's side, and the control panel can be removed from the car with the vacuum lines intact. So much for getting control of the controls.

The heater/AC control box and the wiper assembly can now be removed from the car. The attachment nuts on the firewall side were removed previously, so that leaves only a couple of attachment braces located under the dash holding the heater box in place. Once those braces are removed, the unit easily drops out from under the dash on the passenger side. Note: Be sure to disconnect the vent hoses before attempting removal of the heater box.

All that is left under the dash now is the brake pedal assembly, a fresh air vent on the left side, the emergency brake lever, and the main wiring harness. I unbolt and remove these parts one at a time, photograph each one, and store it.

Finally, the padded dash cover can be removed. This piece is secured to the dash panel via a series of bolts located at the base of the windshield and a few screws that should have already been removed along the front lower lip of the pad. Once the bolts are removed, I can slide the pad forward to remove it and store it flat to prevent wrinkles.

If your dash looks like the dash in photo 12, you've earned a well-deserved break. Take five, then it's back to the grind.

If this is your first foray into dash removal on a Mustang, by now you have figured out that the dash panel itself doesn't come out. It is welded to the cowl and is part of the unibody structure. Later, I will sand the dash panel using 320-grit sandpaper in preparation for a fresh coat of semigloss black.

PHOTO 12: The empty dash compartment. It's time for a break.

ADVANCE TO THE REAR

The next area I am working on is the rear of the car. One of Ford's great ideas back in the sixties was to use the top of the fuel tank as the trunk floor pan. That makes removal of the fuel tank fairly easy. I remove the fuel inlet hose, the fuel line, and several bolts around the perimeter of the tank, and the tank lifts right out. Later, I'll replace the old rusty tank with a shiny new one from American Designers.

The last bolted-on part of this Mustang is the differential unit. I start by removing the brake lines, the emergency brake cables, and, last, the shocks. The differential is removed as a complete unit by first supporting it with a floor jack, then removing the front and rear spring hanger bolts. The jack is lowered, and the differential is removed.

For ease of storage, the leaf springs are removed from the unit, and the entire assembly is pushed into a corner until I have time to clean and inspect the unit. At a later point, the springs will be sent out for rebuilding, and the axle assembly itself will be inspected to determine the condition of the bearings and gears.

NOTES

CHAPTER 7

REMOVING OLD PAINT AND REPLACING RUSTY FLOORS

If you have been keeping up with your paperwork, the master list should now be several pages long, with a new parts list almost as long. If you have begun to accumulate Mustang parts catalogs and earmark a few Mustang parts Web sites on your computer, you should also have a good idea of the cost for all those shiny new parts that look so good on a vintage Mustang.

If it seems like a lot of money, take heart. When compared with the cost and availability of parts for other vintage vehicles, Mustangs can be virtually rebuilt from the ground up on the cheap. That's one of the reasons I didn't bother with a salvage parts list. If you can't purchase it NOS (new old stock) or find it in the aftermarket, Ford probably didn't install it on the car in the first place.

I'll start by discussing the correct seam sealers for this car; continue with the necessary steps, tools, and supplies needed to remove the old paint; and finish with some new floor pans.

REPLACE THE SEAM SEALERS

At this point, the Mustang is a bare-bones shell, and that makes this the perfect time to photograph the body joints and seams in order to note the methods originally used to apply seam sealer throughout the car. Ford liked to use a black semihard tarlike substance to seal the majority of the interior seams on the Mustang and a cream-colored sealer that ages like concrete everywhere else.

In areas not subjected to the elements, such as inside the passenger compartment and inside the trunk, both sealers hold up very well. But in areas exposed to the weather, they have a tendency to harden and crack over time. Ever wonder why the typical Mustang seems to rust from the inside out? In many cases, failed seam sealer is the culprit.

Unfortunately, removing the tar sealer is next to impossible while it is still somewhat soft. It will clog sandpaper if sanded, gum up a grinder disc if ground, and turn to beach tar if sandblasted. So in areas where the sealer is still soft with no signs of cracking or otherwise beginning to fail, I leave it in place and scuff sand it using a Norton Bear-Tex Scuff Pad in preparation for a coat of epoxy later on. Fortunately, this sealer can be painted over, as is evident from the painted sealer found in several areas of the car.

Areas of the sealer that have cracked, hardened, and failed, which will be the majority of the areas sealed with the cream-colored sealer, need to be replaced. Fortunately, this failed sealer is usually rock hard, and removing it with a putty knife is fairly easy. Once every point on the car that contains seam sealer has been photographed and all the failed sealer scraped off, it is time to consider how to replace the sealer.

The world of seam sealers has changed dramatically since this Mustang rolled off the assembly line. Better choices for caulking up the gaps and holes in this car are readily available. Here are a few 3M products that will make life easier:

PHOTO 1: The dash and inner windshield post are painted with a semigloss finish to match the color of the interior, in this case black. Notice that I've marked the areas to be sprayed semigloss black. At a later time, I will be coating everything in here with red epoxy. The photos will serve as a reminder of what parts were originally painted black.

PHOTO 2: The interior of this car was first coated with red oxide primer. During the refinishing process, the exterior green color was oversprayed onto the front seat pan, the wheel wells, and the package tray.

TIP

I use a water pencil to define the borders separating the areas oversprayed with the exterior green color. I also mark those areas sprayed with low-gloss black to complement the interior trim color, such as the inner windshield post and dash. Months from now, when I'm trying to determine how to duplicate the factory paint job, having the lines of color clearly marked on the photographs will make life much easier.

- **Strip-Calk #8578:** This is a nonhardening, water-resistant sealer used for caulking and sealing areas where the parts being sealed are subjected to movement. That would include around the taillamps, the marker lamps, and even the windshield and back glass, should extra sealer be required around the weather strips. This is a black, almost butyl rubber–type of sealer that should not be painted, so these areas should be sealed only once the car has been refinished.

- **Fast'n Firm Seal Sealer #8505:** This is a firm-setting sealer for interior and exterior body joints and seams that can be painted. I use this more than any other sealer because it easily duplicates factory sealing methods.

- **All-Around Autobody Sealant #8500:** Like the Fast'n Firm Seal Sealer, this product can be used to seal any seam on the car, and it can be painted. Both of these sealers remain flexible and are resistant to oil and fuel. They each have different application windows to preserve the restored appearance of the car, so when the time is right, I'll explain where and how to apply these sealers.

INSPECT THE EXTERIOR AND INTERIOR PAINT

The next inspection to make regarding this car is the paint. Ford wasn't into wasting paint. It sprayed only those portions of the car that required a finish and left the rest of the car sporting a coat of red oxide primer.

Inside the car, the dash and the inner windshield post had been sprayed black. That's because the interior of this car is black. The black is a semigloss black, and matching it will not be difficult.

As I continue my visual inspection of the interior, I note and photograph any areas where the exterior color has been oversprayed into the car. In this case, the inner rocker panels and front seat platforms have been oversprayed with the exterior green color, as have the package tray and rear seat floor pan.

REMOVE THE PAINT AND SAND THE BODY

The next major step in the restoration process is to remove the paint by sanding the body of the car. This has to be the most tedious part of restoring an old car because whether the old paint is burned off, blasted off, stripped off, scraped off, or sanded off, the car must be cleaned of the old paint all the way down to the bare metal. Why is sanding so tedious? In this case, the project vehicle has no fewer than three layers of green paint, with some portions of the car having up to five layers of paint. Between those layers of green paint are layers of primer and plastic body filler. Under those layers lies who knows what. Rust, perhaps? To make matters worse, all of these old paint layers are made up of aging acrylic enamel. This was a good finish in its day but can't hold a candle to the high-quality urethane products available today. Besides, spraying a top of the line urethane finish over layers of old enamel is like using Scotch tape to keep the soles of your cowboy boots from falling off. It may look good today, but don't plan any rodeos for tomorrow.

Since I'll be sanding the old finish off this car, here is a list of Norton sanding products to make paint removal easier:

- **Bear-Tex Scuff Pads #58000:** These can be used to scuff painted surfaces anywhere on the vehicle.
- **AVOS grinder disc #26558:** This is a 50-grit, 5-inch disc used with backing pad #3030 on a pistol grip grinder (thread size ⅜-inch–20). This setup makes quick work of removing multiple layers of old paint in hard-to-reach areas.
- **Speed-Lok TR disc #37757:** This is a 3-inch, 36-grit disc for use with Norton backup pad #55105 that is designed for use when sanding those hard-to-reach areas.
- **Surface Blending Pad #9194:** This is a 3-inch course sanding pad, much like a Bear-Tex Scuff Pad, used for sanding areas where a smoother finish is desired than would be achieved with any of the above-mentioned products. For use on the Norton backup pad #55105.
- **Bear-Tex Rapid Strip Disc TR #11781:** This is a 4-inch-round, coarse disc used to remove layers of paint in hard-to-reach areas and still leave a fine surface. As these discs cut away the paint, they conform to the shape of the area being sanded, making them ideal for sanding glass channels and drip rails. Used with Norton arbor #55105.
- **Sticky-back 24-grit sanding disc #23576:** This is an 8-inch sanding disc for use on Norton backing pad (⅝-inch–24) #43112 on a large high-speed grinder.

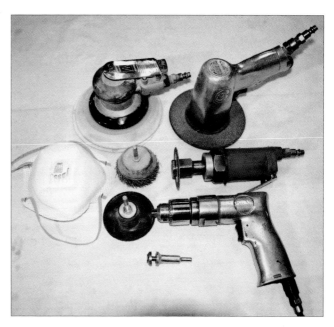

PHOTO 3: Tools to make paint removal easy include (clockwise from top) an orbital sander, a 5-inch mini grinder, a die grinder, a drill, wire wheels, and various sanding disk attachments. Don't forget the dust mask.

- **DA Paper #31481:** This is a 6-inch 80-grit sanding disc best used for removing single layers of old paint. I also like to use this disc to smooth the metal and to remove any minute bits of old paint I might have missed during the initial paint removal phase of this operation.

With the exception of the Bear-Tex Scuff Pads, none of these products will perform without some type of power tool attached. Here are a few power tools you will need to sand the car:

- **Mini grinder:** Referred to as a 5-inch grinder because it is normally used with a 5-inch grinder disc, this unit is ideal for removing paint in those hard-to-reach areas.
- **Random orbital sander:** The one shown in photo 3, with its low profile, is known as a palm sander. I recommend this type of sander because it is easy to handle and control with only one hand.
- **Die grinder:** Can be adapted for use with the Bear-Tex Rapid Strip Disc TR #11781.
- **Drill:** The drill in photo 3 is a pneumatic ⅜-inch chuck unit. Forget the battery operated or electric versions. They just won't hold up to the abuse restoring an old car will put them through. This can be used with the Norton Speed-Lok TR Disc #37757, the Norton arbor #55105, and even a rotary wire brush when necessary.

PHOTO 4: A plumber's torch is used to melt the layers of old paint accumulated around the fresh air intakes on the cowl. Once the paint is melted, a wire brush is used to clean away the paint residue.

In addition to the must-have items listed above, a dust mask is essential because paint removal is nasty work and the old paint may be lead based. I have also been known to use everything from a putty knife to scrape off seam sealer to wire wheels on a drill to a plumber's torch to burn paint out of areas that are almost impossible to properly sand by any other means. One of those impossible-to-sand areas to come to mind is the fresh air intake grilles on the cowl. Three or four layers of paint along the sides of these fins can be as difficult to remove as a brother-in-law from the beer cooler. A little heat will bubble the paint, making it easy to scrape or brush off. To get rid of the brother-in-law, try handing him a tool.

This may sound like a completely useless step, but I'm going to wash this car before beginning the sanding process. Sandpaper lasts longer when it isn't being clogged with grease, grit, grime, and road tar. To clean the car, I use a mild detergent (Dawn) in a pressure washer, rinse the car with clean water, then allow it to dry.

When you are ready to begin removing the paint from the car, you should consider where to start. Since the bulk of the paint on this car will eventually end up on the floor, I like to start at the top and work my way down. I begin on the roof. Previously, I had removed the vinyl top cover and discovered a heavy layer of vinyl top adhesive on the panel. The adhesive is old and brittle, which means I can use 80-grit on the palm sander to cut right through it. I move from the roof to the interior, where the

rotary wire brush and Bear-Tex pads do most of the work. From here I go to the trunk, followed by the engine compartment, and I finish up with the exterior of the car.

Sanding a car is a slow, tedious, dirty process. My method is to pick an area of the car to sand, complete that operation, then take a break from the monotony of sanding by putting aside the sanding tools and tackling some other part of the project. I continue to do this until all of the body has been completely sanded. In this case, I'm going to start by sanding the roof and the interior, blow the car clean using compressed air, then turn my attention to replacing the interior floor pans.

REPLACE THE FLOOR PANS

This is a good point in the restoration to replace the floor pans. The condition of the floor pans is pretty typical for a forty-year-old Mustang. Both sides are rusted, but not so badly as to have holes large enough to step through. That is going to make this repair a little easier.

The first order of business when replacing any sheet metal panel is to compare the new parts to the old parts before some piece that can't be readily replaced gets hacked apart. Most suppliers are known for getting everything right the first time, but now might be a good time to start following Larry's Law, which states: Left is right unless it's right; and if it's right, it's wrong.

For replacement panels, I selected floor pans from American Designers, a company specializing in top-quality sheet metal replacement parts, gas tanks, and radiators. The pans I selected are referred to as full-floor pans since they come as full-length pans for each side of the car. The pans extend from the seam joint located under the rear seat all the way forward and up the firewall about 4 inches. That's more than enough metal to take care of all the rust.

The pans are available in left and right as well as in half-floor pan sections, should only a partial floor pan replacement be necessary. Mustangs are know for rusting out the rear floor pans in particular, so having the option of replacing only that section of the floor makes keeping the old pony in good condition a little easier.

This Mustang is showing signs of rust in both the rear and front floor pan areas, which is why I elected to install full-floor pans. The plan calls for replacing both sides of the floor pan as individual panels. Since one panel replaces exactly as the other does, I'm going to take you through the process of replacing the right-side floor pan only.

The first order of business is to remove the front seat mounting platform. Note: Should this mounting platform require replacing, American Designers makes it, and it is available through most of the retail Mustang parts suppliers mentioned in chapter 1.

The seat platform is spot welded in place, so I begin by locating and marking all of the spot welds with the water pencil. To remove the welds, I use the Blair spot weld cutter #13216. I begin by drilling a ⅛-inch pilot hole in the center of each weld. The pilot holes assist the cutter in cutting a smooth round hole around each of the spot welds to separate the panels. I then use an air chisel with a flat blade to gently free the seat platform from the floor pan.

With the seat platform out of the way, the new floor pan is test fitted by laying it over the old one. Any areas where the new pan does not fit the contour of the old floor pan can be worked with a body hammer and dolly or cut and trimmed until a satisfactory fit is achieved. Secure the new floor to the old floor with sheet metal screws as the panel is worked into place to help the new panel better conform to the shape of the old floor pan.

Why spend so much time fitting the new panel over the old panel? The factory stamped the floor of this car from a single sheet of metal, and it may still hold some residual stress that will be released the moment I start cutting the floor apart. That could result in the driveshaft hump loosing some of its "hump." Prefitting the new pan allows me to fit everything back together even if the hump tries to dehump.

Once a good fit is achieved between the old and the new pans, I mark the outline of the new pan on the old floor pan using the water pencil. I will be using an overlapping flanged seam to join the new pan to the driveshaft hump, so after removing the new pan, I add ¾ inch to the mark on the driveshaft hump to compensate for the flange.

Finally, I drill out all of the spot welds on the old floor pan using the Blair spot weld cutter, then cut the old floor pan along the overlap seam on the driveshaft hump using a die grinder with a 3-inch-diameter, ⅛-inch-thick cutoff

PHOTO 5: New left and right floor pans from American Designers.

PHOTO 6: The Blair spot weld cutter #13216 is used to drill out all of the spot welds holding the seat platform and the floor pan in place.

PHOTO 7: The new floor pan is laid into place over the old floor pan. Notice the lines around the panel. This defines the placement of the panel to ensure that I don't cut out too much of the old panel.

PHOTO 8: Once the old floor pan is removed, the edge along the drive shaft hump is flanged to accept the new panel.

PHOTO 9: Blind holders are used to secure the new pan to the drive shaft hump.

PHOTO 10: The floor pan is laid in place so the location of the frame rails can be marked on the underside. The pan is removed, and a series of ⁵⁄₁₆-inch holes are drilled through the pan for welding to the frame rails.

wheel attached. I complete the removal of the old pan using an air chisel to separate the panel from the frame rails and inner rocker panel.

Once the old floor pan is out of the car, I can clean up the metal around the seams and frame rails using the mini grinder. While I'm in the cleanup mode, I also scuff sand every inch of the new floor pan inside and out so the paint will adhere to the surface. It is a lot easier to sand this panel now while it is out of the car than to sand it once it has been installed.

The next step is to install the new pan. This is where all those holes I drilled while attaching the new panel to the old panel will come in handy. I'm going to use those same holes to position and align the new floor pan. But before I do that, I need to drill a few hundred spot weld holes around the edges of the new pan to give me plenty of weld points for securing the new pan to the car. Each hole should be ⁵⁄₁₆-inch in diameter and spaced roughly 2 inches apart.

I thought the new pan would fit better than it does. But I don't want to forget that I was laying a new panel over an old panel and they don't always fit like a glove. I begin by temporarily securing the new panel to the drive-shaft hump using blind holders. Once that seam is secured, I move forward to the firewall, then to the rocker panel, then to the rear floor seam, attaching the new floor pan to the body of the car.

Got a teenager who can't do anything but hold a phone? Swap the phone for a dolly, and stuff him or her inside the car. The idea here is to have him or her hold a dolly against the seam line of the driveshaft hump while you go under the car and flatten the seam using a body hammer. This should be a fairly easy task and may not be necessary at all. It is simply to ensure that both panels are wed to each other as much as possible.

While under the car, mark the edges of the new floor pan where it meets the frame rails. This gives you a way to identify where to drill for the spot welds that will secure the floor pan to the frame rails. Remove the floor pan by removing the blind holders, and drill a series of ⁵⁄₁₆-inch spot weld holes inside the marks around the frame rails.

The last step in securing the floor pan is to weld it on. I don't want to start welding without first applying 3M Weld-Thru Primer #39786 everywhere the new floor pan will receive a spot weld. This helps prevent rust from forming around the welds.

Where I begin welding doesn't really matter. I pick a spot and make one spot weld. Then I move at least 2 inches away and make another spot weld. This method of welding disperses the heat from the welding process across the entire panel, thereby reducing the chances of heat warping the metal in any one area. I repeat this procedure until all the drilled spot weld holes have been welded shut.

Next, I remove the blind holders one at a time and weld those holes shut as I go. Finally, I complete the welding process by welding the entire seam line along the driveshaft hump using the stitch weld method of welding 1 inch, moving at least 2 inches away, and welding another inch until the entire seam is welded.

Once the metal has cooled, I grind all of the welds smooth, then mark any suspect welds and partially welded holes. What does a suspect weld look like? Usually this weld appears as a bubble of metal resting on top of the panel and is a result of the weld not penetrating the panels being welded. This type of weld must be ground smooth and rewelded. The finished product doesn't have to look as if your uncle, the professional welder, did the job, but it does need to look good enough that you won't be ashamed to remove the carpet in front of company.

NOTES

_____

_____

_____

_____

_____

_____

_____

_____

_____

_____

_____

_____

_____

_____

_____

_____

CHAPTER 8

NO-WELD RUST REPAIR

Now that I have the body sanded clean of all the old paint and have replaced the rusted floor pans, I can turn my attention to other problematic areas of the car. I need to fix rust problems around both rear wheel wells, the right fender apron, and the core support. I'll use a no-weld technique to repair the rust around the wheel wells and to replace the right fender apron and core support with new parts.

REPAIR RUST ON THE REAR WHEEL WELLS

Like finding rust in the trunk floor pans of an aging Mopar, finding rust around the rear wheel wells on a vintage Mustang is a given. Fortunately, on this car the rust in that area is minor. It is serious enough, however, to warrant cutting out the affected metal and replacing it with new metal.

Patch panels that extend from the wheel opening to the door and the wheel opening to the rear body panel are available from most of the Mustang parts sources mentioned in chapter 1. Since the rust on this car is minor, I'll be able to make the needed repairs by forming my own small patch panels from 20-gauge steel using the Eastwood planishing hammer.

In this case, the smaller I make the patch panel the better because it makes shaping the curves and contours of the patch panel that much easier. In photo 2, I deliberately trimmed the size of the patch panel so that it didn't extend down to the seam line where the quarter panel meets the rocker panel. This eliminates the need to form this lip and that in turn simplifies the repair.

Once I have the size I'm looking for, the patch panel is clamped into place over the rusted area, and it is outlined on the good panel using ¾-inch-wide masking tape. Why bother to mark the size of the patch panel with masking tape? When I remove the patch panel, the masking tape line around the repair area tells me without question if my patch panel is large enough to extend beyond the rust. This ensures that I'm working with good metal

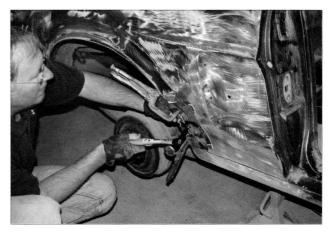

PHOTO 1: The patch panel is initially shaped using the Eastwood planishing hammer, then clamped into place over the rusty metal. Any final shaping is accomplished using a body hammer and dolly.

and not trying to patch metal that has already begun to rust. That would be defeating the purpose.

Once I'm certain the patch panel is the right size, it is time to make my cuts. I will be using Eastwood's

PHOTO 2: The patch panel is trimmed to size and again clamped into place so the perimeter of the patch can be marked using ¾-inch-wide masking tape.

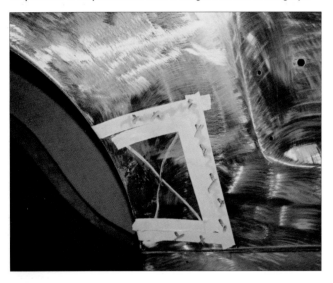

PHOTO 3: A second line of ¾-inch-wide masking tape is laid inside the first tape line. The inside edge of the second tape line will be the actual cut line to remove the rusted metal.

PHOTO 4: The opening receives a flange using the flanging pliers provided in the kit.

No-Weld Panel Repair Kit #31102 to make this repair. The kit contains everything I need, including flanging pliers, countersinking pliers, an assortment of blind holders, and a tube of panel bonding adhesive.

The first step is to cut out the rusted metal and to crimp a flange around the edge of the opening for the patch panel to seat against. To do that, I need to know precisely where to make my cuts. This is where the masking tape outline comes into play for a second time. I lay another line of masking tape just inside the first line of masking tape, as shown in photo 3. The outer line of tape denotes the outer perimeter of the patch panel. The inner line of tape gives me the actual cut line, and that is located exactly ¾ inch inboard from the edge of the patch panel. Confusing? Laying down the second tape line gives me an easy way to mark the ¾-inch wide flange I'll be crimping into the metal using the flanging pliers provided in the kit.

I use a die grinder to make my cut along the outside edge of the inner tape line, remove the tape, then add the flange using the flanging pliers. After that, the patch panel is again clamped into place, checked for fit, and trimmed where necessary.

Next I drill a series of ⅛-inch holes spaced about 1 inch apart around the perimeter of the patch. I use blind holders to secure the patch panel as I drill. Once I have the holes drilled, the patch panel again comes off and all the holes are countersunk to accept the ⅛-inch rivets that will be used to permanently secure the patch to the panel.

Finally, panel bonding adhesive is applied all around the flanged edge, and the patch panel is again installed using the blind holders to secure it. One by one the blind holders are replaced with rivets. Depending on the temperature, I have between 15 and 30 minutes to replace the blind holders with rivets before the adhesive begins to set up. The repair is completed with the addition of extra adhesive applied over the patch panel to bury the rivets and smooth the surface of the repair. I'm leaving rivets in the panel? Isn't that a big no-no? In this case, the rivets are not being exposed to plastic body filler, which has a tendency to crack when applied directly over rivets. The rivets are beneath a layer of panel bonding adhesive, and this type of repair has been proven not to crack.

On the left side of the body, I've detected a few rust dots just in front of the rear wheel. Rust dots begin on the inside of the panel and slowly work their way through to eventually form a pimple of rusted metal on the outside of the panel. It's sort of a precursor to the more serious rust problem found on the right side of the body.

To repair these small rust dots, I cut out the affected metal, a spot measuring roughly 2 x 3 inches, trim a patch panel to fill the opening, and weld it into place. Why weld the patch in place instead of using the adhesive? The location of the repair, which is just inside the wheel opening, and its relatively small size are conditions that make welding the quickest and best way to make this repair.

RUST ON THE RIGHT FENDER APRON AND THE CORE SUPPORT

Leaky batteries equate to rusted battery trays, and in this case almost forty years of leaky batteries equates to a rusted battery tray that caused damage to the right fender apron and core support as well. The good news is that when I first inspected this car, I placed the fender apron on the replacement parts list because some body technician with a big hammer left his calling card all over the panel. I turned to The Paddock Parts for a replacement fender apron. The rust holes in the core support weren't found until I removed the engine. For the new core support, I turned to Aftermarket Automotive Parts Distributing (AAPD).

To replace the right fender apron and core support, I first need to take measurements. Then I will cut out the panels and test the fit of the new panels. Once there is a correct fit, I will drill for the spot welds and install the panels. This is also a good time to finish sanding the engine compartment.

Taking Measurements

Installing the fender apron and the core support panels will be quick and easy, but there are a few details to attend to before bringing out the cutting tools.

Anytime metal is removed from around the engine compartment of a unibody vehicle, one with welded-on fender aprons and core support, the remaining structure is free to move and flop around at will. To recognize and respond to this tendency to shift out of alignment, I need to take accurate measurements of the entire engine compartment. Accurate measurements are also necessary to precisely relocate the panels and are critical to keeping the front structure of this car square. Who cares if the front structure is a little out of square? I will when I attempt to install the fenders and hood. An out-of-square

PHOTO 5: The patch panel is again clamped into place and a series of ⅛-inch holes are drilled around the perimeter of the patch, spaced about 1 inch apart. Blind holders prevent the patch panel from moving as the holes are drilled.

PHOTO 6: Adhesive is applied around the opening before the patch panel is riveted in place. The inside edge of the second tape line will be the actual cut line to remove the rusted metal.

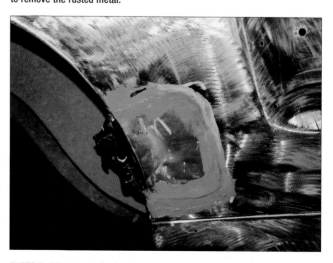

PHOTO 7: A final coat of adhesive is used to bury the rivets and smooth the surface of the repair.

condition will prevent these panels from aligning, and that is the last thing I need when trying to finish up this project.

The good news is that this is a symmetrical engine compartment, meaning when I take a measurement on the right side, I can move to the left side and get the same reading, whether taking a measurement of length or taking a cross measurement. Note: All measurements are taken using fender mounting bolt locations as references.

I start by taking a cross measurement from the left front to the right rear of the engine compartment and compare that with the same measurement on the opposite side, and then write the measurements down. This Mustang measures 60 1/16 inches from the right rear to the left front, and 59 15/16 inches on the opposite side. That equates to being 1/16 inch out of square, and that's well within factory tolerance. How did I arrive at 1/16 inch? The difference between the two measurements is 1/8 inch and half of that is 1/16 inch. To square the engine compartment, I would need to shift the left fender apron to the right exactly 1/16 inch to equal a measurement of 60 inches. Then I would need to shift the right fender apron to the right exactly 1/16 inch to equal a measurement of 60 inches. At that point, I would have a perfectly square engine compartment.

But I'm not going to quibble over a 1/16-inch difference. What I am going to do is jot these measurements down so I can refer back to them later. Where's a good place to jot these measurements down so they are easy to find? Had I been repairing this car because of a collision, I would have used the windshield as a writing tablet. All I'd have to do to be reminded of a particular measurement would be to glance up and there it would be. But because the glass is out of this car, I write my notes on the cowl.

What would I have done had the engine compartment been out of square by more than 1/4 inch? That would be time to call my friendly neighborhood collision repair center to discuss the options for returning this engine compartment back to a square condition.

Next, I measure the length of both fender aprons. I take the measurements from the rearmost fender mounting bolt near the cowl to the forwardmost bolt near the front tip of the apron. This one is 40 1/4 inches on the left and 40 1/4 inches on the right side. While I'm working in this area, I also note the measurement from the rearmost apron bolt hole to the center and to the inboard shock tower bolt hole, then I measure from that same shock tower bolt to the front of the apron. This one measures 18 inches and 25 1/2 inches, respectively.

Next, I measure across the shock towers from inside bolt to inside bolt. This one reads 30 1/2 inches. After that, I measure from the left rear fender apron bolt mount to the center inboard shock tower bolt and repeat this measurement for the right side. The left side measures 41 1/2 inches and the right side measures 41 7/16 inches. Once again, close enough, but had those measurements differed by more than 1/2 inch, I'd be making that call to the collision center.

Out with the Old

Something I learned from the collision repair side of this business is that sometimes the factory didn't have the best interest of the repair technician in mind when manufacturing its vehicles. The tendency was to sandwich panels between structural members, mount extra brackets on them, and even add spot welds that were not accessible once the vehicle was built. That makes removing some of these panels extremely difficult when trying to duplicate factory methods. This problem manifests itself when I try to get the core support out of this car.

The bottom corners of the core support are tucked neatly between the layers of the forward cross member and the frame rails and so will be difficult to get out. To remove the core support, I use an air chisel to cut through and separate both corners from the frame rails. That frees the core support to come out and at the same time preserves the integrity of the frame rails. The welds on the fender aprons, on the other hand, are easily accessed, and both the front and the rear panels come out without a problem. But I'm still a step away from bringing out the die grinder and spot weld cutter. The core support has a couple of external hood-locking pin brackets that need to be dealt with.

To start, I measure the position of these brackets where they are mounted to the core support and transfer those measurements to the new core support. Once I know exactly where each bracket is to be mounted, I can drill out the spot welds and attach the brackets to the old panel using the Blair spot weld cutter, then transfer them to the new core support.

Finally, I am ready to begin removing the panels. As I did when removing the old floor pans, I start removal of the old panels by drilling out all accessible spot welds using the Blair spot weld removal tool. Any spot welds not accessible to the Blair spot weld removal tool are ground away using the die grinder and a 3-inch cutoff wheel, or they are left for the air chisel.

Can't find all the old spot welds? Difficult-to-locate spot welds can be found by sanding the weld area with a Norton 24-grit Speed-Lok disc on a drill. Each spot weld can then be marked to improve its visibility.

Once the old panels are out of the car, the spot welds can be cleaned up and ground smooth using the die grinder or mini grinder. Any areas not accessible to either of these tools will need to be cleaned of the old paint using a 24-grit Speed-Lok disc or 80-grit sandpaper.

TESTING THE FIT

The next step is to test the fit of the new panels. All three new panels are clamped into place and aligned. This is where all those measurements I took earlier become important. I start by measuring across the shock towers. This measurement ensures that the right shock tower hasn't moved and that the rear piece of the fender apron can be positioned exactly where it should be. I measure from the left rearmost fender mounting bolt to the center inboard shock tower bolt on the right side. That measurement should read 41½ inches, and it now measures 41⅞ inches. Next, I measure between the shock towers. That measurement should read 30½ inches, and it now measures 30½ inches.

Did it move? Usually, if a shock tower moves, it moves either inboard or outboard, never forward or backward, because that's where most of its strength is located. A shift inboard or outboard causes an incorrect measurement from the rearmost fender mount bolt to the shock tower bolt and affects the tower to tower cross measurement. If necessary, a cable puller or hydraulic jacking ram can be used to apply pressure to the tower to move it and hold it in position until the fender apron pieces can be welded solid.

Next, I measure the overall length of both fender apron pieces. In this case, the measurement should read 40¼ inches. This ensures that the length of the new fender apron is correct and all the fender attachment bolt holes will align with the corresponding bolt holes in the fender. Finally, the new panels are secured using either #8 sheet metal screws, blind holders, or Vise-Grip pliers.

DRILLING FOR SPOT WELDS

Now that I know everything fits, it is time to remove the sheet metal screws, blind holders, and Vise-Grips and take the new panels back off the car.

PHOTO 8: The spot welds around both fender apron pieces are cleaned and marked to identify where each one is located. After that, they can be drilled out.

PHOTO 9: The new parts are clamped into place for a test fit. What are the arrows for? These are two critical alignment points. The front fender apron piece must align with the both the strut tower and the lower frame rail with enough overlap to provide sufficient welding area.

With the new panels on the bench, I drill out the spot weld holes using a ⁵⁄₁₆-inch drill bit. I space each hole 2 inches apart around the perimeter of both fender apron pieces and across the bottom of the core support. I then scuff sand all three pieces using a Norton Bear-Tex Scuff Pad and apply 3M Weld-Thru coating # 5913 everywhere the panels will be spot welded.

SANDING MADE EASY

Now is a good time to sand the engine compartment. No, I didn't forget I was in the process of replacing the core support and right fender apron, but with more than half of the engine compartment removed, access to sanding the rest of the compartment is a lot easier. I start this process by cleaning the compartment using a strong degreasing cleaner, PPG DX 330 degreaser, and a power washer to remove any grease and grime; then I sand everything with 320-grit sandpaper. When that's done, I can go back to replacing sheet metal.

INSTALLING THE PANELS

With the remainder of the engine compartment thoroughly sanded and a tape measure in my pocket, I start putting the car back together beginning with the rear half of the fender apron. Using the sheet metal screws and blind holders to align the panel, I install the piece and once again check the necessary measurements. Once satisfied that the panel is where it should be, I spot weld it in place. While I still have good access to the engine compartment, I smooth the spot welds using a die grinder or mini grinder.

Next, I move to the front half of the fender apron. I secure the front apron piece using sheet metal screws and blind holders, then install the core support and secure it. Once again the measuring tape comes out, and I make a final check of all measurements. When I'm sure everything is in place and the engine compartment is as square as possible, the front apron piece and core support are welded.

Recall the problem with the core support lower corners being sandwiched inside the frame rails? Sometimes consideration for what is best for the vehicle must take

PHOTO 10: The lower corners of the core support are trimmed to fit around the frame rail. This eliminates the need to hack the frame rail apart. Once welded, this modification will not be noticeable.

precedence over installing parts in exactly the same manner as the factory did. In this case, I had the choice of hacking the frame rails apart to accommodate the core support or trimming the corners of the core support to butt against the rails and secure that joint by welding it solid. I elected to leave the frame rails intact and trim the core support. By carefully welding the corners and grinding the welds smooth, this modification will never be noticed.

NOTES

CHAPTER 9

PERFECTING

THE METAL

I spent a lot of time removing the old paint from the Mustang's body as I cleaned this car down to the bare metal. However, the plan does not call for converting this car into one of those stainless steel, void of a nice paint job rides. I need to perfect the body of this car and eventually put a shiny new green finish over all this bare metal.

Bare metal isn't a good state to leave this car in for another reason. Rust has a way of attacking any metal left in the raw, and the signs of surface rust are already beginning to show. The time has come to coat this car with something that will last as long as the car.

Before applying the initial epoxy coats to the car, the entire exterior surface needs to be sanded to perfect the metal. Next, I need to prepare the car for the epoxy coats by cleaning it, masking the areas I don't want to be oversprayed, and assembling the car. Only then can I apply the first coats of epoxy.

SAND THE METAL

I accomplished the bulk of the sheet metal alignment procedures back when the car was in one piece and still sported a shiny green finish. I also went around the car searching out all the dents I could find, marked them with a water pencil, and took them out using a body hammer and dolly. What I didn't try to do was perfect the metal. That's a little difficult with several layers of old paint and plastic body filler still on the car. Even though all that paint and body filler has now been removed from the car, perfecting the metal is still a difficult task because the metal has been left rough from the grinding process.

My first stop is at the toolbox to find an orbital palm sander and a few Norton 80-grit sanding discs. I'll sand every inch of the exterior of this car with the 80 grit to help smooth the metal and remove a lot of the deeper

PHOTO 1: Project Mustang in the raw. All of the old paint has been sanded off the body as it is being prepped for a coat of epoxy.

scratches caused by grinding away the old paint. This step will not only make the metal smoother, it will also make locating any imperfections that had once been filled with plastic body filler a little easier to find and repair.

Any dents I do find should be minor, since I didn't find any areas of thick body filler on the car when I removed the old paint. If the old filler is thin, less than

¼-inch thick, you don't have a problem. A little hammer and dolly work will easily improve on the metal's shape, and the addition of another thin layer of filler will perfect it.

I was lucky with this car; you might not be so lucky with yours. If you find an application of heavy body filler, up to ½ inch thick or more, on your car, this is the time to determine why that filler was applied so heavily. It could be as simple as laziness on the part of the previous body repair technician, or in a worst-case scenario, you may have found a panel that was damaged badly enough to need replacing but was instead reshaped using plastic body filler. Here is an example: photo 2 is a salvage Mustang door with a serious problem. Not all of the filler has been removed, but I have removed more than ¼ inch just reaching these telltale jerk tool bumps. What the heck is a jerk tool bump? This is actually a bump of stretched metal that occurs when the screw on the business end of a slide hammer is screwed into a pilot hole that was drilled into a dent and a little too much force is used to extract the dent.

If this door had been original to this Mustang, I wouldn't bother with removing any more filler. I'd call one of the suppliers listed in chapter 1 and order a replacement skin. In the long run, I would spend less time replacing the panel than I would spend repairing the old one, and I'd end up with a far better repair.

But just in case you are considering saving a panel in this condition, let's talk about what to do with those jerk tool bumps. If you find holes in a panel where a jerk tool was used and you don't plan to replace the panel, be sure to remove any body filler clogging the holes and weld the holes shut. Do not leave the holes filled with plastic body

PHOTO 2: The open jerk tool holes hiding beneath this heavy layer of plastic body filler is an open invitation to rust. These should have been welded shut before the filler was applied.

filler. Plastic body filler is porous and acts like a wick in the presence of moisture. This is an open invitation for rust to form under the filler.

After the jerk tool holes are welded shut, the actual repair can be improved upon using a body hammer and dolly to further work the metal. Or, if necessary, you can revert back to the jerk tool (slide hammer) in an attempt to get the panel smoother. Don't forget to weld shut any additional holes drilled into the panel.

APPLY THE FINISH COATS

With the car sanded somewhat smooth, it is time to apply the coats of finish. Having worked closely with my PPG representative for some time now, I've decided to make changes to the way I've always accomplished plastic body filler repairs. In the past, I would remove the old paint from vintage rides, do all of the necessary sheet metal repair work, then apply plastic body filler over the bare metal and follow that with at least three coats of primer/surfacer.

The change I'm making is primarily the result of research by PPG into rust prevention, in which a three-step process is used to accomplish sheet metal repairs. I start by completing all of the necessary sheet metal repairs, and then I apply two coats of epoxy primer over the bare metal. After that, I make any needed plastic body filler repairs, then apply a final coat of epoxy primer over the filler. In effect, I sandwich all of the plastic body filler between two layers of epoxy primer. The result should be a rustproof substrate over which to apply the rest of the finish.

Notice I didn't say anything about applying an etching primer. Etching primers are not recommended for vintage rides requiring any type of panel repair using plastic body filler. Etching primers are designed for use on new bare metal panels that will not require any additional repairs.

Before I start applying the epoxy, I need to prepare the car. This means cleaning the car, masking it off, and reassembling it.

CLEANING THE CAR

The first step in this application is to clean the car inside and out. Since the car is basically a bare steel vehicle, no water will be involved. I blow the car clean using an air hose and finish the job by wiping the car down with PPG DX 330 Acryli-Clean degreaser.

I soak a clean shop towel in DX 330 and clean and dry the car one panel at a time. After each panel is cleaned and before moving onto the next panel, I remove the DX 330 residue using another clean shop towel to dry the panel. The bulk of the interior, engine compartment, and trunk area can be skipped, but I clean around all of the openings in these areas.

Why bother to clean the openings? Since I'll be applying the first layer of epoxy to the exterior only, I'll need to do some masking to prevent overspraying onto the areas I'm not going to spray. Having all of the openings clean will help the masking tape stick.

Masking Tricks

To mask an opening such as the trunk compartment, imagine yourself inside the compartment looking out. Using a roll of 1½-inch-wide masking tape, mask around the edges of the opening, leaving half the width of the tape exposed in the opening.

Now imagine yourself on the outside of the compartment looking in. Half the width of the 1½-inch wide masking tape should be visible. This will form the base for masking the entire opening. Next, use ¾-inch-wide masking tape to make a 12 x 12–inch grid in the opening. This will help support the masking paper. Cover the entire trunk opening with masking paper, taking care to seal all the edges and all the areas where the masking paper overlaps another sheet of masking paper.

This masking method can be used to close any opening on the vehicle, but in this case, I'm not bothering to completely close the interior compartment. Instead, I apply masking paper to the dash and rear package tray to prevent overspray from settling in those areas. After I temporarily install the doors, fenders, and hood, I'll take a little more time to mask around those items to eliminate overspraying the back of the panels.

Assembling the Car

Before spraying the epoxy, I need to assemble the car. I need to install the doors, the hood, the fenders, the deck lid, and the quarter panel extensions. To hang the doors, I need to reinstall the hinges.

Why do I want to assemble the car before I spray it? Although as a rule I never assemble a car to paint it, in this case, where the objective is to reach a point where I can complete the body repair work, putting the car back together is the best way to achieve that goal. Besides, I

PHOTO 3: To mask an opening, begin with an application of 1½-inch-wide tape around the perimeter, leaving half the width of the tape exposed in the opening. Then ¾-inch-wide masking tape is used to grid the opening.

PHOTO 4: The end result. This method can be used to close any opening on the vehicle.

want to give you an idea of how to spray a complete car in the event you are considering just making your vehicle look better without doing a total restoration.

Applying the Epoxy Primer

I will be applying two coats of PPG DP74LF Epoxy Primer to the exterior panels only. The color of this coat is the same red oxide color you would expect to find if you sanded through the paint on any unrestored Mustang, so that is going to help maintain the originality of this car.

Why apply epoxy to the exterior panels only? At this point in the restoration, I'm concentrating on filling and smoothing the dents and bumps on this car. I'll have plenty of time later to coat the rest of this car with epoxy.

DP74LF Epoxy Primer can be applied over just about any surface, from sanded bare steel to sanded and prepped aluminum, sanded fiberglass, e-coated metal, original finishes, primer/surfacers, most types of fillers, and just about everything else you could safely put on a

PHOTO 5: Spraying begins at the right windshield post and moves across the roof panel.

PHOTO 6: Spraying continues by coating the left side of the roof and the rear of the vehicle before moving back to the right side.

PHOTO 7: Fifty percent spray pass overlap is achieved by overlapping the previous pass by half.

vehicle. However, you cannot put DP74LF Epoxy Primer over products such as PPG DPX 170/171 wash/self-etching primers. Remember I said to forget the etching primers? This is another reason.

PPG DP74LF Epoxy Primer mixes 2:1 with DP 402LF Catalyst. I apply two wet coats using the Binks M1-G, allowing 10 to 15 minutes between coats, and then I allow the second coat to cure overnight

So where's a good place to start applying the epoxy coats? Ask five different painters where to start spraying, and more than likely you will get five different answers. However, the one thing all painters have in common is that they like to start painting in an area that reduces the chances of leaving a dry paint line. What's a dry paint line? If you look at the mixing ratio of DP74LF, you'll see it uses only two components, epoxy and a catalyst; no reducer is used. The absence of a reducer in the mix means the paint film will dry quickly. So if I began my first spray pass near the center of the roof, for example, and work outward, the first pass I made would be dry long before I could finish the near side of the roof and move to the other side and continue. The result would be a very rough line of paint down the middle of the roof panel, where wet paint was sprayed over dry paint. That's leaving a dry paint line. To avoid this problem, I begin spraying at the right windshield post, then work my way across the roof to the center. I stop, spray both the windshield and back glass opening channels on that side of the car, and finish by spraying the sail panel.

Next, I move to the other side of the car and pick up where I left off, spraying near the center of the roof. I continue across the roof, spray the glass opening channels, and move down the sail panel.

From there, I move to the rear of the car and spray the package tray panel, the tops of both quarter panels, and down the rear body panel. Note: The deck lid will be sprayed separately.

Next, I move to the right side of the car and make the first spray pass starting at the quarter panel and moving all the way to the front of the car before stopping and making the next spray pass using a 50 percent overlap. This method of spraying eliminates the problem of panel-to-panel overlap.

How much is a 50 percent overlap? It's simply overlapping the previous spray pass by half. In other words, if the first spray pass is laid down half on the panel and half into thin air, the second pass is sprayed covering half the

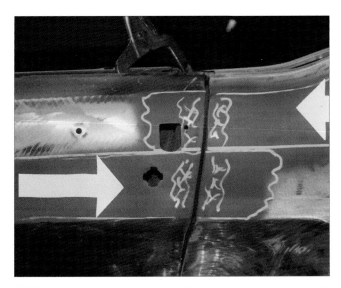

PHOTO 8: Panel-to-panel overlap is caused by spraying each panel individually and overlapping onto the adjacent panel.

PHOTO 9: The first coat is complete when the left side of the car is sprayed.

coverage of the first pass and half onto clean metal. The third pass would begin at the bottom of the first pass, covering the lower half of the second pass and half onto clean metal. So every time a spray pass is made, only 50 percent of the pass is made onto clean material. The other 50 percent is sprayed over the previous pass.

What is panel-to-panel overlap? If you spray the quarter panel, paint is overlapped onto the door in order to get proper coverage on the quarter panel. Moving on to spray the door, paint is overlapped back onto the quarter panel in order to achieve proper coverage on the door. The result is a 4- to 5-inch-wide strip on both panels that receives double the recommended coats of finish. This might not be a problem when you're spraying primer or some extremely opaque color, but it can become a real problem if you're spraying a transparent color such as a pearl or a candy color. The result could be a vertical stripe of darker color everywhere one panel meets another. The 50 percent method eliminates the panel-to-panel overlap problem.

After the right side of the car is sprayed, I move to the front and spray the cowl, the tops of both fenders, and the hood. From there, it is down the left side to complete the first coat. I repeat the process 15 minutes later because I need two coats for my initial layer of epoxy.

You will notice that I stopped spraying everywhere a horizontal panel meets a vertical panel and vice versa. This method all but eliminates the chances of leaving a dry paint line anywhere on the car.

You may also be wondering why I didn't bother to apply epoxy to the interior, the inside of the fenders, or the underside of the hood. The interior is being left until I can roll the car over and finish welding in the floor pans. The underside of the hood and fenders are being left for later because it simplifies the process of getting epoxy on the exterior of the car. When I'm ready to spray the interior, I'll also spray the insides of these other panels. Note: If humidity is a problem in your area, you will need to apply epoxy to the above-mentioned parts before assembling the car to prevent surface rust.

CHAPTER 10

WORKING WITH
PLASTIC BODY FILLER

The first and second coats of epoxy are on the exterior of the car, and although I had to be pulled kicking and screaming into the new era of epoxy first, then body filler, I'm already beginning to appreciate the change. The shiny red coat of epoxy has allowed me to discover problems with the metal that might not have otherwise been found until after the car had been primed and block sanded.

Reaching this stage in the restoration also signals a momentous turning point in that I am now moving out of the major surgery phase and entering into the cosmetic reparation stage—soon to be followed by the recovery phase, when the project gets a great new look. But, alas, a new look for this car is still some distance down the road. Right now, this Mustang needs the epoxy coats to be sanded, the body filler to be applied, and any broken edges of paint to be removed.

SAND THE EPOXY

PPG DP74LF Epoxy Primer has a seven-day recoat window within which I can apply additional products over the epoxy without having to sand the coat. But it has been more than a week since the two coats of epoxy were applied to the car, so my first step will be to scuff sand the exterior body panels using 180-grit sandpaper. That will give the surface a good bite to ensure that the plastic body filler will adhere. Would I apply filler over the epoxy without sanding had I been within the seven-day recoat window? I doubt it. Sanding the car takes very little time and should be considered cheap filler adhesion insurance for a skeptical mind.

I fold a sheet of 180-grit sandpaper in half and use that to gently sand the car by hand. I don't use a sanding block because it cannot conform to the lines and curves of each panel, which could result in the epoxy being sanded through in various places, exposing the bare

PHOTO 1: A clean shop towel is used as a buffer between my hand and the surface of the metal to better feel the bumps and dents on the panel.

metal beneath. Because the plan calls for applying the plastic body filler over a continuous layer of epoxy, the last thing I need is a spot of bare metal.

After I finish sanding, I use a trick I've employed many times in the past. I use a clean shop towel as a buffer between my hand and the surface of the panel to

PHOTO 2: Every imperfection is marked to be sure none are missed when I begin applying the plastic body filler.

help gain a better feel for the panel to aid in locating all of the dents and dings. Once located, each imperfection is marked using a water pencil and will later be filled in with plastic body filler.

Why bother going over the car again looking for and marking all those imperfections? It's worth it if for no other reason than this car will be painted a dark green. The deeper and darker the finish, the more the imperfections on the surface will show.

A LITTLE FILLER

My choice for plastic body filler is Evercoat Rage #106. This is a premium filler that goes on smooth, sands easily, and creates fewer pinholes than most other plastic body fillers. Once I have the plastic body filler applied and sanded smooth, I'll follow that application with a skim coat of polyester glazing compound Evercoat Metal Glaze #416. This is a very thin and creamy filler designed to fill sand scratches, take care of minor imperfections, and—for what I primarily use it for—to act as a final smoothing coat over the plastic body filler.

Plastic body filler can't just be slopped out of the can and applied. It must be prepared, mixed correctly, and then applied. After that, it is on to sanding using 40-grit and 80-grit sandpaper.

PREPARING THE FILLER

Every can of plastic body filler should be shaken or stirred thoroughly before each use. Plastic body filler is made up of a lot of compounds, but the one that keeps it creamy enough for a smooth application is a liquid resin. As the can sits, the denser compounds tend to sink and the lighter resin tends to pool at the top of the can. If the can isn't stirred or shaken before every use, the consistency will not be even throughout the can.

The filler must also be catalyzed using a cream hardener, and the rule is to apply a 1-inch ribbon of hardener to every one to two golf ball–size clumps of filler. To do the actual mixing, I scoop filler onto a 12 x 12-inch-square metal mixing board, add the hardener, and use a plastic applicator to fold the hardener into the filler until the color is consistent throughout. Once the hardener has been added to the filler, the clock starts ticking. On a hot day, the filler will begin to set up within minutes of being mixed. On a cool day, the clock slows, and it can take as long as five minutes before the filler begins to set up.

To get the filler on the panel, I use the same plastic applicator used to mix the filler and apply a smooth, thin coat of filler over the entire repair area. Remember that the heavier and the sloppier the filler is applied, the more sanding will be required to smooth the surface.

SANDING THE FILLER

How do you know that the filler has cured and is ready to sand? If the filler was mixed properly, the surface will dry and turn white if scratched. If the filler wasn't mixed properly, the surface will remain soft and tacky, in which case it should be removed and then reapplied.

The rule for block sanding any panel is to use the longest sanding block possible (see chapter 11 for tips on choosing the right size sanding block) and to always sand in an X pattern. For example, working with a 16-inch-long sanding block using 40-grit sandpaper, I begin the first sanding stroke near the top rear, or upper left corner, of the panel and sand diagonally down and across the panel to the lower right corner of the repair. This technique is used until the entire surface of the filler has been sanded at least once. The process is then reversed as I switch sides and sand in the opposite direction, moving from the

> **TIP**
>
> *I keep a spray bottle of lacquer thinner on the bench to clean the plastic body filler mixing board and plastic applicator after each application.*

upper right corner diagonally across the repair to the lower left corner.

If you have ever sharpened a knife, you know the correct procedure is to move the blade across the whetstone in one direction a number of times, then reverse the process and move the blade over the whetstone in the opposite direction the same number of times. This pattern is repeated, decreasing the number of times the blade is moved across the whetstone until the blade is moved across the whetstone only one time in either direction. This method balances the blade and produces a very sharp edge with which to work. Block sanding uses the same process. I don't suggest trying to count each sanding stroke, but do try to balance the number of strokes made in either direction. The result will be a nice smooth surface.

To get the surface smooth, selecting the right sandpaper is critical. I always begin sanding plastic body filler using 40-grit sandpaper because it cuts through the filler quickly and produces an extremely level surface.

Got a curved surface in need of sanding? The fenders on the Mustang have a complicated double-curved wheel opening that can be easily sanded flat if you aren't careful. The curve rolls sharply inboard just beneath the upper body line, then gently rolls outward as it forms the wheel opening. To maintain the integrity of this curve, the sanding block must follow the roll of the curve as well as follow the length of the curve.

Sound confusing? The shape of the Mustang fenders is similar to the shape of an egg. Now imagine cutting that egg in half lengthwise and laying it cut-side down on a flat square surface. With the egg on the square in front of you, begin sanding it starting at a point closest to you and sanding up and over the egg to end the stroke at the farthermost point away from you. Each stroke after that would begin just to the right of the previous stroke and move up and over the egg to end just to the left of the last stroke. This is an extended and narrow X pattern, but an X pattern nevertheless.

So which block is best for sanding curved surfaces? I start with a 5-inch block to achieve the correct shape of the curve, and if possible I follow up with an 8-inch block and use an extremely elongated sanding stroke to prevent the flattening effect shorter blocks tend to produce. If the 8-inch block is too long to be effective, stick with the 5-inch block. If the 5-inch block is too much block to form the deep curve, try making your own block out of a short

PHOTO 3: The first half of the X sanding pattern. The block is worked diagonally across the repair, beginning near the top left corner and sanding down toward the lower right corner.

PHOTO 4: The second half of the X sanding pattern. The block is again worked diagonally across the repair, beginning near the top right corner and sanding down toward the lower left corner.

TIP

I've watched body technicians use 40 grit until all of the grit was gone and there was nothing left but the paper. I'm frugal, but sandpaper lasts only so long. After it becomes worn, its ability to cut is greatly diminished; and once its ability to cut is gone, all you are doing is polishing the surface. Sanding with 40 grit has one purpose: to plow through the layer of plastic body filler and level the surface. If it can't plow through the layer, it can't level the surface. Once the sandpaper quits cutting, toss it in the trash. It has served its purpose.

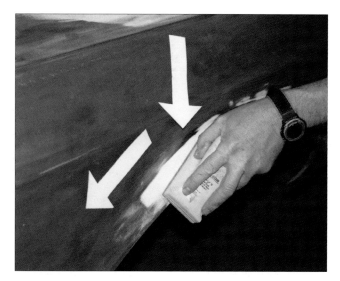

PHOTO 5: Even a curved surface must be sanded using the X pattern of sanding. Here, a 5-inch block is used to sand this wheel opening.

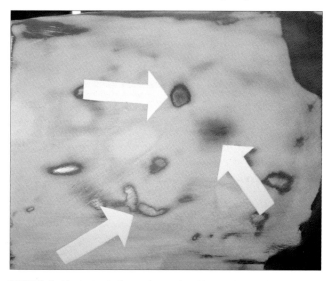

PHOTO 6: Problem areas in the repair must be addressed by applying more filler or tapping down the high spots, applying additional epoxy, and then applying more filler.

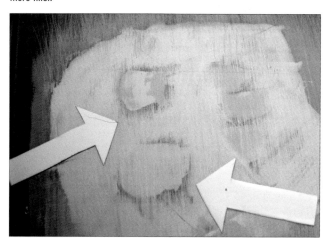

PHOTO 7: Proof that this repair isn't as smooth as could be are in the rings of guide coat left behind. Coating the entire repair with Evercoat Metal Glaze #416 is the best way to perfect the surface of this repair.

length of 1 x 2–inch wood stock. If you are having trouble maintaining or shaping the depth of the curve, try wrapping the sandpaper around a short length of ¾-inch heater hose. But no matter what type of block you end up using, always maintain the X pattern of sanding. It is the only way to achieve a perfectly level surface and maintain a highly curved surface.

BACK TO THE PANELS

Once the surface has been sanded with 40 grit, it is time to move to 80 grit. Sanding the repair with 80 grit accomplishes a couple of things. First, it removes the majority of the deeper sand scratches caused by the 40-grit sandpaper; and second, it refines the surface to help give a better feel for how smooth the repair has become.

But before I bring out the 80-grit sandpaper, I want to apply a guide coat of flat black spray-can lacquer over the repair. A guide coat is going to highlight any problem areas such as deep sand scratches, pinholes, and low spots once I sand the repair with 80 grit. As photo 6 shows, after sanding with 80 grit, a low spot was found on the right side of the repair, evidenced by the dark guide coat left on the surface. That's an easily repaired problem. A little Evercoat Metal Glaze #416 will make short work of the spot. Mix Metal Glaze the same way plastic body filler is mixed, but apply Metal Glaze to the low spots only. Once cured, sand with 80 grit until smooth.

Of course, low spots and sand scratches aren't the only problems encountered when finish sanding a repair with 80 grit. The problems not so easily repaired are the several areas of exposed metal also visible on the repair. Since the exposed bumps of metal are obvious high spots, the first step is to carefully tap each one down using a body hammer. Next, the areas of bare metal must be spot coated with additional epoxy. This is the only way to preserve the integrity of the sandwiching effect I want to achieve with the epoxy and plastic body filler. No need for a dramatic production; just blow the repair clean with an air hose, wipe it down with DX 330, and cover the spots with a coat of epoxy.

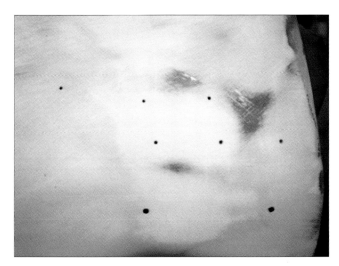

PHOTO 8: No, these aren't worm holes. Plastic body filler tends to fill molding attachment holes. Those holes must be cleared of filler before the repair is primed.

PHOTO 9: One of the problems encountered when applying plastic body filler over a layer of epoxy is that the layer often gets sanded off.

At this point, I don't want to go back to Evercoat Rage because that would force me once again to sand the repair with 40-grit sandpaper. I want to avoid the 40 grit because it has a tendency to remove too much filler. So instead, I use Evercoat Metal Glaze to put a thin patch over the repairs; once it has cured, I'll block sand the patches with 80 grit.

I stated earlier that the addition of a skim coat of Evercoat Metal Glaze over the entire repair helps fill the deeper sand scratches and pinholes as well as provides an extremely smooth surface over which to prime. How does that work? Consider that you have repaired an area using plastic body filler and needed to apply additional filler to a number of problem areas as I just did. The problem areas were repaired and filled using Metal Glaze, and a guide coat was applied. The Metal Glaze was then block sanded smooth using 80 grit. In photo 7, notice that the rings of guide coat were left behind after block sanding the repair smooth. Where did those come from?

When small patches of filler are sanded, the block can't help but sand some of the surrounding filler. The problems come because the patch of filler is higher than the surrounding filler and the block must ride up and over the patch as it sands. That tends to leave a very small area of unsanded filler around the edges of the patch. So although the sanded patch feels smooth in comparison with the surrounding filler, in reality it may not be. It may still be slightly high, a condition additional block sanding may not correct. So what's the cure? Make all additional repairs required, then skim coat the entire repair using Evercoat Metal Glaze and block sand that coat with 80

grit using the same X pattern technique used to block sand the plastic body filler.

Recall the shop towel trick used earlier? Now that all of the plastic body filler repairs have been completed, this will be the last opportunity to check the plastic body filler work before priming the car. It is better to find a wave or bump now than to find it after the primer has been applied.

One final little detail to attend to with this repair is to clear all the molding and nameplate attachment holes of filler. The backside of this panel has a number of filler worms clinging to it. Everywhere a filler worm clings to the panel is a hole. I locate all the worms, remove them, then either drill out the holes or gently punch them out with an awl.

REMOVE THE BROKEN PAINT EDGES

All of this block sanding has resulted in two things. First, the body of this car is about as perfect as it is going to get, and second, the course grit of the sandpapers I've been using have cut right through some of the epoxy previously applied.

In photo 9, you can see that I've sanded through the epoxy and left a ring of bare metal around this repair. You can also see traces of epoxy around the edges of the filler, which means no filler is touching bare metal. It still rides on a layer of epoxy. That's good. I can seal this repair with a final layer of epoxy to complete my sandwich.

But what I don't want to do is apply that last layer of epoxy over the broken edges of the previous layer. I need to feather back all those broken edges using a palm sander, or handheld orbital sander, with 180-grit sandpaper attached to leave a nice smooth surface over which to apply the final coat of epoxy.

Who cares if a few broken paint edges are left behind? All refinishing products have at least some solvents in them. Those solvents are likely to attack the raw, exposed edges of a previously applied coat of finish and penetrate under them. Once the solvents have made their way under the layer, they can cause that layer of finish to lift. In extreme cases, solvent penetration can actually cause a layer of finish to bubble up and wrinkle. If you have spray painted before, you've probably seen this problem. If you've never seen this problem and would like to, try spraying a test panel with enamel, lightly sand it, then cover it with lacquer. Wait a few minutes, and you'll get a prime example.

So the next step is to use the palm sander with 180-grit sandpaper to remove all of those raw paint edges that were left everywhere I applied plastic body filler. Caution! Do not sand the plastic body filler. You've just spent several hours perfecting the repair. Don't ruin it by passing an orbital sander over it.

How can an orbital sander ruin plastic body filler? The tool sands in an orbital direction, which tends to erode and soften the edges of the filler, whereas a block can sand only in a straight line and will not erode the edges of the filler. The result is that a block tends to leave a flatter surface than does the orbital sander.

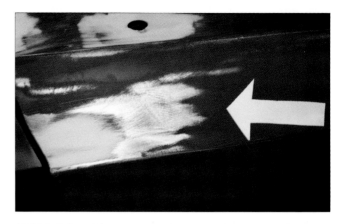

PHOTO 10: Before adding more epoxy, the broken and rough edges of the previous epoxy coat are smoothed using a palm sander and 180-grit sandpaper.

I know it's a bumpy and rough project vehicle when almost every inch of that vehicle requires at least a little plastic body filler repair. I also know I've only touched on a couple of problem areas. But these should be typical to repairing most any panel on a vehicle.

Speed when applying the epoxy and the filler and when sanding the vehicle is not of the essence here. Repairing the two panels shown here required roughly six hours to complete. I still have the rest of the car left to repair. The point is this: don't hurry, don't become frustrated, and, by all means, don't keep pushing when you are tired. The vehicle isn't going anywhere. Of course, everything you did yesterday should be rechecked today, just to be sure. When everything is right with the filler and the panel surfaces are smooth, apply that final coat of epoxy.

NOTES

CHAPTER 11

PRIMING AND
SANDING

The whole idea behind prepping this car for paint was to first remove all visible damage such as the bumps, dents, ripples, and waves and return each panel back to its original condition. That was accomplished previously, with a lot of filling and sanding. The addition of a layer of primer/surfacer over my epoxy-filler-epoxy sandwich isn't going to make much difference to, or dramatically improve upon, the condition of the surface as it now exists.

So if the panel doesn't feel "right" at this point, before the primer coats are applied, it isn't going to feel any more right after block sanding the primer because the problem doesn't lie in the primer coat; it lies somewhere underneath. If that thought makes you uneasy about the condition of your project vehicle at this point, this might be a good time to consider revisiting a little plastic body filler before some minor problem grows into a big shiny problem after the car is painted.

If you are satisfied with the look and feel of your car, it's time to move on to the next steps: applying the coats of primer and doing a lot of block sanding.

A LITTLE PRIMER, PLEASE

The primer/surfacer I selected is PPG Global 2K–Chromatic Surfacer D8005. This is a 2K, or catalyzed primer/surfacer, meaning it will cure only once the hardener has been added. It offers an optimum film build of 1.5 mm per coat when dry as well as a quick cure time. In a "have-to" situation, D8005 can be sanded after 1½ hours of drying time at 70 degrees F. My preference is to allow the primer to cure overnight before sanding.

D8005 mixes 4:1:1, 4 parts D8005 to 1 part D8291 hardener to 1 part D872 reducer. Note: D872 reducer is rated for use at temperatures ranging between 77 and 95 degrees F. Reducers rated for use at other temperatures are also available and should be used when required.

PPG recommends spraying D8005 with an HVLP spray gun, using either a 1.6 or 1.8 mm spray tip. I use the Binks M1-G HVLP spray gun with a 1.4 mm tip at 22 psi and add an extra ½ part D872 reducer to help achieve a better flow. Why the smaller tip size? I think it provides a smoother application.

D8005 can be applied over sanded OEM paint, new e-coated panels, properly treated and sanded aluminum, sanded bare steel, sanded galvanized steel, polyester body filler, fiberglass, and sheet molded compound (SMC). Note: Because I'm applying D8005 over a fresh coat of DP74LF epoxy primer, sanding is not required. The DPLF Product Usage Sheets state this product can be top coated up to one week after application without sanding. After one week, DPLF must be sanded prior to being top coated.

APPLY THE PRIMER

The car is still assembled, so the primer application will follow the same procedure I used when applying the epoxy coats. I begin spraying at the right windshield post, move across the roof panel, spray the rear body and the left side, then move to the front and spray both the hood and the cowl screen panel before finishing with the right side. I apply two coats of primer and allow 5 to 10 minutes between coats.

I'm applying only two coats of primer at this time because I want the opportunity to recheck my work before moving on to the color application stage. To do that, I am going to apply two initial coats of D8005 primer/surfacer, block sand those coats with 180-grit sandpaper, and repair any imperfections I find. At this point, an imperfection is defined as a pinhole or a deep scratch. Either can be repaired by filling the imperfection with Metal Glaze and sanding it smooth using 180-grit sandpaper. Once I am satisfied that everything is perfect, I apply two additional coats of D8005 primer/surfacer and complete the block sanding process using 320-grit sandpaper.

The idea behind using this method is that the 180 grit quickly cuts through the layers of primer/surfacer to expose any problem areas and at the same time leaves the bulk of the surface level and smooth. How? Consider what happens when block sanding plastic body filler with 40-grit sandpaper. The 40-grit sandpaper quickly cuts through the filler to level and smooth the surface of the repair. Any problems such as bumps or low spots are quickly exposed so they can be repaired. Once repaired, the entire surface is skim coated with Metal Glaze and sanded smooth with 180-grit sandpaper. The same process applies to the primer and sanding. Beginning the primer coat sanding process using 180-grit sandpaper is just another way to begin perfecting the surface while at the same time helping quickly locate any minute imperfections that might still remain on the surface.

SAND THE PRIMER

In case this is your first bout with block sanding a primed vehicle, let me warn you: everything within 300 feet of the vehicle will get covered with primer dust. That includes you, the shop, everything in the shop, everything outside the shop, and even the road leading to the shop. It can't be helped, and no, do not attempt to prevent the impending dust storm by wet sanding the vehicle. This primer sands best when sanded dry, and besides, portions of this car are still in the bare metal stage, and water is the last thing you need collecting on the raw metal.

If this is your first time sanding, here is information on how to choose the correct size sanding block and the correct respirator for the job. I also provide you with great techniques and tips to achieve the proper sanding procedure and instruct you on how to correct problem areas of the car.

Choosing a Sanding Block

Which block is the right block? Photo 2 shows an assortment of blocks that are useful when block sanding primer/surfacer. They range in style and size from round to flat to short to long. The question of how to determine which block works best for a particular sanding job is best answered by determining the size and shape of the area being sanded. If the area being sanded is highly contoured, then a round block may be the best choice. If the area being sanded is mostly flat, then the longest, flattest block available is the best choice. If the area being sanded is somewhat flat with mild contours, start with a long flat block, graduate down to a short flat block, and finish with a small round block. Just don't try to block sand a large surface with a block that seems small in comparison with the surface being sanded. It won't come out as smooth as might be desired.

Choosing a Respirator

With a sanding block in hand, the next step is to find the correct respirator to keep from breathing in all that dust you're about to create. If you are looking for some serious protection, try an elastomeric respirator like the 3M 7183 unit. This respirator is approved by the National Institute for Occupational Safety and Health (NIOSH) for sanding, welding, grinding, and polishing, and it incorporates a comfortable head harness to hold the mask securely on your face. The unit comes with a gray body and pink filter cartridges, which makes it easily distinguishable from any other respirator that might be around the shop. When not in use, I store the respirator in an airtight plastic bag. I also replace the disposable filter cartridges after 40 hours of use.

For a little less serious protection, I prefer the 3M 7185 maintenance-free particulate dust mask. This is a double-strap fiber mask that is NIOSH approved for use when sanding or polishing a car or when cleaning the shop. If you can't find the 3M brand, look for a mask with an N95 label on the exhaust port located on the front of the mask. This designation means the mask filters out 95 percent of all solids and liquids in the air, excluding oils and painting products. I use this type of mask for one day and toss it.

SANDING THE PRIMER

Now that I have primed the car, selected the right sanding block, have the correct grit of sandpaper stuck to that block, and can breathe safely, the next step is to spray a light guide coat of flat black aerosol lacquer over the primer/surfacer. While the lacquer is drying, I'll remove the fenders, doors, and hood to reduce this car back down to a shell. Why go to that trouble? Doors and fenders sand more easily when perched on a bench than they do hanging off the sides of a car; the hood sands more easily when you don't have to stretch to reach it.

To sand the primer, use Norton 180-grit rolled sandpaper on a sanding block. Use the longest block possible combined with the longest strokes possible, and always adhere to the X pattern of sanding. To keep all that dust from clogging the sandpaper, keep a soft-bristled brush handy, and use it occasionally to clean the sandpaper as you work.

At this point in the process, I'm concerned more about using the right techniques and achieving the correct results than I am about anything else. I've already spent time explaining the techniques of block sanding primer, including the use of the longest sanding block possible and maintaining the X pattern of sanding, so let's talk about results.

You will notice in photo 4, after block sanding this quarter panel with 180-grit sandpaper, a great deal of the initial layer of primer/surfacer has been removed, and several areas of red epoxy primer have been exposed. This isn't cause for alarm. I knew sanding a mere two coats of primer/surfacer with 180-grit sandpaper would result in most of the primer/surfacer being removed. My real concern here was to be sure the layer of epoxy was not breached. So the moment I sanded through the primer/surfacer and exposed the red epoxy underneath, I knew it was time to stop sanding in that area and move on. This could be compared to trying to scrape the white icing off of a chocolate cake without touching the cake itself. Any low spots on the top of the cake will stay pooled with icing, and you will end up with a brown and white cake.

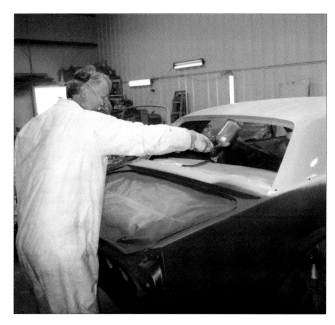

PHOTO 1: Each coat starts at the right windshield post; moves to the roof panel, over the rear of the car, to the left side, and to the front; and finishes with the right side.

PHOTO 2: An assortment of sanding blocks: 1-inch round, 1 x 2 x 3–inch rectangular, 5-inch block, 8-inch block, and 16-inch block.

PHOTO 3: Two 3M respirators for use when block sanding primer: (left) 3M #7185 Particulate Respirator and (right) 3M #7183 Half-Face Elastomeric Respirator.

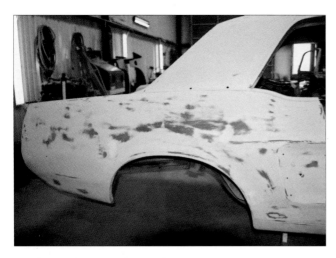

PHOTO 4: Sanding the car with 180-grit sandpaper makes short work of the two coats of primer/surfacer. The exposed red epoxy indicates that very little primer/surfacer is left on the car.

PHOTO 5: Once again, a shop towel is used as a buffer between my hand and the surface of the panel to help locate any existing imperfections.

PHOTO 6: This ring of exposed epoxy indicates a low spot. How? Had this area been flat, the epoxy would not have been exposed, and the primer inside this ring would have been sanded.

If you ignore the strange coloring, you will find the end result to be a very smooth cake over which you can apply a bakery slick icing for a show-winning finish. Isn't that the purpose here, to achieve a show-winning finish?

So in effect, when you start block sanding the primer, the guide coat is telling you to keep sanding while the red epoxy coat is telling you to stop sanding. Sound confusing? Keep reading. The fog will lift.

What am I doing with the shop towel in photo 5? You guessed it. During the sanding process, I uncovered several suspicious-looking spots where the "cake" showed through and the "icing" remained thick. I'm using my hand to tell me if any of these spots are severe enough to be felt or if they are as I suspect and extremely minor.

What made these spots suspect? Photo 6 shows an example. The exposed epoxy almost forms a ring around this small area of primer. If this area were perfectly level and smooth, this ring would not be here because more than likely I would not have sanded through the primer/surfacer to expose the epoxy coat beneath. All indications are that inside this ring lies a very minor low spot.

Photo 7 shows another, more obvious, problem. This small area of unsanded primer/surfacer indicates a definite low spot. This spot is rough to the touch, a sure sign that the block is not sanding this area.

How do you repair these problems? Photo 8 shows the hood of the car. Block sanding exposed a low area just behind the hood grille opening. I corrected the problem by adding a very thin layer of Evercoat Metal Glaze and block sanding it smooth using 180 grit. I was careful to concentrate my sanding efforts on the Metal Glaze filler and not on the exposed epoxy. What if the layer of epoxy had been breached and bare metal was exposed? Refer to the previous chapter and apply more epoxy.

That's really the nuts and bolts of sanding the first two coats of D8005 with 180 grit. I improved on the surface of every panel by filling in the deeper sand scratches with primer/surfacer and by bringing to light a few problem areas that otherwise might not have been found. All the problems shown above were repaired by filling them with a thin layer of Evercoat Metal Glaze and block sanding each one smooth in order to make the car ready for the final two coats of primer/surfacer.

SANDING TIPS

Here are a few tips to help with the sanding process. First, where do you start sanding this car with 180 grit? That has to be on the roof. This panel is going to be covered with a vinyl top, so I can use it as a tutorial to let me know how aggressively I can sand the rest of the body without compromising the red epoxy coat beneath. I sand with a 16-inch-long block over most of the surface, and switch to a 5-inch block when I reach the rolled edges of the panel. I know almost instantly how many sanding strokes it takes to reach the epoxy coat and how much sanding pressure each stroke can take—which brings to mind another good tip.

Novice body technicians often don't realize they tend to bear down on the sanding block as they sand. In the case of body filler, the brain quickly learns that the harder you press, the more body filler is removed, and the quicker an unpleasant task is finished. Most often that's not a problem because the block itself acts as a fail-safe device to prevent the filler from being gouged out in any one area. However, at this stage in the process, it's those small areas where the technician might have, knowingly or unknowingly, borne down a little too hard to sand a minute low spot of primer/surfacer that comes to the forefront.

Let's take the low spot in photo 6, for example. How do I know this area is low? The exposed epoxy almost forms a ring around the unsanded primer. It wasn't found previously possibly because I may have borne down too much on the block as I sanded the body filler. That could have forced the block to sand an area that was already too low. Or possibly it was because the low spot was so small that no matter what I did I wasn't going to find it until after the panel had been primed. I find it at this point only because I understand that blocking primer isn't like blocking body filler. I use medium to heavy pressure to block sand plastic body filler to cut through the harder surface. I use medium to light pressure to sand primer/surfacer because it is a softer substrate than plastic body filler, and my intent is to sand only until the guide coat has been removed; at that point, all sanding in that area stops. It is only then that problems like this come to light.

The problems mentioned above are pretty straight-forward. Photo 9 shows a problem that was never going to be found until a coat of primer/surfacer was applied to highlight it. It is a crack in the fiberglass deck lid that runs along the length of the spoiler, the exact direction that part of the spoiler would be sanded. Sanding would have filled this crack with residue, and the chances of finding it again, before the car was painted, would have been

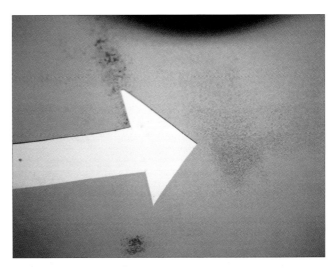

PHOTO 7: **A very obvious low spot, as indicated by the area of primer that has not been sanded.**

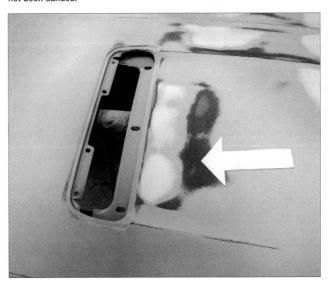

PHOTO 8: **Problem areas such as this low spot and the ones shown in photos 6 and 7 are corrected by applying a thin layer of Evercoat Metal Glaze and block sanding the filler smooth.**

PHOTO 9: **The top of the deck lid spoiler has a tiny crack running along its length. I could have easily missed this crack by filling it with primer dust.**

almost zero. Luckily, I found it, and the only recourse now is to grind a V along the length of the crack and fill the void with structural adhesive. This is the same product I used to repair the deck lid and quarter extensions. Once cured, the adhesive can be sanded using 180-grit sandpaper and primed.

So the bottom line is to treat primer/surface with kid gloves. Sand it lightly, and be prepared to uncover and repair problem areas. This is one of the keys to getting the body of any project as straight and smooth as possible.

APPLY THE NEXT COATS OF PRIMER

Before applying the next coats of primer, I take a little extra time to really clean the surface of the car. Residue from the initial sanding is everywhere. I use the air hose to blow the car clean, and then I soak a clean shop towel with PPG DX 330 to wipe the panels clean, and I remove any remaining residue with a clean, dry shop towel.

Now that the surfaces are smooth and clean, it is time to mix up a second batch of D8005 and make two more trips around the car with the spray gun. I'm not going to reinstall the doors, fenders, or hood on the car yet, so they will be sprayed on the bench.

After the primer is dry, I block sand the car again. I apply a guide coat of black that requires only a light sanding. I carefully block sand each panel until the guide coat of black lacquer is removed and the primer is smooth. I blow each panel clean using the air hose and inspect it for any traces of guide coat that might remain. Any found traces are lightly sanded until they disappear.

NOTES

CHAPTER 12

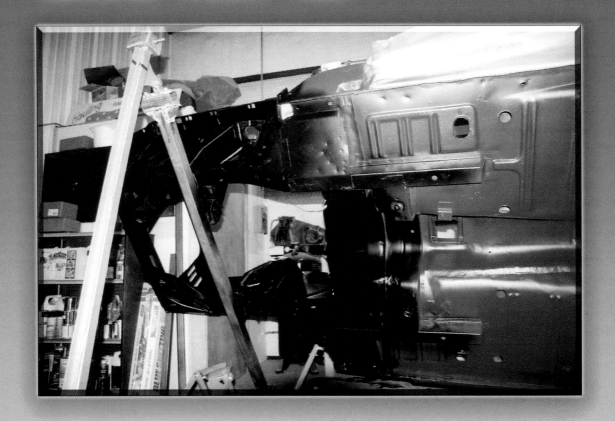

REFINISHING THE COMPONENTS AND THE UNDERSIDE

Believe it or not, this project is moving toward the downhill side. Santa has been dropping off boxes of new parts almost every day; I'm not quite as dirty when I go home in the evenings, which is a sign most of the dirty work has been completed; and there isn't a postage stamp–size spot anywhere on the shiny side of this car that hasn't been touched with either sandpaper or a spray gun.

Now it's time to do something about all those boxes of dinged and abused parts that I removed from the car. Since I don't have an unlimited budget or access to Ford's secret vault filled with vintage parts, most of the stored parts will need to be cleaned, rebuilt, overhauled, refinished, or powder coated before they can be put back on the car.

This is also a good time to refinish the underside of the car. I first need to roll the car over so I can have access to the underside. That will allow me to complete the welding on the floor pans, clean the underside, sand it, apply two coats of epoxy, and paint it.

CLEAN THE COMPONENTS

In an ideal world, we would have a steam cleaner in the storage building next to our lawn mower. But since the world isn't ideal, an alternative is to gather a load of greasy parts and make a car wash run. Most do-it-yourself car washes crank out a little warm water and a lot of soap. But if your pile of quarters is stack-challenged like mine, try soaking the parts in a degreasing solution before heading to the car wash. Any automotive store degreaser will do the job, just don't expect the stuff to leave the parts sparkling clean. It isn't going to happen.

Once the pile of old parts is clean, they will need to be sanded or media blasted to prepare them for a shiny coat of paint. A Norton Bear-Tex Scuff Pad does an excellent job of scuff sanding the parts to prepare them for refinishing, and a little 320-grit sandpaper will do an even better job.

In the case of difficult to sand parts, such as the door hinges and suspension pieces, I prefer to media blast these parts to remove all traces of the old finish. To do that, I have two different blast units. One is a cabinet model that keeps the media, in this case glass beads, contained. The other is a small portable handheld unit from Eastwood that I use outdoors on the parts that are too large to fit into the cabinet model. This unit works best when filled with fine sand.

Media blasting does a good job of cleaning but tends to pit the metal somewhat. That's usually not a problem when cleaning suspension parts, but it might not be desirable when cleaning parts such as door hinges. To do a good job of cleaning parts without worrying about pitting the metal, use glass beads when media cleaning. However, do not try to clean greasy parts in a blast cabinet containing glass beads. The grease will cause the beads to clump and will seriously reduce the effectiveness of the machine.

If it moves, especially if it is connected in any way to the suspension system, it will have bushings, ball joints of some type (control arms and steering linkages), or bearing surfaces. All of these parts need to be cleaned before they can be taken apart and rebuilt. Thinking of tossing the old ball joints and tie-rod ends in favor of new ones? Hang on to them until the new ones are in hand. An F-150 truck ball joint mispackaged in a Mustang ball joint box isn't going to fit the car no matter how large a hammer you have.

If the plan calls for reusing the old bushings, ball joints, or bearings, sand these parts by hand using a Norton Bear-Tex Scuff Pad or 320-grit sandpaper. Do not subject these parts to the media blaster. The grit will attack and erode the wear surfaces, resulting in their eventual failure.

REFINISH THE COMPONENTS

My plan calls for either painting or powder coating nearly every square inch of this car. This means that a gallon and a half of green paint and two quarts of black won't be the only colors on the bench. I'll also need an assortment of specialty finishes, and those include reflective silver for the lamp housings, cast-iron gray for many of the mechanical components that can't be powder coated, zinc-rich coatings to protect all those tiny brackets and retainers, plus a can or two of semigloss black to take care of all those detail brackets and braces. Where do you find reflective silver and cast-iron gray? Try the Eastwood catalog—it has more coatings and colors than a NASCAR race.

Why bring up the subject of refurbishing old parts at this point in the restoration? If you are like me, having an opportunity to step back from the car and work on something else for a while offers some relief in the form of a change of pace. Besides, I hate staring at all those boxes of grimy parts just waiting for me to do something with

them. So when a change of pace is needed, I start cleaning, rebuilding, or refinishing.

Where am I going to put all those parts once they have been refurbished? I keep a number of large plastic storage bins stacked against one wall of the shop, and as a part is restored, it goes into a bin.

PAINT THE METAL PARTS

If the part is made of metal, more than likely the piece was originally painted semigloss black. Many of those parts will be greasy, and all of them will be dirty. My first step is to clean the parts using a pressure washer and to degrease the parts with DX 330. Once cleaned and degreased, each part is scuff sanded using a Bear-Tex Scuff Pad.

To refinish these parts, I mix PPG Deltron 2000 DBI 9600 semigloss black at a 1:1 ratio with PPG DT 885 reducer and apply two coats to each part using the Binks M1-G with a 1.3 mm tip, allowing 10 minutes between coats.

Of course, any time I pick up a spray gun, I need to protect myself. To paint these smaller parts, I wear painter's coveralls, latex gloves, and a 3M 7193 half-face respirator.

PAINT THE PLASTIC PARTS

Plastic parts are prepped for painting the same way metal parts are prepped, by cleaning, degreasing, and scuff sanding, with one exception. Plastic parts, particularly plastic parts found in the interior of the car, should be cleaned and degreased at least twice to remove the accumulation of interior cleaning products, must of which contain silicon, before being scuff sanded. Paint will not stick to silicon, even if the part has been sanded, and the telltale sign that silicon is present is the tendency of the fresh paint to bubble on the surface of the piece being painted. If this occurs, the piece must be cleaned and degreased again.

POWDER COAT
THE COMPONENTS

This is a refinishing step I normally reserve for metal parts that will be subjected to a lot of abuse, such as many of the suspension parts. Powder coating is an almost bulletproof finish, but it is one that requires more preparation than refinishing with paint.

Any part being powder coated must be perfectly clean and capable of withstanding a temperature of 450 degrees F for up to an hour. I cover this subject in depth in chapter 16, so for now I'll concentrate on the finishes that come out of a spray gun.

REFINISH THE UNDERSIDE

One of those areas where the finish will come out of the spray gun is the underside. First, I am going to weld the floor pans onto the underside. Then, I am going to refinish the underside by cleaning it, sanding it, applying epoxy, and painting it.

ROLLING THE CAR

Some time ago, I attended a Specialty Equipment Market Association (SEMA) show where everything imaginable that had to do with automobiles was laid out for my viewing pleasure. One of the latest ideas in accessing the underside of a vehicle was a machine sold by the Eastwood Company designed to allow anyone with a drill and an impact wrench to roll a vehicle up onto its side. I liked the concept but never had a chance to put one of these units to the test until now.

The principle of operation is simple. The unit consists of a pair of tubular steel rolling rails that are bolted to the front and rear wheel hubs on one side of the vehicle, and an elevating piece that is bolted to the opposite front wheel hub. A drill is attached to the elevating piece, and presto, the car rolls up on its side.

The problem I encountered using this unit is that this Mustang has nothing under it that even remotely resembles a suspension, much less a wheel hub, to bolt the unit on to. To get around this dilemma, I constructed two brackets out of 2 x 2-inch-square steel tubing that could be bolted under the car in place of the suspension to give the unit someplace to mount. The rear bracket is T shaped and was mounted where the right rear spring would normally mount; the bottom of the T extends outward near the center of the wheel well to take the place of the rear axle hub. The front bracket is I shaped and mounts where the lower control arms would normally mount. This bracket extends across the width of the front of the car to allow the rolling rail unit to be attached on one end and the elevating device to be attached to the other end. That allowed me to attach the unit and roll the car over to an almost 90-degree position.

PHOTO 1: The car turner attached to Project Mustang. Notice the attachment bars extending out from the suspension points. Because this car has no suspension, support brackets had to be fabricated from 2 x 2–inch-square steel tubing.

If you don't have access to a machine of this type, about the only other alternative to rolling the car over is to mount the car on a rotisserie. This is a much larger and bulkier machine, but it will do the job quite effectively.

WELDING THE FLOOR PANS

With the car rolled up on its side, my first task under the car was to finish welding the new floor pans that I had installed earlier. I welded a continuous bead along the length of both sides of the driveshaft tunnel where the new floor pan panels overlapped the old floor pan, then ground those seams smooth. I don't have a problem with adding a little body filler to a weld seam inside the car to improve the appearance of that seam, but I don't, however, like to apply plastic body filler to the underside of any vehicle. Plastic body filler can be a little fragile when it comes to being hit by rocks kicked up by the tires, and the last thing I need is to have an area of cracked or chipped body filler under the car where it will be exposed to the elements. So with that thought in mind, a little more time was spent welding and grinding the weld seams under the vehicle so that eventually I can apply a coat of epoxy and have an almost invisible repair.

CLEANING THE UNDERSIDE

After seam welding but before epoxy coating, the underside of this project needs a thorough pressure washing and sanding. I am lucky in that the underside of this car is void of any extra undercoating that would have to be

PHOTO 2: The new floor pans are welded solid on the underside of the car. No body filler will be used here, so a lot of time is spent grinding and smoothing the welds.

PHOTO 3: If this machine has any drawbacks, it is that some areas under the car are not accessible. Notice that the right rear wheel well has not been coated with epoxy.

removed or any excessive grease from a leaky engine, transmission, or rear axle assembly.

How do you get rid of unwanted undercoating? A plumber's torch, putty knife, and wire brush will do a pretty good job. Paint stripper and a pressure washer will also get you there, it's just a little messier. Note: Don't use the plumber's torch if the interior is still in the car. Car interiors don't do a slow burn, they go Poof!

Now is a good time to use up any remaining degreaser left over from parts cleaning because the underside needs to be as clean as possible before bringing out the sandpaper. I spray the entire underside of the car with degreaser, and let it soak for a while before putting the pressure washer to work.

Sanding the Underside

Once the underside has dried after being pressure washed, the next step is to sand the underside. Sanding is accomplished using several Norton Bear-Tex Scuff Pads and a box or two of Norton Speed-Lok discs #9185 attached to a drill. It isn't necessary for me to remove all traces of the old paint. My goal is to sand every inch under here, leaving the surfaces scuffed and dull. That ensures that the epoxy to be applied next will stick.

After sanding the underside of the car, every nook and cranny must be blown clean of trapped dirt and sanding dust. That includes inside the frame rails. It never fails that the moment a spray gun is passed near a frame rail, trapped dirt blows out of the rail and settles everywhere the paint is wet.

Applying the Epoxy

The next step in preparing the underside of the Mustang for a coat of epoxy is to mask off everything I don't want oversprayed. I mask off the rocker panels, the quarter panels, the rear wheel openings, and the rear body panel. As long as the car is rolled up on its side, I'm also going to spray the engine compartment, so I've also masked off the cowl grille panel.

Since I covered the details of mixing and spraying epoxy primer in chapter 10, I'll dispense with that explanation and go straight to the mixing bench and load the Binks M1-G HVLP spray gun. I apply two coats of DP74LF red epoxy to mimic the red primer Ford had applied back in 1968, and allow it to dry overnight.

After the epoxy has dried, I inspect the vehicle for proper coverage. If you look at photo 3 where the rear turning mount is located, it is obvious that no epoxy has been applied to the right rear wheel well. If this Eastwood rotator has any drawback, that is it. To coat the right rear wheel well, the car will have to be placed on jack stands once again, and the turning mechanisms will have to be moved to the other side of the car. That will allow me to roll the car in the opposite direction and coat any missed areas. Remember the one-week recoat application window for the DP74LF epoxy? It comes in handy here.

The engine compartment also gets two coats of epoxy, and if you are looking at photo 4 and wondering if I sprayed under the right fender apron, the answer is no. This is another one of those areas I'll spray when I roll the car over the other way.

Overnight is plenty of time to allow the two coats of epoxy to dry, so the next step is to apply seam sealer around the perimeter of the new fender apron pieces. The seam sealer of choice is 3M's All-Around Autobody Sealant #8500. This seam sealer cleans up with water, so if the application seems too heavy, wipe off any excess sealer with a damp shop towel. Allow 3M 8500 to cure for at least 30 minutes before painting. All I'm doing here is sealing the seams to prevent moisture from penetrating between the panels and causing rust later on. The beads of sealer are very thin, and when this area is painted semi-gloss black, the seam sealer will not be evident.

PAINTING THE UNDERSIDE

The engine compartment on this Mustang came from the factory painted black. This was not a high-gloss black, so the finish of choice for the engine compartment will be PPG Deltron 2000 DBI Semigloss Black 9600. This is basically a single-stage finish in that it does not require a clear coat and dries to a semigloss finish. The name may indicate that this product is meant for painting interiors, but it is durable enough to stand up to the rigors of an engine compartment and will give me that same semigloss look the factory applied back in 1968.

DBI mixing ratio is 1:1, 1 part DBI Interior Color to 1 part PPG DT 885 reducer. Apply three coats using a 1.3 mm tip on an HVLP, and allow 5 to 10 minutes between coats.

After applying the DBI black to the engine compartment, I remove a portion of the masking paper on the cowl. This provides a point of contrast to demonstrate where to mask the cowl in order to break the line between the Augusta green to be applied later and the black being applied now. That point is at the seam line where the cowl grille panel is welded to the firewall. Everything below this seam receives three coats of black, and everything above the seam will eventually receive three coats of green. But the green is for later; for now, let's concentrate on the black.

PHOTO 4: The engine compartment is also coated with epoxy.

PHOTO 5: The joint seams in the engine compartment receive a thin coating of 3M All-Around Autobody Sealant #8500 to prevent moisture from penetrating the seams and causing them to rust.

PHOTO 6: The engine compartment is painted semigloss black. Notice the separation line between the black and the epoxy coat on the cowl. Everything above this line will receive a coat of green paint.

Not only is everything below the cowl seam inside the engine compartment painted black, but also the color extends to the outside of the core support, the outer fender aprons, and outer corners of the cowl. The black also extends down the firewall to the joint seam where the floor pan meets the firewall. But don't mask off any of these areas. The factory was content to allow overspray to filter back onto the floor pan and frame rails; so am I.

I'll let the paint cure for a day before lowering the car back down to the jack stands and switching sides with the car turner. I'll roll the car over in the opposite direction, coat any missed areas of the underside with epoxy, and complete the engine compartment area with more DBI black.

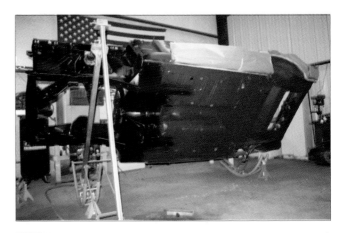

PHOTO 7: The semigloss black extends down the firewall and fades away as it reaches the front unibody frame rails. The outside of the fender aprons also receive a coat of semigloss black.

NOTES

CHAPTER 13

REFINISHING THE DOORS, THE INTERIOR, AND THE TRUNK

Once the components and the underside have been refinished, I can turn my attention to the body of the car. I first develop a refinishing strategy to decide which color to paint the car. Then I move on to the preparatory steps prior to painting the car. These include getting the right paint color and the other painting supplies as well as preparing the areas for painting, including cleaning the car and masking and covering the areas that I do not want to paint. Only then can I apply epoxy and paint to the doors, the interior, and the trunk.

THE REFINISHING STRATEGY

How important is it to return a project vehicle back to its original color? I get a lot of debate over this question. Some people are adamant that changing the color is akin to heresy, whereas others say it really doesn't matter. My thinking lies somewhere in between. I would opt to refinish a vehicle back to its original color if the vehicle were somewhat rare and changing the color would affect the value of the vehicle, and if the car's owner is pleased with the original color.

When would I change the color? If you read *Project Charger*, you know I changed the color on that car from a light green to an extremely eye-catching Plum Crazy purple. This was a plain-Jane car with very little hope of increasing in value, no matter how shiny the coat of green paint. But then several modifications were made that changed the perception of the car, so it only made sense to brighten the color to enhance its value. It is my opinion that the car receives a lot more thumbs-up painted purple than it ever would if it had been refinished the original light green.

So I'd have to say if the plan calls for putting the vehicle back as close to original as possible, or if the owner is happy with the original color, then I would opt for the OEM color. If the plan calls for restoring the vehicle to look like the one you owned way back when or the one you wished you owned way back when, by all means build the ride of your dreams and paint it the color you

love. After all, you are the one who is destined to sit behind the wheel.

And this Mustang? For a fleeting moment, the idea that a red Mustang would look nice took wings, but in less time than it takes to click your heels and repeat "resale red" three times, I was back to the original color.

And the original color would be? Research into the VIN done by Marti Auto Works indicated that this Mustang came from the factory painted Augusta green, also referred to as Highland green: the same color it sported the day it came into the shop. Now that I know what color this Mustang is to be painted, it is time to formulate a spray plan.

I normally spray paint my project vehicles while they are disassembled, and this car will be no exception. With that thought in mind, the first parts of this car to be sprayed will be the inside of both doors, the interior and trunk compartments, followed by the exterior of the body and all of the individual pieces such as the hood, the fenders, and the deck lid. That means decisions about the type of finish and the amount of paint needed to complete the entire project must be considered. As I've already mentioned, the color selected for this Mustang is the same Augusta green that the car was originally painted. So do I use lacquer, enamel, single-stage urethane, or base coat/clear coat to reapply the Augusta green?

Lacquer is out if for no other reason than Ford used enamel to paint the car in the first place. Although enamel was originally used, it too is out because I prefer a finish that will stand up better to a little abuse. Singlestage urethane is a possibility because it offers an extremely durable finish that is easy to apply. But it's out too because I prefer to color sand all of my finishes to get them as slick as possible, and color sanding a metallic finish is a bad idea. Why? Sanding a metallic finish results in shaving off the tops of the metallic particles in the paint and can leave a mottled and blotchy look behind. Not something I like to see in any paint job. So that leaves base coat/clear coat. I will apply three coats of Augusta green base color and top that with three coats of polyurethane clear. The result will be an almost bulletproof finish I can color sand to my heart's desire.

GATHER SUPPLIES

The best place to start is by making sure all the needed refinishing products are on hand and ready to be applied. Because I'm going to start the refinishing process by painting the inside of both doors plus the interior and trunk compartments, I need to have epoxy, semigloss black, Augusta green, and some clear coat products on the bench. What, no sealer? At this point no, and I'll explain why as I move deeper into the refinishing process.

I purchased a gallon of DP74LF epoxy some time ago and used most of that applying the initial layer of finish on the exterior and as a final layer on the underside of the car. That left me with almost a quart of epoxy, which will be more than enough to coat the inside of the doors and the interior and trunk compartments.

I've also previously applied some of the semigloss black I'll be using to spray the dash and a portion of both doors. This is the same PPG Deltron 2000 DBI Semigloss Black 9600 I used to spray the engine compartment previously. I initially purchased two quarts of DBI black and still have plenty left in the can. At a later date, I'll use any leftover black to refinish suspension components that will not be powder coated.

That leaves the Augusta green base color and the clear coat products to discuss. To be sure I have enough paint on hand to refinish the entire car, I ordered 1½ gallons of Augusta green PPG Global BC 43644 and 1 gallon of PPG DCU Concept 2002 polyurethane clear coat.

Will 1½ gallons of Augusta green be enough to complete this car? Definitely. After all, I won't be applying Augusta green to the underside of the car, the engine compartment, or even very much of the interior. But because this paint is a special mix, I would rather end up with too much paint than not enough and have to go back and purchase more. So 1½ gallons will ensure that I have enough base color to apply up to three coats everywhere this car needs to be painted green and still have paint left in the can when this project is finished.

As for the clear coats, I'll apply two coats to the trunk compartment and to a portion of the inside of both doors. The exterior of the car will get three coats. I didn't include the interior compartment on the list of areas requiring a clear coat, and I'll explain why in a moment.

CLEAN THE INTERIOR AND THE TRUNK BEFORE PAINTING

Ever try using an air blower to clean an interior or trunk compartment after sanding? It may stir the air and even push out some of the larger chunks of old seam sealer and sanding dust, but it just won't clean things enough to allow for painting. That requires the use of a good vacuum. I vacuum every inch of the inside of the car, including all corners, access holes, and hidden areas because that's where most of the debris tends to hide. I complete the cleaning process by donning a pair of latex gloves and wiping down both compartments with DX 330 degreaser. The gloves protect my skin as well as prevent the oils from my skin from contaminating the surface and causing the finish not to stick.

PREPARE THE DOORS FOR PAINTING

I lay the doors on the workbench face up so the outer panels can be masked off to prevent overspray from settling on the primed outer surfaces. Once masked, the doors can be turned over for painting.

All doors have openings to access the window regulator and latch assemblies. In 1968, Ford didn't bother to rust treat any portion of the inner door, so now is a good time to remedy that problem. I give the inside of both doors a heavy coat of Eastwood Rust Encapsulator #16060 Z.

MASK THE BODY FOR PAINTING

While the rust inhibitor is drying, I mask off the exterior of the body to prevent overspray from settling there. Now, where's my roll of masking paper?

PHOTO 1: Before the doors can be painted on the inside, the outside must be masked off to prevent overspray from settling on the primed outer surfaces.

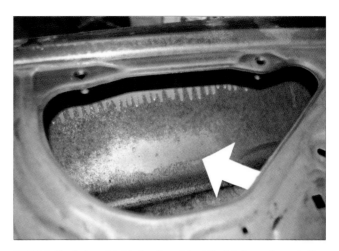

PHOTO 2: The factory didn't bother to rust treat the interior portions of either door. Before being painted, the inner areas of both doors will receive a coat of Eastwood Rust Encapsulator.

Masking the exterior of this car requires masking off every exterior panel plus the engine compartment. Bear in mind that if it isn't masked off, more than likely you will have to scuff sand that area to remove overspray later on. Base colors such as black and green don't create much overspray, but epoxy and clear coats tend to go everywhere and get on everything. So be generous when masking. Even the small openings into the trunk and the interior must be closed to prevent overspray from passing through these openings and settling on the exterior. In photo 4, you can see that the taillamp openings, the fuel inlet, and the quarter extension mounting holes have been masked off.

PAINT THE DOORS, THE INTERIOR, AND THE TRUNK

I'm about to apply three very different refinishing products, and normally I would use three different spray guns: one for applying the epoxy, one for applying the base coat, and one for applying the clear coat. But in this case, many of the areas I need to reach are difficult to access. So to make life easier, I'm going to use the Binks M1-G to spray the epoxy coats. The Binks M1-G will do a good job of applying the heavy-bodied and fast-drying epoxy. Then I will switch to a DeVilbiss SRi 630 mini HVLP spray gun to spray the color coats and clear coats. The SRiW 630, with its smaller size, is the perfect spray gun for applying color and clear coats to all those hard-to-reach places around the dash and inside the trunk compartment.

If you own only one spray gun, don't worry about not being able to maneuver the gun to reach all of those hidden

PHOTO 3: The exterior of the car is masked to prevent overspray from settling on the primed surfaces.

PHOTO 4: If it is opened to the interior of the car, it gets masked. Here the taillamp openings, the fuel inlet, and the quarter extension mounting holes get masked.

areas. The fan size can be easily adjusted down to a small dot to help concentrate the spray area. Don't forget to clean the spray gun thoroughly after using each of the three products.

PHOTO 5: The inside of both doors receives a coat of red epoxy.

PHOTO 6: After the first epoxy coat has dried, every seam inside the car is sealed using 3M All-Around Autobody Sealant #8500.

Once you have decided which spray gun you are going to use, it's time to apply the finishing coats on the doors, the interior of the car, and the trunk compartment. I will be applying a coat of epoxy, black paint, Augusta green paint, and clear coat to these parts.

Applying the Epoxy Coat

Under any other circumstance, I would mix DP74LF epoxy at a 2:1 ratio, 2 parts DP74LF epoxy to 1 part DP402LF hardener, just as I did when I sprayed the body of this project for the first time. But because I will be following this application with a layer of semigloss black over the dash area and Augusta green in other places, I'm going to modify the mixing ratio by adding an additional ½ part DT 885 reducer. That will give me a better flow out and ultimately a smoother surface. Having a smoother surface will let me omit the seal coat.

Why omit the seal coat? In this case, the factory didn't get too picky when it came to controlling the overspraying. The black was oversprayed onto the red oxide base primer, as was the Augusta green. Not applying a seal coat will allow me to duplicate that overspray pattern inside the car without having to worry about covering the sealer. The result should give the final interior finish that factory look.

I start applying the epoxy by spraying one coat to the inside of the car and both doors. After the first coat of epoxy has dried for an hour, I follow up by sealing all the seams in the car using 3M All-Around Autobody Sealant #8500.

Next, I replace the tar sealer that the factory used to coat many of the body joints with 3M 5910 Rocker Panel Spray. This is actually an aerosol spray coating used primar-ily on the rocker panels of late model vehicles to prevent rock chips. It's a heavy-bodied product that leaves a lightly textured finish when sprayed but is almost invisible until painted. It will work great for my purpose, which is to replace the old tar substance on the floor pans and in the trunk with something that creates basically the same tex-ture as the tar sealer but outperforms it hands down.

Painting It Black

The mixing ratio for the DBI Semi Gloss Black is a simple 1:1, 1 part DBI black to 1 part DT 885 reducer. I use the DeVilbiss SRiW 630 mini HVLP spray gun to apply the semigloss black to the dash inside and out, both wind-shield posts, the kick panel areas just beneath the dash, and the inside of both doors. I apply three coats to all of these areas, allowing each coat to dry at least 15 minutes before applying the next coat.

Applying the Paint

The three coats of black paint applied to the doors and to the inside of the car need some time to cure before these panels can be safely masked off. I set the spray coat timer for two hours and go find the photos I took of the trunk and interior compartments during disassembly to be sure I get the overspray pattern around the door openings cor-rect. Once the panels are dry, any area that was painted black needs to be completely masked off using masking tape and masking paper.

The next step is to paint the inside of the car, the doors, and the trunk with PPG Global BC 43644 Augusta green. This is a premium base color that mixes at a 1:1 ratio, 1 part BC to 1 part DT 885 reducer. I apply three medium-wet coats using the DeVilbiss SRiW 630 mini

PHOTO 7: The trunk compartment and package tray receive three coats of green, whereas the inside of the door openings are only oversprayed green.

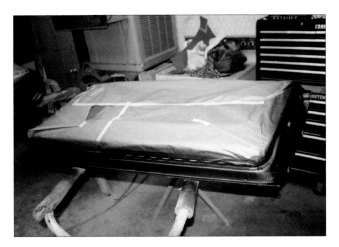

PHOTO 8: The portion of the doors to remain semigloss black is masked off so the outer portion of the inside of both doors can be sprayed Augusta Green.

HVLP spray gun set at 28 psi at the inlet, and allow each coat to dry for 15 minutes before applying the next coat.

Duplicating the factory overspray for the green paint inside the car isn't that difficult. The factory refinished the entire trunk compartment and package tray with Augusta green and allowed green overspray to fall where it may around both the door openings and the quarter glass openings. The trick is in knowing how to make a base coat/clear coat finish look like factory oversprayed enamel.

To accomplish this task, I'm going to spray the trunk compartment, the rear package tray area, and inside the door openings with base coat and apply the clear coat to only the trunk compartment and the top of the package tray. That will leave the door opening areas coated with base color only, and that will give those areas an oversprayed look without the white ring normally associated with having oversprayed a clear coat onto a panel.

That leaves the edges of the doors to paint green. The first step is to mask off the semigloss black. I use the door weather strip channels as a guide and mask off everything inside the weather strip. That gives me a color change break that is hidden underneath the weather strip.

The last phase of this refinishing step is to paint the door hinges green. I've already disassembled the hinges and sandblasted the pieces clean. To make sure the correct hinge halves stay together and don't get mixed up, I wire the mated halves together. The wire also makes a great hanger for painting the individual pieces.

Applying the Clear Coat

The clear coat product I've chosen is PPG DCU 2002 Concept Polyurethane Clear. This is also a premium product and is designed for application over the green base color already on the car.

DCU 2002 mixes at a 4:1:1 ratio, 4 parts DCU 2002 to 1 part DT 885 reducer to 1 part DCX 61 hardener. I use the DeVilbiss SRiW 630 spray gun set at 28 psi at the inlet and apply two medium-wet coats, allowing the first coat to dry for 15 minutes before applying the second coat. DCU 2002 will be dust free in about 70 minutes and completely dry in about 3 hours. Isn't 70 minutes a long time for the clear to dry and cure? Yes, but the slower drying time gives me two distinct advantages over faster-drying clear coat products. First, the slower the clear cures, the less brittle the final product will be. That's important when the plan calls for putting the car back on the road. Second, the extended drying time allows the clear to flow out and lay extremely smooth on the surface of the car. That reduces the time spent color sanding and buffing the finish.

NOTES

NOTES

CHAPTER 14

REFINISHING THE BODY

A pplying the final finish to this car is so crucial that before the paint goes on I need to ensure the fit of all the panels, take care of a lot of masking, apply the seal coat, then, at last, put color on this car and buff it to a bright shine.

REASSEMBLE THE CAR

It feels like déjà vu all over again and again. I have DP74LF epoxy, semigloss black, and Augusta green base color waiting on the bench. Clean spray guns hang in the gun rack, and the body of this project car is just waiting for a coat of paint. So why don't I load a spray gun and paint the body of this car? I have this fear of parts not fitting the way I want them to fit once the car has been painted and assembled, and the only way to quell that fear is to leave the paint in the can and mock up this car one last time.

It takes a little time, but mounting the hood, fenders, doors, deck lid, and quarter panel extensions back on the car is the only way to be sure I have everything fitting the way it is supposed to fit before I paint the car. These old muscle cars were notorious for uneven gaps between panels and misaligned body lines. Checking the gaps and lines one last time while the car is still in primer affords me the opportunity to make changes without causing any unnecessary delays. I don't want to reach a point several months from now where I find two panels that don't align and realize my only recourse is to make a repair and refinish part of the car again.

One of the more demanding areas of alignment is around the trunk where the quarter panel extension spoilers meet the deck lid spoiler. I initially spend a lot of time making sure all of these parts fit the way they should, but after repairing, sanding, priming, and block-ing, the corners of these extensions can become round-ed off, and no amount of adjusting or aligning will com-pensate for that kind of problem. Since every part of this car is being refinished before being installed back on the car, I'll paint and install the deck lid before paint-ing and installing the quarter extension spoilers. That affords me a final opportunity to verify the alignment of these pieces.

PHOTO 1: Project Mustang is assembled one last time to verify the fit of all the panels.

PHOTO 2: One of the more demanding areas of fit involves the deck lid spoiler and the quarter panel extensions. All three pieces must align, or the fit will never look right.

Note: The fenders are shown in the photos with a guide coat still on the primer, and the quarter panel extension spoilers are shown with some green enamel paint on them. If an alignment problem had become apparent during the mock-up, all efforts to correct the problems would have been centered on those panels. After all, they are the furthest away from being refinished, and reworking those pieces would not affect the work-flow of the project.

PHOTO 3: The major openings into the car are masked off by first creating a grid of masking tape over the opening.

PHOTO 4: The grid is then covered with masking paper to seal the opening.

PHOTO 5: The inside of both doors gets masked off by first taping around the rolled lip of the outer panel. That leaves the lip exposed so it can be painted when I paint the outside of the door, and it also gives me the perfect stopping point.

The hood, fenders, doors, deck lid, and quarter panel extensions are put back on the car, and all the alignments are checked. Once the major parts of this car meet the alignment requirements, the car is taken back apart. The hood, deck lid, and fenders are stored where they will not be subjected to damage, but the doors are a different matter altogether. They are laid face up on fold-out workbenches so they can be painted along with the car body, which is next on the to-do list.

TAPING AND MASKING TIME

The first step in painting the car is to mask any areas where you do not want the paint to go. Masking begins by using masking tape to form a grid across the door opening. I use 1½-inch-wide masking tape around the perimeter of the opening, leaving about half of the width of the tape exposed in the opening; then I use ¾-inch-wide tape to form the actual grid. What isn't obvious in the photograph is that the entire grid is laid out with the tape placed sticky side out. Having the masking tape positioned sticky side out gives me the perfect backing for holding the masking paper in place. That's easy to do when working from the inside of the vehicle, but not so easy to do when working from the outside, which I must do. Once the grid is laid out, I close off the door opening using 12-inch-wide masking paper.

I repeat this grid-building process as I close off the other door opening, the windshield opening, and the back glass and trunk openings, then finish the process by masking off the engine compartment, the rear wheel openings, and the back side of both rocker panels. I also mask any access holes and other small openings that might allow overspray to reach the interior of the car. I end by masking off the previously refinished portions of the insides of both doors.

Photo 5 offers a detail of how the doors were masked for painting. Notice that the lip of the outer panel where it rolls around the door frame was left exposed. After masking the inside of the door, this lip was sanded with a Bear-Tex Scuff Pad so that when the door is turned over for painting, I am able to reach the spray gun under the door and refinish the lip. Once the masking paper is removed, the line between the previously painted inner portion of the doors and the freshly painted outside of the doors will disappear completely.

PHOTO 6: The first coat of finish goes on. In this case, the coat is PPG2K Chromatic Sealer D8085, and I'll apply one coat.

PHOTO 7: (Left) The Binks M1-G HVLP spray gun and (right) the DeVilbiss GFG 670 compliant spray gun.

SEAL COAT THE BODY AND THE DOORS

Before I mix and apply the seal coat, I take a little time to clean the shop from top to bottom and wet down the floor to eliminate dust in the air. I clean the car with DX330 degreaser.

I wasn't concerned about not using a seal coat when I sprayed the inside of the doors, the interior, and the trunk compartment. Thinning the epoxy coat an additional 10 percent, as I explained previously, left the surface smooth enough for an acceptable finish. However, the outside of both doors and the exterior of the body need a good seal coat to ensure that the final surface is far more than merely acceptable. I want the Augusta green to lay flat and smooth, and to do that a seal coat is required.

The sealer of choice is PPG 2K Chromatic Sealer D8085. This is a light gray sealer that will provide an excellent base over which to apply the base color coats. D8085 mixes at a 6:1:3 ratio, 6 parts D8085 to 1 part D897 hardener to 3 parts DT 885 reducer. I'll be using the Binks M1-G HVLP spray gun set at 22 psi at the gun inlet to apply the seal coat.

Once I'm ready to paint, I'll be wearing an Eastwood Pro Air 40 Full Face Mask Pro #34050, a clean painter's suit, and latex gloves. After the sealer is in the gun and I'm ready to begin painting, I wipe the car down with a tack cloth to ensure that the car is perfectly clean. Of course, I start painting where I started spraying every other coat of finish applied to this body, at the right windshield post, and apply a single wet coat to the body following the same sequence as I did with the epoxy.

D8085 needs to cure a minimum of 30 minutes at 70 degrees F before top coating, and the next finish must be applied within 72 hours. If not, the sealer must be sanded with 320-grit sandpaper before applying the next coat.

APPLY THE BASE COLOR COATS TO THE BODY AND THE DOORS

The 72-hour drying time for the sealer gives me plenty of time to prepare the car and spray gun for applying the base color coats. I need to find the right setting for the spray gun and spray a test panel to ensure that the correct fan shape is set before I can paint the body of the car green.

SETTING THE GUN

First, I need to clean the spray gun. I'm using the same Binks M1-G spray gun to spray the color coats that I used to spray the seal coat because I'm familiar with the way this gun sprays, and that will help me lay down some very smooth coats of color. That being so, I can't leave any traces of the gray sealer inside the gun that might inadvertently find their way onto my green color coats. To clean this gun, I pour clean lacquer thinner into the cup, pull the spray trigger, and allow the thinner to flow through the gun and out the spray nozzle. When the thinner flows clear, with no traces of gray sealer, I remove the cup and spray nozzle to clean them individually, clean the outside of the gun, then assemble the cleaned gun.

Either of two quality spray guns can be used to apply the paint and clear coats: a Binks M1-G HVLP gravity feed spray gun or a DeVilbiss GFG 670 gravity feed compliant spray gun. Is one better than the other? I fell in love with

PHOTO 8: The control features common to most gravity feed spray guns: (1) controls the size of the spray fan; (2) regulates the air flow; (3) the spray nozzle (most can be changed to allow for spraying different refinishing materials; the nozzle in this gun is a 1.2 mm); and (4) the spray trigger.

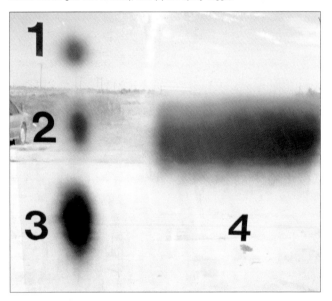

PHOTO 9: Glass pane held up to the light and used for spraying a test panel. Being able to look through the test spray tells all about how the gun is spraying.

the GFG 670 the first time I sprayed clear through it. It seems to do a better job of atomizing the clear than does the Binks. That means I spend less time color sanding the clear to remove orange peel and more time reading *Auto Restorer* magazine.

To properly set either of these guns for spraying, I begin by adjusting the top knob (part 1 in photo 8) full in clockwise, then backing it out counterclockwise one-quarter turn. This knob controls the size and shape of the spray fan. Next, I turn the lower adjustment knob (2) counterclockwise several turns to loosen it. This is the airflow control knob, and it controls the amount of air pass-

ing through the spray nozzle (3). Caution! This knob is spring loaded, and if loosened too much the knob will pop off. Next, I depress the trigger (4) fully and turn the lower knob (2) clockwise slowly until the trigger begins to move. The gun is now set for spraying a test panel.

TIME FOR A TEST PANEL

The next step is to mix the Augusta green base color using the same 1:1 ratio as before, taking the time to spray a test pattern to get a feel for how the gun is spraying.

Once the spray gun is set correctly and you have your spraying techniques down pat, the base coat should spray easily and lay smooth once applied. But then the actual act of painting a car never seems to be as easy as it sounds. Problems have a way of rearing their ugly heads once a paint gun is in hand, and there is no turning back. Fortunately, most problems arise as a result of poor preparation, and that always starts with failing to properly set the gun for spraying. That's why I always spray a test panel. I want to be sure there are no gremlins hiding in the paint cup waiting to ruin my paint job.

A trick I learned from a friend in the truck repair business is to use a pane of glass as a test panel. Why glass? If you hold the glass up to the light, as shown in photo 9, it is easy to see exactly how the gun is spraying. For example, if the spray pattern appears heavy at the top and thin at the bottom, this would indicate a clogged air nozzle. If the pattern produces heavy drops of paint, that indicates not enough air pressure at the gun inlet or the gun is being held too close to the work. Fine drops indicate too much air pressure at the gun inlet or the gun is being held too far away from the work. But the correct air pressure combined with the right distance from the panel, usually 6 to 8 inches away, and moving at roughly 1 foot every 2 seconds across the panel yields acceptable results. The glass pane can also be used to set the spray fan size by turning the upper knob (2) either clockwise, to shrink the size and shape of the spray fan, or counterclockwise, to lengthen the spray fan. Small round dots, as shown in sample 1, photo 9, are great for spraying into tight areas but not so great for spraying the exterior of a project vehicle. For that, you want an oval-shaped fan roughly 5 to 6 inches tall and 2 to 3 inches wide, as shown in sample 3, photo 9. Once the correct fan shape is achieved, a test pass is made, as demonstrated in sample 4, photo 9. This pass should exhibit a smooth, even texture. If it doesn't, the gun needs more cleaning, or you need more practice.

APPLYING THE COLOR COATS

Now that I have cleaned the spray gun, adjusted the spray gun to the proper spray setting, and painted a test panel, I am finally ready to paint the body and doors. Once the seal coat has cured, I'll spray three medium-wet coats of base color using the Binks M1-G spray gun set at 22 psi at the gun inlet and allow each coat to dry for 10 minutes before applying the next coat. Be sure to follow the same basic spraying sequence used previously to apply the primer and seal coats.

Unlike the seal coat, which is applied using a wet coat application, the color coats are sprayed using a medium-wet coat application. So why spray the seal coat wet and the base color coats medium-wet, and how do you differentiate between the two methods?

Generally speaking, sealers are not meant to be sanded. Therefore, they should be applied wet to allow the coat to flow out and lay smooth on the surface. Color coats should be sprayed medium-wet primarily because if sprayed wet, the coat would run or sag.

Wet and medium-wet coats also differ in the speed at which they are applied. To apply a wet coat, you need to slow down each pass of the gun enough to visibly see the gloss of the finish just behind the gun. The gloss fades quickly, but seeing that gloss is the best indication of a wet coat. By contrast, a medium-wet coat demonstrates very little of the gloss characteristic trailing behind the spray gun, and what little gloss does appear fades into a flat finish almost immediately. Therefore, medium-wet coats can be applied more quickly.

The question of color match when painting individual pieces at different times always seems to come up, so I'll address that here. It isn't a problem. The paint being used to spray the body and all the parts come out of the same can of Augusta green. I use the same air pressure, about 22 psi at the gun (Binks M1-G), the same number of color coats, three, and do my best to duplicate the actual spraying techniques each time I spray. So if you use the same paint, the same equipment, and the same techniques, the parts will match.

APPLY THE CLEAR COATS

Once I finish painting the car, I need to allow it to cure for a minimum of 15 minutes before applying the clear coats. For the clear coats, I use PPG DCU 2002 Concept Polyurethane Clear. This is the same premium-grade 2K

PHOTO 10: The final product. The body of Project Mustang has three coats of Augusta Green and three coats of DCU 2002 Concept Clear.

TIP

Not completely comfortable with walking up to a car with a gun in your hand and painting it? That's what masking paper was made for. To become more familiar with the spray gun, mask off part of a wall in the shop and practice spraying. It is the best way to learn, and your mistakes can be wadded up and tossed into the trash, not left on the side of the project vehicle, where they will need to be sanded off.

clear coat product I used to spray the trunk compartment and the inside of both doors.

I initially apply two coats of DCU 2002 using the DeVilbiss GFG 670 spray gun, allowing 15 minutes drying time between coats. I allow the second coat to dry a minimum of 30 minutes at 70 degrees F before applying a third and final coat. That gives me a total of three coats, more than enough to ensure that the finish can be color sanded to a perfectly smooth finish. Why the delay between the second and third coats? The first two coats have a significant amount of solvents present within the layer of clear. The 30-minute delay allows those solvents to dissipate before the third coat is applied.

DETERMINE THE THICKNESS OF THE FINISH MATERIALS

How thick will the finish be when all is said and done? Here is the breakdown of applied materials. The second DP74LF epoxy coat applied after the body repair work was completed has a film build of 0.5 mil. After block

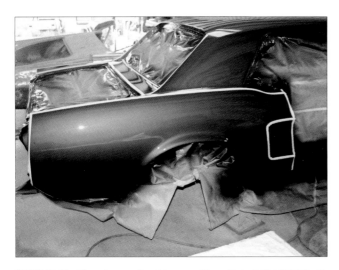

PHOTO 11: All of the edges are taped to prevent burn-through. The finish is relatively fresh, and sanding or buffing through an edge is very possible. The tape is a preventive measure.

sanding, the D8005 primer/surfacer has a film build of roughly 2.0 mil. The D8085 seal coat has a film build of 1.0 mil. The three coats of PPG Global BC 4364 base color coat have a film build of roughly 1.2 mil. Finally, the three coats of DCU 2002 clear have a film build of roughly 4.0 mil before sanding. That is a total of 8.7 mil of refinishing material on the car. Excessive? A few years ago, the answer would be yes. Today, applying 8 to 10 mil is pretty much the norm. Any more than 10 mil is excessive and may result in the finish cracking over time and should be reduced by sanding off the old layers before adding more paint to the vehicle.

How do you know if you have too much material on your ride? Actually, you have only a few choices when it comes to accurately determining the paint thickness on a vehicle. You can slip your neighborhood paint dealer a few bucks to use his extremely expensive digital thickness gauge to measure the material buildup on your car—provided he has coughed up the bucks to buy the machine in the first place; or you can purchase the digital gauge yourself and charge your friends to measure the paint thickness of their cars. If that doesn't work, you can go the low-tech, somewhat inaccurate, way and get a ballpark figure using a magnetic paint thickness gauge.

The magnetic contraption works by measuring the magnetic pull of the metal beneath the paint to (it is hoped) give you a reading of the thickness of the paint. Even on a good day, this type of gauge isn't very accurate, and on a bad day, it won't give you a measurement at all, especially if the vehicle has body filler on it.

There is one other way to roughly measure the thickness of the finish as it is being applied to a vehicle, and that is to spray a single test panel with each of the various layers of material being applied, then measure the thickness of the test panel with a micrometer. It can be extremely accurate, but it won't take into consideration the amount of finish removed from the vehicle during the block sanding or color sanding processes.

SAND AND BUFF THE CLEAR COATS

The last step in the refinishing process is to color sand and buff the clear coats. *Color sanding* is more of a body shop term than an actual process because the layer being sanded is actually the clear coat and not the color coats beneath. The same goes for buffing. This is also a body shop term because once the car has been color sanded, it must be compounded and not necessarily buffed, to bring out the shine. *Buffing* is a term more aligned with refining an already existing shine.

SANDING THE CLEAR COATS

I allow the clear coats to cure for 24 hours before doing any color sanding. Before I sand, I need to apply masking tape to all of the edges. Although I have three coats of clear over the Augusta green base color, giving me a relatively thick coating, the finish is still fresh and the edges are fragile. It doesn't take very many passes with a sheet of sandpaper to cut right through the clear on one of these edges and expose the base color. If that happens, I will have to repaint that portion of the car. How do I know if I've breached the clear and exposed the color coats? That portion of the finish will actually change colors. In this case, the exposed green will appear darker than the surrounding finish.

Once the tape is in place, I am ready to sand. I use a 3M Hookit II Hand Pad #5291 with 3M 1000-grit sandpaper #0869. I color sand this car wet by first soaking the 1000-grit sandpaper in a pail of clean, desalinated water (bottled water), and then I use a sprayer to keep the panel and the sandpaper wet as I sand.

How do I know when to stop sanding? Study the transition area between the sanded and unsanded portions of the panel shown in photo 12. The edges of this panel have not been sanded, and that area still retains the high gloss and slight orange peel look associated with a fresh clear coat. The rest of the panel has been color sanded using 1000-grit sandpaper. Observe how flat and smooth that area of the panel appears. Any traces of the orange peel effect have been sanded away. This is the type of surface I'm looking for. No orange peel and extremely smooth and flat.

Once all of the flat surfaces of the body have been thoroughly sanded using 1000-grit sandpaper, I switch to 3M 1500 grit and repeat the sanding process. The result is an extremely flat and smooth surface with almost no sand scratches that is ready for compounding.

What about the taped edges? Generally speaking, the edges can be left alone and not sanded at all. But if sanding up to an edge becomes necessary to remove orange peel work, take each sanding stroke from the inboard side of the edge outward to the edge to ensure that you never unintentionally sand across the edge.

Buffing the Clear Coats

Now that I've finished sanding, I can remove the tape from the edges, and I am ready to buff the car. This is where all the hard work of color sanding pays off. I use a 3M Superbuff buffing pad #5700 on a variable speed electric buffer to bring out the shine. Don't try using a buffing pad on a high-speed grinder. Most grinders turn at roughly 12,000 rpm, enough speed to literally melt the finish on your car. Most variable speed buffers turn at a maximum of 3,200 rpm and can be regulated down to a slow crawl, an option you'll find handy when it comes to compounding deep curves and hard-to-reach areas of the car.

The buffing pad must be clean. It can be washed beforehand if necessary and should be cleaned occasionally during the buffing process using a buffing spur. The compound of choice is 3M Perfect It 3000. This is a fast-cutting, swirl-mark resistant compound designed for use on clear coat finishes.

The actual technique of buffing is relatively simple. Never operate a buffer with the pad placed flat on the paint surface. Tipping the buffer up at a slight angle gives you more control over the machine and allows you to concentrate on one specific area at a time.

The buffer causes the shine to come out almost instantly, but the trick is to look beyond the shine and search out any minute sand scratches that might be left on the surface. That's easy to do when buffing a darker surface, not so easy to do when buffing a lighter surface.

PHOTO 12: The contrast between the sanded portion of this panel and the unsanded portion is easy to see. I'm looking for a very flat, very smooth surface with no traces of the orange peel effect common to clear coats once the panel has been sanded.

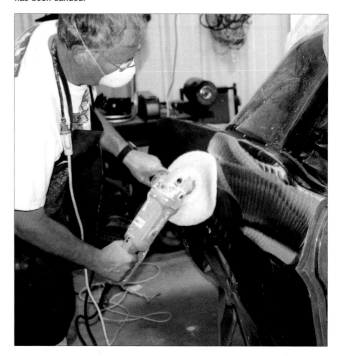

PHOTO 13: Operate the buffer at a slightly tipped angle to the surface being buffed. This gives you more control over the machine. Also notice the dust mask, the buffing apron, and the position of the electrical cord. Having the cord draped over my neck is a sure way to prevent the cord from being tangled in the spinning pad.

> **TIP**
>
> *A strong light can be your best friend when inspecting the surface for sand scratches or other imperfections.*

PHOTO 14: The correct positioning of the buffer places the pad so it buffs from a position on the panel to off the panel.

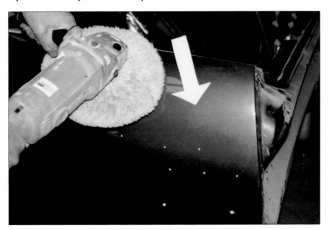

PHOTO 15: The wrong positioning of the buffer. Here the pad is held so that it buffs from a position off the panel onto the panel. The result could be buffing through the top edge of the quarter panel.

Most buffers turn clockwise, which means you can safely buff up to an edge as long as the direction the buffing pad is turning is such that it buffs from a position on the panel to off the panel. Confusing? Here is an example: In photo 14, the buffer is tipped so that the working surface is at the top of the machine. As the pad turns, it moves from a position on the panel to off the panel.

The buffing shown in photo 15 is a no-no. The buffer is held in a position that allows the pad to buff from a position off the panel down onto the panel. The body line at the top of this quarter panel is subject to being buffed through, exposing the color coats beneath.

Anything else you should know about buffing? Inspect the surface for sand scratches, wash the panel, and dry it. Mark any found imperfections such as sand scratches with masking tape, then repeat the buffing process in that area. Periodically reapply the compound, and never allow the buffing pad to dry out. This would cause the pad to heat and possibly burn the finish.

The final step is to wash the entire surface of the car clean to remove excess compound. Compound residue etches into fresh paint if left on the surface.

NOTES

CHAPTER 15

WIRING THE CAR AND INSTALLING THE DOORS

One of the last components to be removed from the car during the teardown phase was the main wiring harness. Years of stereo installations, wiring repairs, and day-to-day use and abuse were not kind to this black tape–wrapped menagerie of wires and terminals. The severely aged plastic insulation crackled and snapped like cold cereal in a bowl as I went about removing the harness. Once it was out of the car, I knew this mess of patched and spliced wires was destined for File 13 and a new harness would be in order, or, more precisely, on order.

THE PAINLESS PERFORMANCE WIRING HARNESS KIT

If you have ever used a Painless Performance wiring harness kit, you already know it has taken what normally appears to be a mangled and tangled mess of wires, seemingly going everywhere and connecting to everything, and condensed it down to a clean and efficient single harness that is clearly marked and labeled for easy installation.

My first step is to spread the new harness out on the floor to gain a quick understanding of what I have. The Painless Performance harness is broken into specific wire sections, including the rear body, the front lighting, the dash, and the engine wiring, with each bundle neatly tied, labeled, and separated from the main harness. Within each separated bundle, every wire is color coded to match the original wire and is named and numbered. That makes this harness almost self-installing.

But just in case a little instruction is needed, the kit also comes with an easy-to-read wiring manual. In the back of the manual is a wiring list covering each and every wire in the kit. For example, if I need to find the right rear turn signal wire, I can go to the back of the manual, look for the heading Turn Signal Switch, and determine that the right rear turn signal wire is a 14-gauge orange wire with a black stripe and is numbered 948, with "right rear turn signal" printed next to the number. I also know that the bundle of wires where I

PHOTO 1: Once out of the box and spread across the floor, the Painless Performance wiring harness doesn't appear so daunting. The black box on the right is the fuse block, the heart of this assembly.

found wire number 948 is that portion of the harness meant for the rear of the car. How sweet it is.

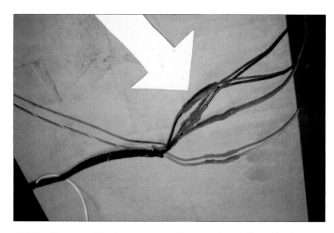

PHOTO 2: The rear wiring harness gets spliced into the existing wiring harness. Each connection is soldered and wrapped with heat-shrink tubing before being wrapped with dry vinyl tape.

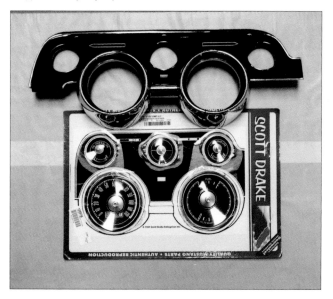

PHOTO 3: The gauge cluster gets a new face and new lenses from California Mustang.

Once all the wiring has been completed, I am free to install the doors on both sides of the car. This starts with installing the hinges. Once the doors are installed, they need to be aligned. I then finish the doors by installing the latches to secure the doors and the door handles.

INSTALL THE HARNESS

Painless Performance recommends leaving the original harness in place and routing the new harness around it. In this case, the car is completely gutted, so there is no need to route the new harness around existing components. Instead, I separate the harness into its four sections—the dash wiring, rear body wiring, front body wiring, and engine wiring—and wrap the first 6 feet of the rear-body wiring loom with dry vinyl wiring harness

wrapping tape #25000 from Eastwood. This is basically a black electrical tape but without the adhesive, thus the name dry. Once the loom is taped, I tuck the main harness into the gauge cluster opening of the dash and feed the rear-body wiring loom through the left door hinge post, along the left rocker, through the left quarter, and out into the trunk.

I am working on a California Special Mustang, which has taillamps that are completely different from that of the stock Mustang, so the wires for the taillamps on the new harness don't exactly match the wires on the old harness. To simplify the wiring of these lamps, I clean and make any necessary repairs to the existing lamp sockets and splice the last few feet of the old loom into the new loom. Each splice is securely soldered and sealed using heat-shrink tubing. The result is a professional-looking splice that can be easily hidden by completing the dry vinyl tape wrapping of the loom.

Moving back to the dash area, the front-body wiring bundle needs to be dry vinyl tape wrapped for about 3 feet, just enough to extend the bundle through the firewall and into the engine compartment on the left-hand side. The same goes for the engine wiring bundle. I wrap the first few feet with dry vinyl tape so it can be fed through the firewall into the engine compartment via an opening near the center of the firewall.

That leaves the remainder of the dash portion of this harness filling the gauge cluster opening. For the time being, that's a good place to leave it. Next, I turn my attention to rebuilding the dash and giving all those dash wire connections someplace to go.

REBUILD THE DASH

Several steps need to be taken to rebuild the dash. The gauge cluster will be restored first. Next, the mechanical components, such as the brake pedal, the brake lever, the air vent, the heater and air conditioner box, the vents, the radio speaker, and the windshield wiper motor, will be installed. This is followed by connecting the vacuum lines. The next major step is to connect the dash wires. The dash is completed by installing the dash pad.

REBUILDING THE GAUGE CLUSTER

The rebuild starts with restoring the gauge cluster. I turn to California Mustang for a reproduction cluster bezel, gauge lenses, and faces. I also had the option of changing the appearance of the gauges by converting them to the now popular white faces, but I elected to stay with the original black faces, if only to maintain the originality of the car.

The first step is to disassemble the cluster and give it a thorough cleaning. The easiest way to clean the delicate components within the cluster is to purchase an 8-oz aerosol can of compressed air used to clean computers. I also use cotton swabs dampened with rubbing alcohol to help reach those difficult areas.

To install the new gauge faces, I first peel away the backing from the new face, then wet it thoroughly with a solution of 1 tablespoon dish washing liquid to 1 cup of water mixed and poured into a spray bottle to prevent the face from sticking as I position it. Next, I use tweezers to gently position the face on the gauge and a cotton swab to push the liquid from underneath. Once the new face is in place, I allow the gauge to dry overnight.

After refacing all the gauges, each indicator needle gets a fresh coat of bright orange paint. Before painting the needles, I cover each gauge with masking paper to ensure that the orange paint goes only where it is supposed to go. I prefer PPG #60436 Chrysler Hemi Orange because it gives the needles a distinct look. To apply the paint, I use a small touch-up brush. Notice in photo 4 that I also removed the clock hands and refinished them individually.

Once the indicator needles have dried overnight, the cluster can be reassembled. Don't forget to remove the "pony" emblem from the old cluster bezel and install it in the new one.

INSTALLING THE MECHANICAL COMPONENTS

The situation in photo 6 may look like the beginning of a wiring nightmare, but if you close your eyes and think about where everything should be located, this dash is really quite simple. The visible pieces of the dash assembly include the glove box, the radio, the ignition switch instrument cluster, and the heater control panel. Behind the above-listed components is the wring harness, the brake pedal assembly, the emergency brake lever, the left side fresh air vent, the heater and air conditioner box, the defroster vents, the radio speaker, and the windshield wiper motor. These are the primary pieces of the dash assembly, listed in the exact order they were removed from the car, and they must be installed back in the car in reverse order with the exception of the wiring harness, which has already been installed.

PHOTO 4: The indicator needles for each gauge are refinished in a bright orange. In this case, I used Chrysler Hemi Orange, PPG #60436.

PHOTO 5: The "pony" emblem shown here does not come with the new bezel. It must be removed from the old bezel and installed before assembling the cluster.

The mechanical components of the dash are laid out in the approximate positions they will occupy in the car to take the guesswork out of what goes where. Starting on the left side of the dash, I have the emergency brake handle, the fresh air vent, the brake pedal assembly, and the wiper assembly. Not much can go wrong with any of these components, so all of these parts receive a good cleaning, sanding, and refinishing with PPG Deltron 200 DBI Semigloss black 9600 paint before being installed back in the car.

I checked the wiper motor for proper operation during the initial inspection of the car, so I already know it works just fine. But that isn't so for the heater box that occupies the right side of the dash. Inside this unassuming plastic box lies the heater core and the air conditioner evaporator.

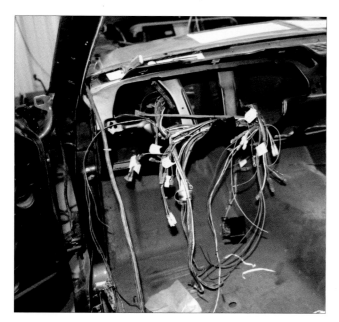

PHOTO 6: A nightmare of wiring made simple. After all the individual wiring bundles are routed throughout the car, all that is left is the dash wires.

PHOTO 7: The basic mechanical components of the dash are laid out in the approximate positions they will occupy once installed in the dash. This takes the guesswork out of the installation sequence.

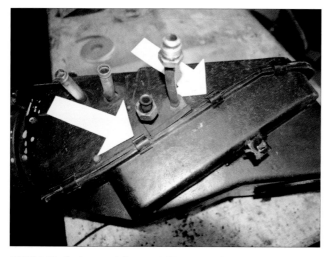

PHOTO 8: The heater case halves are held together with these metal clips.

Yes, I did operate both units before disassembling the car and yes, everything worked just fine, including the vacuum-operated doors that switch from the floor vents to the dash and defroster vents. What I could not determine by simply operating the system was the condition of the heater core. For that I need to disassemble the heater box and have the heater core professionally tested.

The clips shown in photo 8 hold the case halves together. I remove all of these clips and separate the case halves to expose the heater core, shown in photo 9. I drop the heater core off at the local radiator shop for cleaning and testing. What if it leaks? Forget the aluminum flake leak stopper or even attempting to have the core repaired. It is old. If it leaks, replace it with a new one, generally costing less than $100.

The air conditioner evaporator core, shown in photo 10, is also located inside the heater box. This unit rarely fails and needs only to be inspected for damaged cooling fins, cleaned, and reinstalled. Once both cores have been cleaned and refurbished, the case can be assembled for installation.

INSTALLING THE VACUUM LINES

Once the behind-the-scene components listed above have been installed, it is time to consider the vacuum lines. The heater/AC control panel mounts to the left of the steering column and has five vacuum lines connected to it. These lines snake through the dash, and all but two terminate at various points on the heater box. The remaining two lines, one ¼-inch diameter, the other ⅛-inch diameter, exit through the firewall near the center of the dash. The ⅛-inch hose goes to the vacuum-controlled water valve on the inboard heater hose, and the ¼-inch line goes to a small vacuum receiver located on the right fender apron. Don't overlook this receiver. It is there to provide enough vacuum volume to properly operate the flapper doors on the heater unit.

CONNECTING THE DASH WIRES

With the vacuum lines routed, the last task here is to route and connect as many of the dash wires as possible. Those include the wires leading to the starter switch, the heater/AC control panel, the heater motor and controls for the heater box, the wiper motor, the brake light switch, and the courtesy lamps. The only components not being wired at this time are the radio, the console, the steering column, and the gauge cluster.

INSTALLING THE DASH PAD

As the dash assembly nears completion, the next piece to be installed is the new dash pad. The Dashes Direct pad provided by AAPD is a factory original-type pad that slips over the metal dash and is secured using screws at each end and along the base of the windshield opening.

After installing the padded dash cover, the dash itself is finished out with new trim pieces from AAPD, shown in photo 12, and the newly restored gauge cluster. I now have a dash that looks factory new.

WIRE UNDER THE HOOD

I don't want to leave the subject of wiring this car without mentioning the two engine compartment harnesses. The engine wiring harness enters the compartment near the center of the firewall and contains wires for the electric choke, the distributor, the AC compressor, the temperature sensor, and the oil pressure sending unit. The other harness near the left side of the firewall routes to the front lights and the ignition circuit. Since neither the engine nor the front sheet metal has been installed, I temporarily route both of these harnesses along the left fender apron to keep them out of the way.

HANG THE DOORS

I left the doors off of the car until now to make installing the dash components a little easier. With the bulk of that work done, I can turn my attention to installing the doors. That starts by installing the hinges, followed by aligning the doors, and finishing with installing the latches and the handles on the doors.

INSTALLING THE HINGES

The hinge halves were previously refinished, so all that is left is to install the new Paddock Parts bushings and pins. This is a straightforward process with the exception of the universal length hinge pins that must be trimmed to the proper size. I install the new bushings and pins and mark the pins for length before cutting each one using a die grinder.

Once the pins are cut to length, I use the die grinder to notch the end of each pin, then use a cold chisel to flare the notched end, securing the pin to the hinge. After that, it is a matter of installing the hinges on the cowl before installing the doors on the car.

PHOTO 9: The heater core must be professionally tested for leaks before being installed back in the car.

PHOTO 10: The air conditioner evaporator core should be cleaned and any damaged cooling fins straightened before being installed back in the car.

PHOTO 11: The new dash pad from AAPD. Identical to the original, it slips over the metal dash and is secured by a series of screws along the rear of the pad and by bolts in each corner.

INSTALLING THE DOORS

Because both doors align using the same procedures, I'll go through the steps using the right passenger side door. Photo 14 shows a trick used by professionals to prevent chipping the paint during door installation. Paint stir sticks are cut in half and taped to the door opening to give the door a place to sit while you are bolting on the hinges.

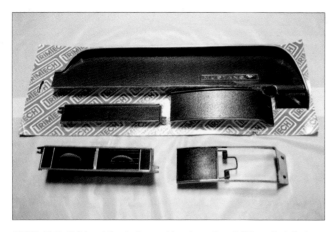

PHOTO 12: To finish out the dash, new trim pieces from AAPD are installed.

PHOTO 13: The Paddock Parts hinge pins are universal fit and will need to be cut to length. Each pin is marked (see the arrow) before cutting.

PHOTO 14: A body-shop trick to prevent scratching the fresh paint is to tape paint stir sticks around the door opening. The door can rest against the sticks and not touch the body of the car.

I start by putting the door in place on the car and snug-tightening the hinge mounting bolts. Next, I open the door, remove the paint stir sticks, and gently close the door, making certain the door does not touch the body of the car at any point.

ALIGNING THE DOORS

If you are faced with car doors that touch the body, there are several adjustments you can make. If the door sags at the rear, it can be lifted by shifting the top hinge slightly forward. This movement will also widen the gap at the top rear of the door. If the door sits too high at the rear, it can be lowered by shifting the bottom hinge slightly forward. This movement will also widen the gap at the bottom rear corner of the door.

You say the gap between the door and quarter panel is even but the door sits too high at the rear? If you have achieved an even gap between the door and the quarter panel, the door needs to be lowered at the hinges. Make this adjustment by loosening all six hinge bolts on the door and allowing the door to drop slightly. The same goes if the door gap is good where it meets the quarter panel but it sits too low: loosen the hinge bolts and raise the door slightly.

Is the door in good alignment with the quarter panel at the bottom but sits too far inboard at the top? Adjust the door inward slightly at the lower hinge. This will bring the top rear of the door outward. If the door is in good alignment where it meets the top of the quarter panel but sits too far in at the bottom, adjust the door inward at the upper hinge. If the reverse of either of these conditions exist, making the opposite hinge adjustment will be true.

INSTALLING THE LATCHES AND THE DOOR HANDLES

Now that the doors are in good alignment, the real test of how they fit can come only with the latches installed. To make opening the doors a little easier once the latches are installed, I'll also install the inside door handles.

> ### TIP
>
> *When installing the hinges on the cowl, leave the attachment bolts loose to allow the hinges to be shifted into place once the door is mounted on the car.*

PHOTO 15: If the door sits too low at the rear, shift the upper hinge forward slightly. That will cause the rear of the door to rise.

PHOTO 16: Adjusting the lower hinge inward will push the top rear of the door outward.

I have three concerns about aligning the door latch with the striker plate. First, if the door is pulled down when latched, the striker plate must be raised until the body lines on the door match the body lines on the quarter panel. Second, if the door lifts when latched, the striker plate must be lowered until the body lines align. Third, if the door either sticks out when latched or is sucked in too far when latched, the striker plate must be moved in or out, depending upon the position of the door when closed.

INSTALLING THE LEFT DOOR

All that is left now is to install the left door and ensure that the gaps around that door match the gaps around the right door. How will I accomplish that? Take a look at photo 17. I use the Eastwood Panel Gap Gauge to accurately measure each gap, so the left door can be positioned to match the right door. Then, I use the same techniques for aligning the left door as I did to align the right door.

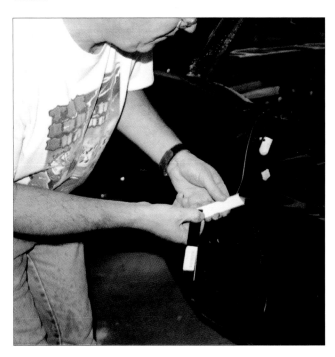

PHOTO 17: Eastwood's panel alignment gauge works much like a feeler gauge and is a must-have for matching panel gaps from side to side.

NOTES

NOTES

APPLYING THE COATINGS, REBUILDING THE SUSPENSION, AND INSTALLING THE BRAKE LINES

When it comes to restoring and refinishing the parts of this car that will be exposed to a lot of use and abuse, I have only two choices. The first is to apply powder coating. The second is to apply two coats of single-stage urethane. So how do I know when to apply which product?

First off, only those parts that can withstand temperatures of 400 degrees F for 30 minutes or more and will fit in the oven can be powder coated. That means parts such as the power steering valve assembly, the steering gearbox, and the tie-rod ends shown in photo 1 should never be powder coated. These parts contain gaskets, O-rings, and rubber boots that dictate never exposing the parts to high heat. These parts should be sanded, masked, and refinished with a single-stage urethane product.

On the other hand, parts such as the exhaust manifolds, the engine pulleys and brackets, the wheel spindles, the brake drums, and the backing plates are

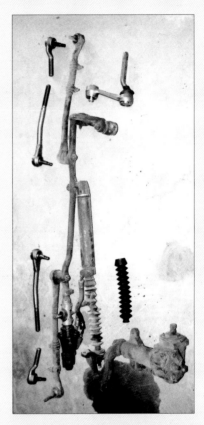

PHOTO 1: Steering components like these that contain gaskets, O-rings, and rubber boots should never be powder coated.

ideal candidates for powder coating. These parts have no O-rings, gaskets, or rubber boots that can be harmed from the heat, and that makes them ideally suited to the powder coating process.

As for rebuilding the suspension and installing the brake lines, these two processes go hand and hand. I'll begin by assembling the steering components of the suspension and finish by adding brakes to the completed assemblies.

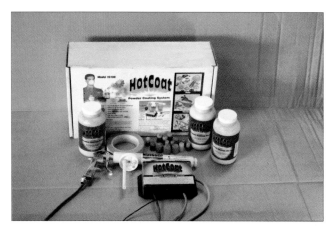

PHOTO 2: Eastwood Deluxe Hot Coat Powder Coating System. This package contains everything you need to produce a professional-looking powder coat finish.

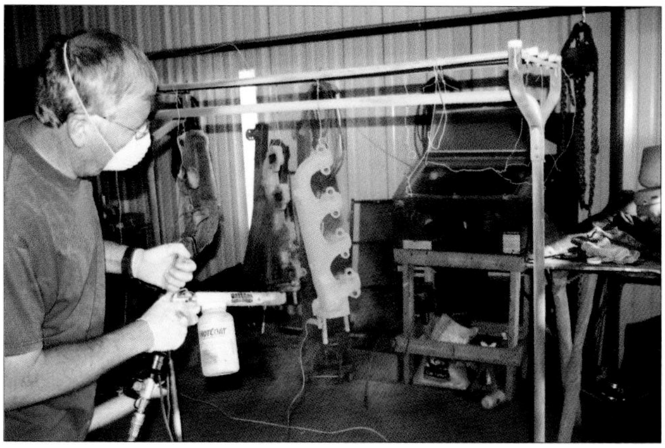

PHOTO 3: The best way to coat a part for baking is to suspend the part on a painting rack to ensure complete coverage.

MAKE SURE THEY'RE CLEAN

If the powder coating process has any drawbacks, it has to be that the parts must be perfectly clean before being coated. That means each part to be powder coated must be stripped of all old paint, which in my case means the parts will go through an Eastwood blast cabinet #22107 or be chemically stripped using an aircraft-grade paint stripper.

THE POWDER COATING PROCESS

The items needed to complete the powder coating process include the Eastwood's Deluxe Hot Coat Powder Coating System #10112, shown in photo 2, dry powder colors, a means of suspending the parts for coating, and an electric oven. Don't try this with a gas oven. Open flames and powder coating don't mix. The powders can explode. Try explaining that to your homeowner's insurance company.

The powders I've selected include Eastwood Hotcoat Powder Semi Gloss Black #10108 and Hotcoat Powder Cast Iron #10095. I've used both of these powder colors before, so I know from experience that the semi-gloss black will closely match the semigloss black color used to spray the engine compartment, and the cast iron color will give the exhaust manifolds and the brake drums that new look.

The actual process of powder coating is simple. I clean the part being coated down to bare metal as outlined above, degrease it with PPG DX 330 Acryli-Clean degreaser, then suspend it for spraying, as shown in photo 3.

I then load the powder coat gun with the appropriate color per the instructions accompanying the kit, connect the part to a power source provided in the kit to electrically charge it to attract the powder, then coat the part.

I apply the powder carefully and evenly over the part, taking care not to touch the part once the coating process begins. Should I inadvertently touch the part and dislodge any of the applied powder, it is best to stop the coating process, blow the part clean of any remaining powder, and begin again.

Once the part is thoroughly coated, I place it in the 450 degrees F preheated oven for about 30 minutes. To get the part to the oven, I usually leave the suspension wire on the piece being coated and use that to transport and hang the part from the upper rack in the oven. As the

TIP

Once the parts are cleaned down to the bare metal, I like to bake them in the oven for 30 minutes at 450 degrees F to help leech out or burn off any contaminants that might be lurking in the pores of the metal.

TIP

I use a tall painting rack to hang the parts and a length of clean (uncoated) wire to suspend the part under the rack. Why use uncoated wire? Using a coated wire such as a painted coat hanger can contaminate the powder during the baking process and cause it not to stick.

part bakes, the dull-looking powder slowly heats and transforms into an almost liquid state, giving the part being coated a freshly painted appearance.

This process is called powder coating for a reason. The powders are so fine that breathing on them can cause a dust cloud. When I'm powder coating, I always wear a dust mask rated at N95 (3M #7185) to prevent accidentally ingesting the dust, and I put on latex gloves to prevent contaminating the piece with oils from my skin.

For those parts with threaded holes, planed ports, and tolerance-fitted surfaces, such as on an intake manifold, the kit comes with various sizes of heat resistant plugs, as well as a roll of heat resistant tape. I insert the plugs into any threaded holes and other places where coating is not desired and tape off the machined surfaces before coating.

When the task of powder coating is finished, cleanup is a snap. After properly securing and storing the powders, I don the dust mask and use an air nozzle to blow the applicator gun clean of any residue. After that, I sweep the application area clean and dispose of the excess powder residue in a sealed plastic bag.

APPLY THE LIQUID COATINGS

For applying urethane to all those parts that can't be powder coated, I selected PPG DCC Concept Acrylic Urethane Single-Stage Gloss black 9600. This is a three-component urethane finish that does not require a clear coat to bring out the shine.

Concept can be applied over most finishes including OEM enamels, lacquers, epoxy, and urethane primers, to name a few. Concept mixes at a 4:2:1 ratio, 4 parts Concept to 2 parts reducer to 1 part DCX61 hardener. Apply two wet coats, allowing 10 to 15 minutes between coats and at least 8 hours to cure.

REBUILD THE FRONT SUSPENSION

Early Mustang front suspensions are relatively basic in design and can be lumped into the category of an SLA (short arm, long arm) suspension. What does SLA mean? Look at the control arms displayed in photo 5. The upper control arms (A-shaped arms) are short in comparison with the lower control arms (bottom), thus the names short arm and long arm, or SLA, suspension.

PHOTO 4: The cast iron powder color gives these exhaust manifolds that new look.

PHOTO 5: Before being installed, the components making up the bulk of the front suspension are laid out in the relative positions they will be once on the car. This is an SLA, or short arm, long arm–type suspension.

Also displayed in the photo, starting at the top and moving down, are strut arms and bushings, upper ball joints, and upper control arm bushings. I replace the old bushings, ball joints, and lower control arms with new parts from National Parts Depot. Parts not shown in photo 5 but also needed to complete the front suspension assembly include coil springs, spindles, brake backing plates, brake drums, new tie-rod ends, inner and outer wheel bearings, new brake pads, and shock absorbers.

I always begin a front suspension rebuild by refurbishing everything associated with that part of the car. The steering components, such as the steering gearbox's steering-control valve, the steering linkage, tie-rod ends, and the idler arm, shown in photo 1, are considered part of the front suspension, so these are the first parts restored and installed back on the car.

Next on the list for installation are the control arms and the coil springs. Both the upper and lower control arms are installed but left loose to allow for movement when installing the coil spring. A pair of coil spring

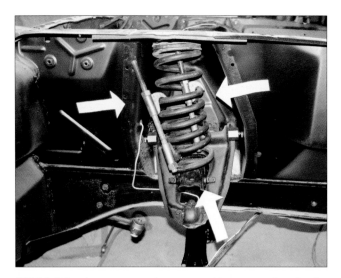

PHOTO 6: Coil spring compressor clamps are used to compress the coil spring for installation. Because of the limited space for installing the spring, one clamp is placed on the outside of the spring, and the other is placed on the inside of the spring.

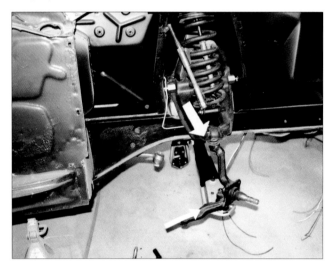

PHOTO 7: Before the compressor clamps can be removed, the spindle is bolted into place.

PHOTO 8: The brake components are assembled and checked for proper operation before installing the brake drum.

compressor clamps (photo 6, top arrows), available at most automotive parts stores, are then used to compress the spring for installation. The top of the spring is protected by a squeak-dampening rubber insulator, and the bottom of the spring sits on a rubber bushing atop the lower spring mounting plate (lower arrow, photo 6).

Once the spring has been compressed enough to slip into place, the upper and lower control arms are connected at the ball joints via the spindle, as shown in photo 7. Once the two control arms are connected, the spring compressor clamps can be removed.

The last steps are to bolt on the brake backing plate and add the new brake shoes (you might want to refer to the teardown photographs for the correct position of the shoes), the brake drum, and, finally, the tie-rod. I always save the tie-rod connection for last because this allows me to swivel the spindle/brake assembly as needed during installation.

BRAKE LINE TIME

Connected to both front brake assemblies are the brake lines. Considering the age of this car, replacing the old flexible brake lines is a given. The steel brake lines can be scuff sanded using a Norton Bear-Tex Scuff Pad to bring back the shine, then painted with Eastwood #10030Z zinc coating.

This is also the time to consider cleaning the inside of the steel brake lines by spraying Gumout Fuel Injector/Carburetor Cleaner through the lines to flush out any brake fluid residue. I allow the cleaner to flow through the lines until all traces of any dark sludge are gone, and then I use an air nozzle to flush the lines clean of any remaining cleaner.

Why didn't I replace the steel brake lines with new ones? Occasionally I do. But the brake system in this car is in very good condition: no dark fluid, no thick gunk in

> **TIP**
>
> *When replacing the tie-rod ends, how do you determine the approximate length of the tie-rod assembly once the new ends have been installed? The original assembly is laid on the floor and measured. In this case, the overall assembly measures 18 inches. I match that length when installing the new tie-rod ends on the adjuster sleeves.*

the brake cylinders, and no signs of trauma such as kinks or dents were visible on any of the lines.

At this point, I install the brake master cylinder and proportioning valve and attach the refurbished steel brake lines. I also attach the brake warning–lamp wire (purple #968 from the Painless Performance kit) to the proportioning valve at this time.

The steel brake line running from the master cylinder to the rear axle can also be routed at this time, but because the rear axle assembly has yet to be installed, I cap the end of the brake line to prevent contamination. Only after the rear axle is installed can the brake system be filled and bled of residual air trapped in the lines. That's a task I'll reserve for later.

PAINT THE DECK LID

If it seems as if I'm skipping all over the map to work on this car, I assure you that there is a method to all this madness. I'd like to install the rear axle, but it hasn't returned from the mechanic's shop where I sent it for inspection. That means I have time to work on a few other items lingering on the to-do list, such as painting and installing the deck lid, while I patiently wait for my name to be called at the mechanic's shop.

The deck lid for this California Mustang is made of fiberglass instead of metal. But that doesn't mean I'll make any changes to the way this panel is refinished. Base colors and clear coats can't tell the difference between the two materials and therefore will lie just as smooth on fiberglass as they do on metal.

If there is any difference at all, it has to be the problem of static electricity. Fiberglass tends to generate static electricity any time it is wiped clean. Who cares about eliminating static electricity? Anyone holding a paint gun in his hand should be. Static electricity causes dust and anything else floating in the air to become attracted to the panel being painted, and we all know what dust and trash in a fresh paint job looks like. It isn't pretty.

What can be done to eliminate static electricity? The part can be grounded by attaching one end of an electrical wire to one of the hinge mounting bolts and the other end to a strong ground point such as a cold water pipe in the shop. In extreme cases, I've even had to ground myself using one of those stylish, grounded antistatic wristbands seen on all of the computer gurus these days. If none of those efforts stop the popping, I resort to PPG

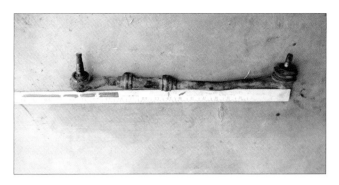

PHOTO 9: Another body-shop trick: measuring the length of the old tie-rod assembly gives me an approximate length for use when replacing the old tie-rod ends.

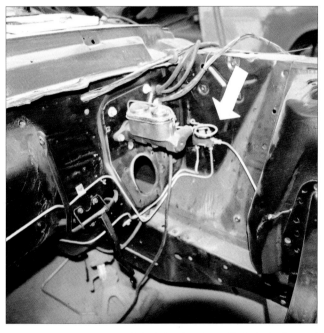

PHOTO 10: The brake master cylinder is installed along with the brake lines and the proportioning valve.

PHOTO 11: Like water on a glass. All it takes is good equipment and some time spent behind the spray gun to get good results.

PHOTO 12: Deck lid hinge springs can be extremely dangerous to install, as they tend to pop and fly around if not held securely during installation. Here, I'm using a pair of Vise-Grip pliers to control the spring as I slip it into the center adjusting notch on the hinge support.

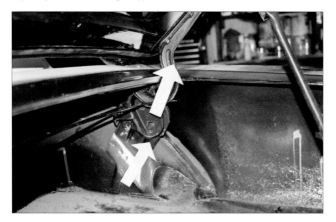

PHOTO 13: The deck lid hinges have up and down adjustments (lower arrow). Initially, adjust the hinge fully upward to prevent chipping the paint during the deck lid installation. The upper arrow points to the forward and back adjustment points on the hinge.

PHOTO 14: How many times do I need to mount these extensions? I hope this is the last time. I need to be sure that the critical points such as the peak of the spoiler (top arrow) aligns with the deck lid and that the body line (lower arrow) aligns with the body line of the quarter panel.

DX 103 Multi-Prep. This is a product especially formulated to help eliminate static electricity. I just load a little into a spray gun and apply a thin mist coat to whatever is being painted.

Once I have dealt with the static electricity issue, the deck lid can be painted and the clear coats can be applied using the same refinishing procedures discussed in chapter 13 to refinish the body of the car.

INSTALL THE DECK LID AND THE REAR SHEET METAL PANELS

One of the problems associated with installing the deck lid is tensioning the hinge springs. I use a pair of Vise-Grip pliers to leverage the springs during installation.

Here is an adjustment most vehicles don't have. The hinges can be shifted up or down, depending on the fit of the deck lid. I always adjust the hinges full upward when installing them. If the deck lid sits too high at the back glass once it is installed, it is a simple matter of adjusting the hinges down until the deck lid fits. Why do it this way? It lets me start with a wide gap between the deck lid and the back glass filler panel instead of a tight gap that might result in scratched or chipped paint.

After the deck lid has been installed, it is time once again to mount the quarter panel extension spoilers and test the fit. I'm looking for two things here, as indicated by the arrows in photo 14. First, I want the peak of the quarter panel extension spoiler(s) to align with the peak of the deck lid spoiler. If it doesn't, more deck lid alignment may be necessary. Second, I want the body line of the quarter panel extension(s) to align with the body lines on the quarter panels. When I have these two points in perfect alignment, the extensions can be removed from the car and refinished.

That leaves the taillamp finish panel, the rear valance panel, and the rear bumper to be installed back here. But because the rear valance panel will be in the way when mounting the rear axle springs, I need to first install the rear axle that I am waiting to get back from the shop.

INSTALL THE REAR AXLE

Just like anyone stepping out for a good time on a Saturday night, the rear axle needed a good scrubbing before leaving the shop. So before packing the unit off to

PHOTO 15: After the springs have been cleaned and painted, new squeaker pads are added, and new clamps are used to hold the springs together.

PHOTO 16: Just like new. The shiny rear axle and repainted springs make the underside of Project Mustang look as good as the topside.

the local professional, I gave it a thorough pressure washing. I always request an initial inspection before doing any work on the unit. The unit may be found to be in excellent condition or a complete rebuild may be in order. A clean bill of health will only set me back a few bucks, whereas a complete rebuild can set me back several hundred bucks. But no matter which way I have to go, it will be money well spent. After all, no one likes to hear a worn out rear axle whine and grind while trying to impress the local cronies with how nice the car drives.

The rear leaf springs on this car also require some attention. The riding height is typical for a Mustang, and the springs measure what I call the "correct unsprung height" of about 9½ inches, which is a typical height for most Mustang leaf springs in good condition. However, I will disassemble both leaf assemblies, clean each spring, replace the squeak pads and the spring clamps, as shown in photo 15, and give the entire assembly a fresh coat of cast iron gray paint before installing everything back under the car.

NOTES

_____

_____

_____

_____

_____

_____

_____

_____

CHAPTER 17

INSTALLING THE VINYL TOP COVER, THE HEADLINER, AND THE GLASS

continue rebuilding the car by installing several pieces that will make a big impact on its final appearance. I am now ready to install the vinyl cover on the roof panel, the cloth headliner, and all of the glass pieces.

INSTALL THE VINYL TOP COVER

For several weeks now, I've had the new vinyl top cover from the Paddock Parts laid out across the top of the car to help relax some of the wrinkles caused by the compact packaging and get it ready for installation. Compared with some roof panels, this is a very small area to cover, but nevertheless, fewer wrinkles mean an easier installation. Of course, an easier installation isn't the only reason for laying the cover out on the car; I also need to be sure I have the correct cover.

Installation begins by making sure I have enough 3M Super Trim Adhesive Yellow #8090 on hand to glue this cover down securely. 3M 8090 comes in an 18-oz aerosol can, and I'll need a minimum of two cans to do a roof panel this size.

The first step is to carefully position the cover on the roof panel and take a couple of measurements from the seam lines to the drip rails. The seams on the cover must be straight when finished, as shown in photo 2, and they must be an equal distance from each drip rail. To be sure I take accurate measurements, I start by measuring from the rear of the roof panel forward and place two lengths of masking tape at 22 and 42 inches, where the cover drapes over the drip rails. At 22 inches, the distance inboard from the drip rail to the seam line is 4½ inches. At 42 inches, the distance from the drip rail to the seam is 4¾ inches.

Getting these measurements exact on both sides of the roof takes a little time, but when both sides measure the same, I know the cover is perfectly centered on the roof. Once that's done, I clamp one side of the cover in place using Vise-Grip pliers and wooden stir sticks to prevent damaging the cover, and then I fold the free side of the cover back over the clamped side and apply a generous coating of 3M 8090 to both the inside of the cover and the exposed half of the roof panel.

PHOTO 1: Laying out the new vinyl top cover helps relax many of the wrinkles that developed while the cover was boxed for several months.

PHOTO 2: Measurements are taken from the seam lines to center the cover on the roof panel.

> **TIP**
>
> *To prevent adhesive from spraying onto areas other than the roof panel, I use a plastic drop cloth to cover and protect the cowl, the trunk, and both sides of the vehicle.*

Now comes the hard part: sticking the new cover to the roof panel without getting any wrinkles or air bubbles. I always seem to have extra plastic body filler

PHOTO 3: One of the most difficult areas to smooth is here, where the cover drapes over the sail panels.

PHOTO 4: The cover must be trimmed around the molding mounting studs at both the windshield and the back glass openings.

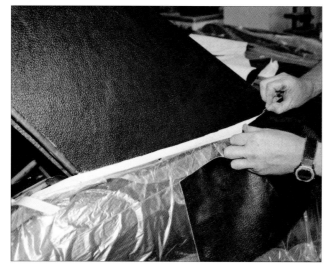

PHOTO 5: Masking tape is used to mark the cut line where the cover meets the quarter panel.

spreaders around the shop, and they make great squeegees to help stick the cover to the roof panel. I start near the center of the roof and work outward, taking care to smooth out the wrinkles as I go.

The critical areas are where the cover folds down onto the sail panels and around the drip rails. These areas are prone to wrinkling and bunching so will require a lot of TLC to get the cover to lay flat. Trimming away the excess vinyl with a safety razor around the drip rails helps the cover to conform to the roof panel and reduces the chances of creating wrinkles in that area.

The lips of the windshield and back glass openings have metal studs used for securing the molding retainer clips that must be worked around. In photo 4, I'm carefully trimming the cover around each stud, then using the plastic body filler spreader to ensure that the cover is properly adhered where it folds over the opening lip. This is a critical step when working around the windshield opening because while you're driving the car, the wind can easily force its way under the cover, causing it to separate from the roof panel.

Once the entire cover is in place, I use a safety razor to trim away the excess vinyl. Notice the masking tape used to define the line where the sail panel molding separates the cover from the quarter panel. Once the cover is trimmed and properly adhered to the car, I can install the sail panel molding. Why install this molding now? The mounting studs are secured by two nuts inside the sail panel. Once the headliner is installed, the mounting studs are not accessible.

INSTALL THE HEADLINER

The new headliner had arrived from the Paddock Parts, so I'm able to install this next. The first step is to lay the old headliner on the floor next to the new headliner so I can confirm that I have the correct replacement headliner. I then transfer the headliner bows one at a time from the old headliner to the new headliner to ensure that I get each one in the correct location. If you recall back when I removed the old headliner from the car, I left the headliner bows in the old headliner. Because none of these bows are the same length, leaving them in place in the old headliner was insurance against installing them in the wrong position in the new headliner.

The bad news is that on the day Ford engineered the installation of the Mustang headliner, it seemingly was extremely unhappy with the guys doing the install. That is the only reason I can come up with that explains Ford's lack of mechanical fasteners to help hold the headliner in place. Ford relied primarily on adhesives to secure the edges of the headliner and used mechanical fasteners only to help hold the sail panel portion of the headliner in place. What all that means is that I'll be securing the new headliner to the roof panel using 3M Fast Tack Trim Adhesive #8031, several pairs of Vise-Grip pliers, an assortment of wooden stir sticks, and a few choice words not to be repeated here.

Headliners are installed by working from the rear to the front and finishing with the sides. I start by securing the headliner around the back glass opening using Vise-Grip pliers and wooden stir sticks. The pliers hold everything in place, and the stir sticks prevent the pliers from damaging the headliner and provide more surface area for gluing the headliner. Once this is accomplished, I move to the front of the car and repeat the operation by securing the front of the headliner all the way across the windshield opening using the Fast Tack Trim Adhesive. Once the adhesive securing the front and the rear of the new headliner has had time to cure, which usually takes a couple of hours, I repeat this securing operation by gluing and clamping each side of the headliner using the Vise-Grip pliers and wooden stir sticks.

Ford was kind enough to engineer the use of a pinch-on windlace that runs the length of each side of the inner roof. Fortunately, that is enough to ensure that the headliner stays in place once it has been properly adhered. The last step here is to use a safety razor to trim away the excess headliner where the roof rail weather strips mount and to install new weather strips from California Mustang.

Finally, the area of the headliner covering the inner sail panel can be secured using the mechanical fasteners Ford was kind enough to incorporate into the inner structure of the car. What are they? Just sharp metal teeth protruding from the inner sail panel designed to hook into the headliner and hold it in place.

Now for some good news. New headliners tend to have wrinkles after being installed. The best way to remove the wrinkles is to close both doors and go work on some other part of the car. The wrinkles will slowly fade away as the new headliner accustoms itself to its new home. Once most of the wrinkles have faded, the dome light, the rear view mirror, and the sun visors can be installed.

PHOTO 6: Both the new and the old headliners are laid out on the floor so the headliner bows can be transferred from the old to the new.

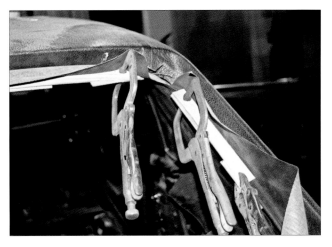

PHOTO 7: Vise-Grip pliers and wooden stir sticks are used to clamp the headliner in place while the adhesive cures.

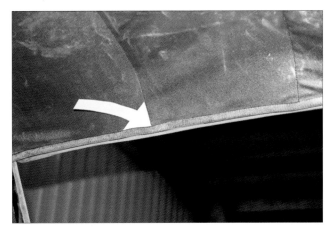

PHOTO 8: A windlace is used to secure the sides of the new headliner.

PHOTO 9: Before installation, the quarter windows and mechanisms are laid out, cleaned, and inspected.

PHOTO 10: The arrows indicate the mounting and adjusting points for the quarter window assembly.

INSTALL THE GLASS

There are many pieces of glass that need to be put back on the Mustang. As you may recall, these glass pieces were carefully stored in a box to prevent them from breaking. I now carefully retrieve all of the glass pieces and prepare to reinstall the quarter windows, the door glass, the windshield, and the back glass. I also need to gather all of the components that were used to hold the glass in place.

PUTTING IN THE QUARTER WINDOWS

I start by installing the quarter windows. All of the components that I removed earlier are laid out in the approximate position they will be placed inside the quarter panel, and then they are cleaned and inspected for wear. The two items numbered 1 in photo 9 are new guide rollers to be mounted in item number 2, the regulator. Once mounted, these rollers slide into the run channel shown as item number 7.

As for installation, the sequence goes as follows: the regulator (2) goes in first. Next is the regulator support panel (3), followed by the glass assembly (6). Both number 3 and number 6 install through the glass opening at the top of the quarter panel. Next, the regulator run channel (7) and the regulator support panel lower mounting bracket (4) are installed. Finally, the short belt weather strip shown above number 3 and the vertical weather strip (5) are installed.

Now comes the tricky part. With the glass installed and moving freely along the guide tracks of the regulator support panel, the upper arm of the regulator must be installed in the roller channel mounted on the bottom of the glass assembly (mounted on the opposite side of number 6). Once that is done, I can tighten the four regulator mounting bolts, temporarily install the crank handle, and roll the glass full up.

With the glass rolled up, I can tighten the remaining mounting bolts, as shown in photo 10. Do these bolts serve any other function? Yes they do. The top bolts (1 and 2) allow the glass to shift either forward or backward, depending on the fit of the glass once the door glass has been installed. The lower bolts (3 and 4) serve as adjustments to shift the glass inboard or outboard at the roof rail. That's why I rolled the glass full up, seated it in the roof rail weather strip, then tightened the bolts. I may have some minor adjustments to make once the door glass is installed, but it won't be much.

INSTALLING THE DOOR GLASS

The first steps to installing the door glass are to disassemble the vent glass assembly and replace the weather strip with new pieces I got from California Mustang. The correct order for disassembling the assembly is shown in photo 11. I start by removing the nut, the spring, and the lower swivel bracket (1) from the vent glass frame. This allows me to push the glass (2) down into the frame, release the upper pivot pin, and remove the glass from the frame.

Next, I remove the old run channel weather strip (3) from the frame. A small screw located near the top of the weather strip must be removed before the strip can come out of the frame.

Finally, I remove the glass weather strip (4) from the frame. This weather strip has a metal-reinforced backing along the rear vertical portion of the strip and is best removed from the frame using a small flat-blade screwdriver. Then I polish the frame using a spiral buffing wheel and stainless compound from the Eastwood Company's Buffing Shop Kit #13109. I clean the glass using #00 steel wool.

Once all of the weather strips have been replaced, I assemble the unit in the reverse order I disassembled it.

I can now, finally, install the door glass. As indicated in photo 12, this Mustang uses a framed glass assembly (3), so the glass can be cleaned using #00 steel wool, and the frame can be polished using the spiral buffing wheel and stainless compound. The regulator (1) and the rear run channel (4) are cleaned before installation and lubricated with lithium grease. This is a white grease and is the best choice for lubricating components exposed to grit and grime.

Before installation, the regulator should be inspected for broken gear teeth, a broken spring, and worn rollers. If any of the above parts show excessive wear or are broken, replacement regulators are available from most of the Mustang supply sources mentioned in chapter 1.

I haven't talked about installing the outside door handles and key lock assemblies when installing and aligning the doors, so if these parts haven't already been installed, do so now. The left door handle takes a lot of abuse; if it is scratched or if the push button seems loose, consider replacing the piece. I elect to replace both the left and right door handles with new ones from California Mustang.

ADJUSTING THE DOOR GLASS

Ford has always been good about providing adequate room for adjustments. Mustang doors are no exception. The numbered arrows in photo 13 point to the primary points of adjustment to help align both door glasses to the body of the car. I start with numbers 1 and 2. These are long double-nut bolts that allow the vent glass assembly to be shifted forward, backward, in, or out. With both bolts left loose, I close the door and position the vent glass assembly tight against the roof rail weather strip. Satisfied with the fit, I open the door and tighten the bolts.

But the adjustments don't stop here. If, after tightening the bolts, the vent glass assembly has been pulled too far inboard, the lower bolts must be loosened and screwed inward. This pulls the bottom of the vent glass

PHOTO 11: The door vent glass is also laid out, cleaned, and inspected, and the weather stripping replaced before installation.

PHOTO 12: The door components are laid out in the approximate positions they will be inside the door.

PHOTO 13: The arrows indicate the mounting and adjusting points for both the vent glass and the door glass.

PHOTO 14: The dollar bill test: If the bill cannot be pulled out, the glass is too tight against the body. If the bill is easily pulled out, the glass isn't tight enough against the body to prevent wind noise.

PHOTO 15: When both glasses are in alignment the gap between them should be about ½ inch wide.

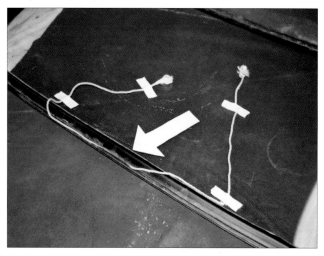

PHOTO 16: This cotton cord is tucked into the gasket mounting channel all the way around the glass.

assembly inboard and causes the top of the assembly to tilt outboard.

To test your adjustments, use the dollar bill test. If the bill can't be pulled from between the glass and weather strip, the seal is too tight. If it is easily pulled, the seal isn't tight enough. If the dollar bill can be pulled only with some difficulty, the adjustments are just right.

Now, back to photo 13. With the vent glass assembly properly aligned, I can roll the door glass full up and tighten the two bolts holding the short regulator run channel indicated at number 3. Item number 3 also has an up and down adjustment. Its function is to level the glass when rolled full up. If the glass does not seat into the top of the vent glass and along the roof rail weather strip, I can change the position of the glass by adjusting the run channel either up or down. If the glass rolls up too far, I can adjust the glass stop found near the top of the rear run channel. This stop was removed during teardown to allow the glass to come up and out of the door.

Number 4 in photo 13 is another inboard/outboard adjustment screw. If the glass leans too far inboard when rolled up, I can tighten this screw to bring the bottom of the rear run channel inboard. This will cause the top rear of the glass to lean farther outboard.

Recall I left the quarter glass in a semi-adjusted state? I can now roll the door glass and quarter glass full up to check the gap between the two pieces of glass. This gap should be roughly ½ inch wide, as shown in photo 15. It's out of whack? To gain better alignment, loosen the two upper bolts, shown in photo 10, and shift the quarter glass until a good alignment with the door glass is achieved. Finally, I tighten all bolts, then roll both windows up and down to be sure that they are operating properly and that the gap between them remains even.

INSTALLING THE WINDSHIELD AND THE BACK GLASS

Both of these glasses are mounted in rubber gaskets as opposed to being soft set using a urethane glass adhesive. Not sure about the difference between these two methods of installation? A rubber gasket–mounted glass uses a soft rubber gasket that can be purchased from any of the Mustang parts suppliers mentioned thus far, and it forms a continuous circle around the glass being installed. This gasket has two channels cut into it: one for the glass to slip into to hold the gasket in place, the other for the lip of metal making up the glass opening on the vehicle.

A soft-set installation uses no gasket. Instead, the glass is laid in place on top of the glass opening lip by first putting down a heavy bead, usually ½-inch thick, of urethane adhesive. This adhesive never completely cures to become rock hard but rather remains somewhat soft and pliable, thus the name *soft set*.

I start installing the back glass by laying it on a clean surface. I find a padded surface because I want to avoid scratching the glass. Next, I position the gasket around the glass by slipping the glass into the widest channel cut into the gasket. These gaskets are glass specific so there is no way you can get it wrong. The gasket fits only one way.

Next, I take a length of cotton cord long enough to circle the glass and work it into the outer channel all the way around the glass. Notice in photo 16 that the cord wraps around the glass and then overlaps itself to ensure a complete circle around the glass.

From here, this is a two-person job, and it starts by laying the glass into the glass opening. When laying the glass into the opening, slip the gasket over the bottom lip

TIP

If the quarter glass is positioned too close to the door glass when both are rolled up, the door glass will have a tendency to rub against the quarter glass when the door is opened and closed. The cure is to widen the gap by shifting the quarter glass back slightly.

of the opening flange to help the glass settle into the opening. With one person on the outside applying medium pressure against the glass, the other person can begin pulling the cotton cord from the gasket channel. As the cord comes out, it forces the lip of the gasket to lift up and over the metal lip of the glass opening, causing the glass to draw into the opening. It helps to gently pat the outside of the glass with the flat of the hand as the cord is being removed. Continue this operation around the entire glass to fully seat the glass.

Repeat this operation with the windshield, and you are done.

NOTES

_____

_____

_____

_____

_____

_____

_____

_____

_____

_____

CHAPTER 18

REBUILDING AND INSTALLING THE ENGINE

The 289 cubic-inch-displacement (CID) engine for the Mustang has occupied an engine stand for several months now. The plan calls for disassembling this engine and delivering only the internal components to the machine shop for repair and rebuilding. I happen to enjoy engine assembly work, so that is one of the reasons I send out only those parts of the engine that require professional attention and leave the rest of the parts on the bench. If having greasy fingernails isn't your cup of tea, by all means load up the entire engine and deliver it to the machine shop of choice as a complete unit. I would recommend asking the machine shop not to paint the engine once it's assembled. This is a task I would reserve for myself to ensure that I didn't get an aerosol can finish. Once you receive the parts back from the machine shop, you are ready to assemble the engine and install it in the car.

MACHINE SHOP REPAIRS

If you are like me and prefer to do your own assembly work, the pieces you will need to provide to the machine shop include the block, the crankshaft, the main bearing caps, the pistons and rod assemblies, and the heads. I would place all of these parts in the "professional repair only" category because the block will more than likely require oversize boring, which will in turn require new oversize pistons to be pressed onto the old rods. The crankshaft will probably require undersizing, which means new oversize bearings, and the heads will require at least some new valves, all new valve guides, and possibly new valve springs and resurfacing.

Obviously, I've left out a number of detail procedures that any good machine shop will perform, but you get the idea. The work done in a machine shop isn't work a garage restorer can successfully undertake without spending a large fortune on equipment and training.

So what is all this over- and undersizing the engine may require? I'll start with the block itself. The 289 CID

engine from the Mustang has eight cylinders, each one with a bore size of 4.000 inches. As the engine operates, the pistons move up and down in the cylinders. As they reciprocate, they are constantly being pushed outward against the walls of the cylinders, and over time this outward force causes what would normally be a perfectly round cylinder wall to wear away and widen slightly. If you could see an exaggerated view of the cross section of a well-worn cylinder wall, you would see that the cylinder is no longer a perfect circle but rather has become egg shaped. This wear can result in a loss of power and engine oil consumption. Boring the cylinder slightly oversize, in most cases .010 to .040 inches, is normally enough to remove the egg shape and return the cylinder to a perfect circle. That will return the power to the engine and eliminate the oil consumption. Of course, all of this cylinder boring means the old pistons must be scrapped and new oversize pistons purchased. It also means new oversize piston rings will be needed to fit the new oversize pistons.

Next is the crankshaft. The crankshaft for the 289 has a total of nine journals, four for the piston rods and five for the main bearing caps. Each one of these journals is perfectly round when new but can become worn or grooved from normal engine use. Each journal must then be undersized in a lathe to return it to a round condition. In most cases, .010 to .030 inches undersizing of each journal is sufficient.

Of course, any undersizing of the crankshaft requires oversizing of the bearings to maintain the proper fit of the main bearing and rod caps. The real trick to all this undersizing of the crankshaft and oversizing of the associated bearings is to ensure that the correct oil clearance is maintained at each journal. I'll go through how I verify the correct oil clearance later, but for now, let me explain that oil clearance is nothing more than a microscopic space left between the crankshaft journal and the bearing. This space is filled with engine oil that forms a barrier between the two surfaces to prevent the crankshaft and bearings from overheating, expanding, and seizing. Not getting oil between the crankshaft and a rod cap, for example, is like clamping a pair of Vise-Grip pliers to the crankshaft and expecting the engine to run. It isn't going to happen.

The heads should also be sent to a machine shop for rebuilding. There are two basic concerns related to restoring an engine head back to a serviceable condition. First, the mating surface where the head mounts to the engine block must be perfectly flat. Between the head and the engine block is a head gasket. It is there to seal off each cylinder from the adjoining cylinders. If the head is not perfectly flat, the gasket can be easily breached and burned away due to the extreme heat and compression built up in each cylinder. This breach can cause a loss of compression in one or more cylinders, and suddenly your V-8 can become a V-6. The machine shop will "surface" both heads to ensure that this mating surface is perfectly flat.

The valve train is next. Exhaust valves get removed and thrown away. No ifs, ands, or buts. The extreme heat these valves are subjected to can severely erode them as well as render them brittle and subject to cracking or breaking.

Intake valves can be removed, reground, and reinstalled provided their condition warrants repair and not replacement. That's where experience comes in. It doesn't take a good machinist long to examine an intake valve and determine its usefulness.

Finally, each valve operates within a hardened steel sleeve inside the head known as a valve guide. Valve guides wear out just like everything else, so most machine shops

opt to install new guides to prevent oil from seeping between the valve and the guide and dropping into the combustion chamber. Ever crank a well-worn engine after it has sat for a day and observed a puff of white smoke coming out of the exhaust? In many cases, that puff of white smoke indicates oil is seeping past the worn-out valve guides and entering the combustion chamber.

ASSEMBLE THE ENGINE

Once I receive the engine parts back from the machine shop, I can start assembling the engine. I'm offering the *Reader's Digest* version of engine assembly, so always refer to the assembly manual for your particular application before installing any component into your engine.

Engine assembly begins with having the right replacement parts, gaskets, bearings, and piston rings on hand when you start. Where are all of these pieces going to come from? The machine shop that did the machine work is the best source. It knows the appropriate oversize and undersize component requirements for the engine and will get the right replacement parts.

Now that I have the engine parts and the right replacement parts, I am ready to assemble and install the engine parts, working from the bottom of the engine to the top of the engine. Once the engine is completely assembled, I will paint the engine Ford Guardsman Blue. The next major part I can install is the transmission, followed by the smaller accessories. I then finish by wiring the engine.

INSTALLING THE PARTS AT THE BOTTOM OF THE ENGINE

I start assembly by mounting the engine block on an engine stand and rotating it to an upside-down position to expose the crankshaft journals. The crankshaft is the first part to be installed. For that, I need the new main bearings, and they come packaged with four identical bearing sets and one shouldered bearing set. The shouldered bearing is the thrust bearing, and in the case of a Ford 289 engine, it mounts on the center journal. Its purpose is to prevent back and forth movement of the crankshaft within the block as it turns. What's wrong with a little back and forth movement? It can cause excess wear on the rod bearings and timing chain.

Installing the remaining main bearings is straightforward because each one easily slips into position on the journals. Once the bearings are in place, the rear main oil seal and crankshaft can be installed along with the main bearing caps. Each main bearing cap is numbered as to position, starting at the front of the engine and working back through all five journals. Don't forget to apply assembly lubricant to each bearing surface and to torque each journal to the correct specifications.

Following is a list of all the correct journal torque specifications:

- Rods bearing bolts: 19-24 ft lbs
- Main bearing bolts: 60-70 ft lbs
- Crankshaft pulley bolts: 70-90 ft lbs
- Flywheel bolts: 75-85 ft lbs

Before going any further, let's talk about ensuring proper oil clearance at each journal. Factory specifications call for .0005 to .0024 inches of clearance between the crankshaft and the main cap assembly. To determine the actual clearance at each journal, a plasti-gauge is used. A plasti-gauge is a very thin, round length of plastic and is available at any automotive parts store. To measure the clearance, the main bearing cap is removed and cleaned of assembly lubricant, a short strip of plasti-gauge is placed on the crankshaft journal, and the bearing cap is replaced and tightened to the correct specifications. The cap is then removed to expose the crushed length of plasti-gauge, which is then measured for width. In this case, the plasti-gauge placed at the number 1 cap measured .0015 inches, well within tolerances. This test is repeated for the remaining journals. What happens if the journal isn't within tolerance? It is back to the machine shop. The crankshaft sizing may not be correct, and that will require the attention of the machinist.

Next to be installed are the pistons and connecting rods. I start by laying out all eight piston and rod assemblies in their correct order. Each rod and cap assembly is numbered 1 through 8 and must be properly matched and installed in the corresponding cylinders. For example, rod and cap number 1 goes in cylinder number 1, rod and cap number 2 goes in cylinder number 2, and so on. In the case of the 289 engine, the cylinder count starts on the right bank (passenger side) and counts back, one, two, three, four, then moves to the left bank and counts back five, six, seven, eight.

With the piston and rod assemblies laid out in the correct order, I install the new piston rings on the new pistons, followed by the new rod bearings. Then I use a piston ring compressor to compress the rings around the piston, and then I install the assembly in its assigned bore.

PHOTO 1: The basic parts required for an engine rebuild include reground crankshaft, restored heads, new camshaft and lifters, new pistons and rings, new oil pump, new bearings, new timing chain and gears, and new gaskets.

PHOTO 2: This shouldered thrust bearing mounts in the center journal, and it is there to prevent the crankshaft from moving back and forth within the block.

PHOTO 3: Every cap, whether a main bearing cap or piston rod cap, is numbered as to placement within the engine. The number 3 cap happens to be the thrust-bearing cap.

PHOTO 4: Plasti-gauge, available at any automotive parts store, is used to measure the oil clearance between the crankshaft and its corresponding journal. In this case, that clearance is .0015 inches, well within specifications.

PHOTO 5: The timing marks on each gear, as indicated by the arrows, must align in order to time the camshaft to the crankshaft.

PHOTO 6: The tightening sequence for each head bolt begins with the centermost bolts and works outward toward each end.

Once installed, I again use plasti-gauge to verify the oil clearance, .0008 to .0024 inches at each rod journal, and then torque each rod cap to the correct specification.

The last major item in the block assembly is the camshaft. The machine shop will have installed new cam bearings, so cam installation is a matter of lubricating the shaft and gently inserting it into the block.

Next, the camshaft needs to be timed to the crankshaft. Both the crankshaft timing gear and the camshaft timing gear are marked for proper timing, and these marks must align or the engine will be out of time. What does engine timing mean? Engine timing means the intake and exhaust valves must be timed with the pistons so that each cylinder compresses the incoming fuel/air mixture, then exhaust the burnt mixture on the correct piston stroke. This is essential for the engine to run properly. The timing of the engine is now set so that when the harmonic damper is installed, the timing indicator will read top dead center (TDC). Do not rotate the crankshaft again until the distributor has been installed.

Next to be installed is the oil pump, the front timing cover, and the oil pan. The engine is now ready to be rolled over to access its top.

INSTALLING THE PARTS AT THE TOP OF THE ENGINE

The top of the engine has four major components: two heads, one intake manifold, and a distributor. Installing the heads and intake manifold is pretty straightforward, so let's go through it quickly.

The head gaskets go on first, followed by the heads being gently dropped straight down onto the block. To properly locate the heads, each side of the block has two locating dowels, one at the front and one at the rear. Do not scoot the head around on the gasket while mounting. The gasket can be gouged, ruining its ability to create a seal.

With the heads in place on the block, I insert the head bolts and torque each one to the required specifications. As shown in photo 6, I start with the centermost bolts and work outward.

Following is a list of all of the correct bolt torque specifications:
- Intake manifold bolts: 20–22 ft lbs
- Exhaust manifold bolts: 15–26 ft lbs
- Cylinder head bolts: 65–70 ft lbs

Next, I install the lifters, after having soaked them in clean oil until they filled with oil; the pushrods; the rocker arms; and, finally, the locknuts. I do not tighten the rocker arm locknuts at this time. I'll tighten and adjust each one after both the intake manifold and distributor have been installed. Why did I soak the lifters until they filled with oil? The valves cannot be properly set if the lifters have not been primed with clean oil.

The intake manifold is installed next, followed by the distributor. Referring back to chapter 6, photo 4, I know the rotor on the distributor must be pointed to a twelve o'clock position (toward the carburetor) to coincide with firing the number 1 cylinder.

With the distributor installed and set to fire the number 1 cylinder, I can adjust the valves starting with the number 1 cylinder. Why this cylinder first? The timing mark on the harmonic damper is already set at top dead center (TDC), where the valves on the number 1 cylinder are in a closed position at the end of the compression stroke, which is necessary for setting the valve lash, or valve stem, to rocker arm clearance.

To set the valve lash, I tighten the rocker arm nuts on the number 1 cylinder until the pushrod can no longer be turned by hand, and then I give the nut an additional one-quarter turn. I repeat this procedure for both valves.

How do you determine when each cylinder is at TDC to set the valves? Scribe a mark on the harmonic damper at TDC as shown on point A in photo 7. Now divide the damper into quarters and mark the remaining points B, C, and D, moving counterclockwise around the damper. Each point indicates the TDC position of a particular cylinder when the damper is rotated to the timing mark indicator.

As an example of how this works, rotate the damper counterclockwise one-quarter turn to line up point B with the timing indicator. Following the Ford 289 engine firing order of 1 5 4 2 6 3 7 8, set the valves on cylinder number 5. From there, rotate the damper another quarter turn counterclockwise to line up point C with the timing indicator, and set the valves on cylinder number 4. Continue this pattern following the firing order until all valves have been set.

PAINTING THE ENGINE: A LITTLE FORD BLUE

Ford painted its engines with the exhaust manifolds, the hoses, the sensors, and the accessory brackets off of the engine, so I leave them off at this time. To paint the engine, I start by cleaning the engine thoroughly using PPG DX 330 degreaser. Next, I scuff sand the entire

PHOTO 7: To set the valves on each individual cylinder, the harmonic damper is divided into four wedges. Point A is located at TDC, B a quarter distance around the damper counterclockwise, and so on. Each point indicates TDC for a particular cylinder.

PHOTO 8: The completed engine painted Ford Guardsman Blue.

TIP

With the timing set to TDC on the number 1 cylinder, the distributor can be removed from the engine during painting.

assembly using a Norton Bear-Tex Scuff Pad. After sanding, I clean the engine again using DX 330. I then mask off the carburetor opening, the fuel pump mounting plate, and all exhaust ports, and then install the old spark plugs. They make great plugs to keep paint off the threads and out of the cylinders.

To refinish the engine, I start by applying a coat of PPG DP74LF Epoxy Primer and follow that with two coats of PPG DCC Concept Acrylic Urethane single-stage finish in Ford Guardsman Blue. This means cleaning the Binks M1-G three times, but as I said before, I'm familiar with the way this gun sprays, so I prefer to use it. DCC mixes at a 4:2:1 ratio, 4 parts DCC to 2 parts DT 885 reducer to 1 part DCX61 hardener. I use the Binks M1-G spray gun to

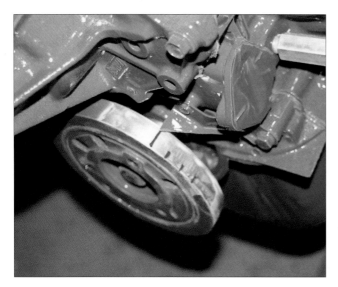

PHOTO 9: The timing marks on the harmonic damper are masked prior to refinishing. This makes finding the marks during the engine timing phase a little easier.

PHOTO 10: The pulleys are numbered as to installation sequence, starting with the harmonic damper pulley and finishing with the water pump pulley.

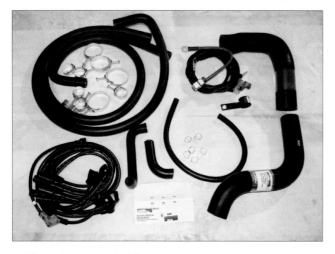

PHOTO 11: Correctly marked hoses, clamps, and cables are a must when returning a vehicle back to its original condition. These products from Marti Auto Works fit the bill.

apply two wet coats, allowing 15 minutes between each coat and a minimum of eight hours for the coats to completely cure. Why the extended drying time? It gives the paint time to harden before I start adding components to the engine.

Before painting the engine, I had masked off that portion of the harmonic damper where the timing marks are located. After painting the engine, the tape is removed and each timing mark, starting with the TDC mark and progressing 10 degrees, 20 degrees, and 30 degrees before top dead center (BTDC), is clearly marked on the damper. You'll appreciate having the marks when using a timing light to set the distributor timing.

INSTALLING THE TRANSMISSION

Next on the list is the Ford C6 transmission. I had delivered this unit to a local repair facility for a thorough cleaning and inspection. Installing a new torque converter was recommended because the old one was filled with used fluid. I bolt the transmission to the engine and install both pieces into the car as a unit.

INSTALLING THE ENGINE ACCESSORIES

Remember the photos taken of the engine prior to teardown? Now is a good time to bring them out and study the placement of the front engine accessories. This is not an easy engine to dress out because it has all of the available options. Photo 10 offers the correct sequence for installing all those parts and pieces. In case the glare in the photo is a little strong, here's the sequence for installing the accessories: harmonic damper pulley, AC bracket, AC compressor, power steering pump, power steering belt idler pulley, alternator, and fan pulley.

One of the final steps to dressing this engine out to correct period specifications is to use the correct heater hoses, radiator hoses, hose clamps, battery cables, and spark plug wires. To cover that need, I turned to Marti Auto Works. Each item is labeled with the correct FoMoCo printing; is the correct period color, style, and type; and will give this engine that factory-new look.

Note: If you are building your pony to concours specifications, which means rebuilding the car exactly how the factory built it in the first place, be sure to route the left bank spark plug wires 7, 5, 6, 8 in the holders. The idea here is to keep wires number 7 and 8 spaced apart to prevent them from coming into contact with each other and causing a crossfire condition. Ford would have done this from the factory, but if your FoMoCo has replacement plug wires, you might want to verify this placement.

WIRING THE ENGINE

The last task to accomplish here in the engine compartment at this time is the wiring. I route the engine wiring loom from the firewall along the right side of the intake manifold, where the individual wires can be branched off to connect to the electric choke, the distributor and coil, the temperature and oil pressure sensors, and the air conditioner compressor.

The last components to be installed are the carburetor, the various linkages, the vacuum lines, and the fuel lines.

NOTES

_____

_____

_____

_____

_____

_____

_____

_____

_____

_____

_____

_____

_____

_____

_____

_____

_____

_____

CHAPTER 19

INSTALLING THE
FRONT SHEET METAL

With the engine in the car, I can turn my attention back to making this project look more like a car and less like a refugee from the salvage yard. Between hanging the headliner and cleaning the grease from under my fingernails after rebuilding the engine, I had refinished both of the fenders, the headlamp housings, and the hood. Now I am ready to install the hood, the fenders, the exhaust system, the fuel tank, the trunk floor safety panel, and the taillamps.

INSTALL THE HOOD AND THE FENDERS

Take note that installing the hood and front fenders is not a one-person job. Draft your wife, husband, son, daughter, or a kid down the street, or sit a six-pack on the roof and wait for one of your buddies to show up and help. Do not attempt to install any of these parts alone. Going it alone is a scratch waiting to happen, and at this stage in the project, the last thing anyone needs is a fresh scratch.

I also need to paint the underside of the fenders. Once the hood and fenders have been installed, these panels need to be aligned. Then I can install the hood latch.

INSTALLING THE HOOD

Whenever possible, such as when working on a unibody car like this one, I prefer to mount the hood before I mount the fenders to ensure that the fenders aren't leaned against and accidentally scratched after they are mounted. When installing the hood, I don't get too excited about adjusting it to fit perfectly. After all, without the fenders on the car, there really isn't much I can do in the way of hood alignment. I just make sure the hood is adjusted far enough forward at the hinges to ensure that it doesn't touch the cowl screen panel when closed, and then I snug the bolts.

PAINTING THE UNDERSIDE OF THE FENDERS

A small detail often missed when installing fenders on a Mustang is the appearance of the underside of the fenders. This area is often oversprayed with the color of the car or left rusty and dinged. I like to give this area a coat of DP74LF epoxy, then cover that with a couple of coats of the same semigloss black color I used to spray the dash and engine compartment (PPG Deltron 2000 DBI 9600). Remember that the epoxy allows a seven-day period of time for you to apply additional products without having to sand the coat. If it has been more than seven days since you sprayed the underside of the fenders with epoxy, they will need to be scuff sanded using a Norton Bear-Tex Scuff Pad before painting them.

As a final step, I like to coat the tops of the undersides of the fenders with a heavy layer of 3M 8883 Rubberized Undercoating. This helps absorb some of the sting from rocks being kicked up by the tires and stops most of the little "outies," or bumps, seen on the tops of fenders that don't use fender skirts or plastic inner liners.

A good time to mount the headlamp housings is while the fenders are still on the bench after you have painted them. The mounting bolts are a little easier to reach, and the pieces are a little easier to align to the fenders. I also route the headlamp socket wiring harness pigtail through the housing while I'm at it.

INSTALLING THE FENDERS

Once the hood is mounted, the fenders can be installed. I go through the actual mounting process using the right-hand fender and start by masking the leading edge of the door, as shown in photo 1. This is insurance against

PHOTO 1: Fender installation begins by taping the leading edge of the door to prevent chipping the paint. The first bolt installed goes at the top rear (top arrow).

PHOTO 2: Align this gap first, the hood to the cowl, to about ½ inch wide.

scratches or chipped paint. I carefully position the fender in place on the car and start tightening the rearmost top bolt (top arrow photo 1) and the forwardmost top bolt at the core support. This bolt will be replaced with a cushioned adjuster bolt from California Mustang later, but for now any fender-mounting bolt will do.

Next, I align the top rear of the fender with the door, snug-tighten the rear bolt inside the engine compartment, and then carefully open the door. This is another time when having two sets of eyes comes in handy. One person can open the door, while the other watches the gap between the door and the fender. Any indication that the door is about to touch the fender calls for pulling the fender outboard at the bottom to give more clearance.

Inside the doorjamb, just above the upper door hinge, is a mount for another fender bolt (left arrow, photo 1). A ½-inch, ⅜-drive socket on a long extension guides the bolt into place. I snug-tighten this bolt and once again check the alignment of the fender to the door. This bolt controls the alignment of the upper body line and the body line crease located a few inches below it. When these two points align perfectly, I tighten the bolt and move to the front of the fender.

ALIGNING THE FRONT PANELS

Next is one of those points where part A must align to part B while part C is adjusted to fit part A but not before it aligns with part B and only if part D is in alignment with part A. Or is it part B to align to part D? Now even I'm confused.

Let's go through the alignment process one step at a time. Part A is the hood, so I start by aligning the hood to the cowl panel (part B), as shown in photo 2. All I'm looking for here is an even gap about ½ inch wide where the two panels meet. Once adjusted, I want to close the hood because this is where things get sticky.

I'm looking to see if the rear edge of the hood sits flush with the top of the fender (part C). If it is too high, as shown in photo 3, I'll open the hood and loosen the rear hinge mounting bolt, as indicated in photo 4, then push the leading edge of the hood up. This causes the hinge to tilt downward slightly at the rear. I'll tighten the bolt and check the hood alignment again and continue this adjustment routine until the hood becomes flush with the fender and cowl screen panel when closed. Should the hood sit lower than the top of the fender at the rear, I'll loosen the same hinge bolt and pull the front of the hood down slightly. That will lift the rear of the hinge and cause the hood to sit higher at the rear.

How do you adjust the sitting height of the hood at the front? Replace the bolt that was installed at the core

> ### TIP
>
> *If the hinges are worn and you can't get enough adjustment to level the hood, try placing a metal body shim under the rear hood hinge mounting bolt to raise the back of the hood, or place the shim under the front hood hinge mounting bolt to lower the back.*

PHOTO 3: A common problem is the position of the hood in relation to the fender and the cowl screen panel.

PHOTO 4: To lower or raise the rear corner of the hood, loosen this bolt and shift the hinge either up or down.

support earlier with a new cushioned hood-stop bolt from California Mustang. These new hood-stop bolts can be adjusted up or down depending upon the need. Why didn't I install these cushions first instead of the bolts? The cushions are difficult to tighten and loosen, as is often necessary when adjusting the fenders to fit. However, the bolts are easy to tighten and loosen, and once the fenders are perfectly aligned, as they are now, the bolts can be tossed.

The next alignment point is where the leading edge of the hood meets the front tip of the headlamp housing (part D). If these two parts don't align, the hood can be adjusted either forward or backward at the hinge. Of course, there are consequences to making these types of adjustments. For example, moving the hood forward on one side widens the gap between the fender and the hood at the front. Moving the hood back on one side closes this same gap. Either instance can be a good thing or a bad thing. If it is a good thing, then the fit and alignment of the front panels will have improved. If it is a bad thing, then the position of the fender must be adjusted either inboard or outboard at the front, depending upon the need.

Bear in mind that shifting the position of the front of the fender either inboard or outboard can have an effect on the alignment of the rear of the fender where it meets the door. How's that? Here's an example: moving the fender slightly outboard at the front causes the top rear of the fender to move inboard ever so slightly. This makes the door appear to stick out from the fender. What's the cure? Loosen the top two rear fender bolts tightened previously, and move the fender outboard slightly.

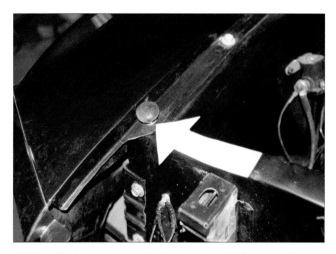

PHOTO 5: The front fender mounting bolt is replaced with a new, adjustable, cushioned bolt from California Mustang.

PHOTO 6: Alignments always have consequences. If the hood is adjusted forward at the hinge, the gap where the hood meets the fender at the front will widen.

PHOTO 7: Opposite consequences. If the hood is adjusted backward at the hinge, the gap where the hood meets the fender at the front will narrow.

PHOTO 8: Any gap that exists here, between the fender and the rocker panel molding, can be closed by shifting the lower forward fender mounting bolt either inboard or outboard.

An area of the fender I've neglected thus far is the bottom rear. Down here, there are two mounting bolts. Both are located underneath the fender, one near the rear of the fender, and one just back of the wheel opening. I start by installing the rearmost bolt. Installing this bolt may require the use of shims. Any space between the fender mounting plate and the body structure must be filled by adding shims. Why? Failure to add shims here would force the fender upward when the mounting bolt is tightened. I just spent a lot of time getting the fender to fit the car, and I don't want to ruin it now by neglecting the shims.

The forward lower bolt under the fender uses a small bracket that must be installed at the same time the dust shield is installed inside the fender. What's the function of this bolt? It controls the inboard or outboard position of the rear of the fender. Controlling this positioning ensures that when the rocker panel molding is installed, no gap will be present where the fender meets the rocker panel. It's unsightly if not adjusted properly.

Now it's time to close the hood and check the gaps between the hood and the fenders. I'm looking for even gaps all around the hood, and I want the leading edge of the hood to be even with the leading edges of the headlamp housings. When the gaps are perfect, the latch can be installed. How perfect is perfect? Mustangs are notorious for having panels that don't fit and align with each other. Sometimes really close is about as perfect as you are going to get.

INSTALLING THE LATCH

Next, I want to install the latch. I start by installing the center grille support bracket. This panel holds the latch catch bolt and must be in place before the latch will work. If the radiator and AC condenser on your project have not been installed, install these parts before mounting the center grille support bracket.

Next, I mount the latch on the hood but only finger tighten the mounting bolts. I then carefully close the hood until the latch drops over the catch bolt. With the mounting bolts left loose, this should bring the latch into alignment with the catch bolt. Now I can open the hood without letting the latch move, and I can tighten the mounting bolts.

I push the hood closed to check its alignment. Caution! Do not slam the hood. Should the latch be misaligned with the catch bolt, the hood will be pulled to one side or the other. The result could be chipped paint on the fender or the hood or both. So I gently push the hood closed and watch both sides to be sure the hood isn't being pulled to one side or another. If it pulls to the right, the latch position on the hood needs to be shifted slightly to the left. A pull to the left indicates the latch needs to shift slightly to the right. The hood fits perfectly but seems loose in the latch? Then the latch needs to be shifted straight up to draw the hood down a little. The

> **TIP**
>
> *When installing the right-hand fender, don't forget to mount the antenna before installing the dust shield.*

hood is hard to close? Shift the latch straight down until the hood closes with ease and does not have a hard pop when triggering the latch.

That should do it where aligning the front sheet metal is concerned. The only thing left is to once again check the fit of all the panels. Sometimes installing and adjusting the latch can cause a minor shift in the position of the hood at the rear corners. I make any necessary adjustments in that area and finish the job by fine-tuning the height of the new hood bumper cushions that were installed earlier.

INSTALL THE EXHAUST SYSTEM

The next item to be installed on the Mustang is a new exhaust system from AAPD. This is a basic single-exhaust system that consists of only four parts: the Y pipe that collects the exhaust from the engine and guides it into the intermediate pipe, the intermediate pipe, the muffler to quiet the noise associated with exhaust fumes, and the outlet pipe to take the exhaust gas out and away from the car. Three 2½-inch muffler clamps and two tailpipe hanger clamps later, the new exhaust system will make this pony purr like a kitten.

INSTALL THE FUEL TANK AND THE TRUNK FLOOR SAFETY PANEL

Aging fuel tanks can contain everything from old fuel residue to flakes of rust. To eliminate this problem, I turned to American Designers for an exact replacement tank. I transfer the fuel gauge sending unit from the old tank to the new tank and drop the new tank into place inside the trunk.

Haven't heard about the rear collision concerns as they relate to the early model Mustangs? I have. Open the trunk on any vintage Mustang and remove the floor mat, and you will find the fuel tank. That's right; the fuel tank is the trunk floor. The concern is that under specific conditions, the tank can rupture during a rear-end collision and spill raw fuel into the passenger compartment of the vehicle. I'm not trying to be an alarmist, just passing along problems that have occurred in the past.

Is there a solution? Yes, and Antioch Mustang Stable has it. Its solution was to design a fuel tank cover made of heavy plate steel. This isn't a wimpy sheet of metal. The

PHOTO 9: This new exhaust system from AAPD is a bolt-on assembly that will keep the Mustang purring quietly.

PHOTO 10: A new fuel tank from American Designers.

heavy gauge Tank Armor plate weighs in at a whopping 40 pounds. Once properly installed, the Tank Armor plate isolates the fuel tank from the interior of the car, eliminating any possibility of fuel splashing inside the car in the event of a rear-end collision.

PHOTO 11: The Tank Armor plate from Antioch Mustang Stable will effectively separate the fuel tank from the interior of the car.

PHOTO 12: The taillamps on the California Special look a lot like the taillamps on a T-Bird. Maybe Ford had a better idea here.

To install the Tank Armor plate in a vehicle that already has the tank mounted, remove the bolts securing the fuel tank to the car, and then remove the rubber fuel filler neck. The Tank Armor plate comes with all the necessary attachment hardware as well as an insulated gasket to surround the fuel tank filler neck opening. Install the insulated gasket around the fuel filler neck opening on the tank, then, with the help of a strong back—a cold six-pack usually lures in a strong back—gently drop the plate into place over the fuel tank, taking care to ensure that the insulating gasket seals the opening between the filler neck and the plate. Replace the rubber fuel neck, and bolt down the plate. You have just improved upon the safety of your pony.

INSTALL THE CALIFORNIA SPECIAL TAILLAMPS

Next on the punch list for completing the Mustang is the taillamps. If you think the taillamps on the California Special Mustang look a lot like the taillamps on the 1965 Thunderbird, that's because they are basically one and the same. But that doesn't mean that this Mustang's taillamps can't be improved upon from the condition they were in when I started this project.

I start by disassembling each unit and cleaning the individual parts with a little soap and water. After that, it's off to the shop buffer to polish the chrome bezels and plastic taillamp lenses. I use the Eastwood 80 Ply Thick Buff 8 x ½ Loose #13269, along with white rouge compound for polishing the chrome, and the string buffing pad #13029 and plastic compound for polishing the lenses.

The reflective coating on the taillamp housings should also be replaced at this time. I use Eastwood's Reflective Aluminum Aerosol #10005 Z.

Finally, inspect the taillamp wiring pigtails for cracked insulation, frayed ends, and rusty terminals. The pigtails on this car prove to be in perfect condition, but had they not been, a trip to the vintage salvage yard for a set of replacement pigtails would have been in order.

The last thing to do before assembling the lamps is to coat each bulb socket with lithium grease. This is a white grease that will keep the sockets lubricated as well as prevent rust from forming around the bulb terminals.

> **TIP**
>
> *Seal the fuel tank opening with a clean shop towel to prevent gas fumes from escaping from the tank, and by all means don't light up until the job is finished.*

> **TIP**
>
> *How do you keep the reflective paint out of the bulb sockets? Leave the old bulbs in place while applying the coating, and then replace them before assembling the units.*

NOTES

CHAPTER 20

INSTALLING THE EMBLEMS, THE BUMPERS, THE STRIPES, AND THE CARPET

You know a project is nearing completion when the shiny parts go on and the carpet is laid down. I'll start with installing the smallest of the shiny parts, the new emblems, and continue with the larger pieces such as the grille and valance panel, then work my way up in size until the bumpers are hung. After that, I'll turn my attention to putting stripes on this car, then finish by installing parts of the interior such as the steering components, the carpet, and the interior trim.

ATTACH THE EMBLEMS

Because I didn't replace either of the fenders, the attachment holes for the emblems are still there, so installing the new Mustang script emblems is a matter of inserting new tube nuts in the mounting holes and then gently pressing the emblems through the tube nuts. What are tube nuts? Most body shops refer to them as barrel nuts, but the proper name is tube nut. This is a small, tube-shaped piece of spring steel that is inserted into a mounting hole and is designed to grip the mounting studs on the emblem being installed. Tube nuts are available in various sizes and lengths and can be used to install a variety of different emblems and name plates. Ford has made extensive use of this mounting device, and they are available from any of the Mustang parts suppliers mentioned in chapter 1.

What if the fenders on your project are new and don't have any mounting holes? To correctly locate emblem mounting holes, you need a reference point from which to take measurements. That's usually found on the old fender previously removed from the car. Using a discarded fender from the car as a reference, take the first measurement horizontally from the nearest edge of the panel to the nearest emblem mounting hole. Take the second measurement from the nearest vertical edge to the same mounting hole. Transfer those measurements to the fender needing holes and repeat for any remaining mounting holes. Apply masking tape to the fender to help mark each mounting hole, as shown in photo 1, and leave

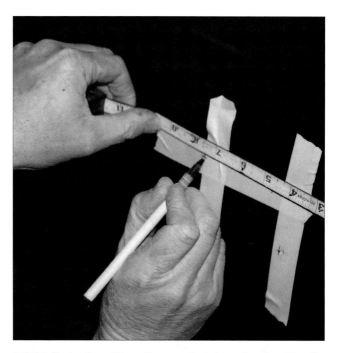

PHOTO 1: The locations of the emblem mounting holes are transferred from the opposite side of the car, then measured and marked before drilling.

the tape in place until all the holes have been drilled. The tape will also prevent the drill bit from wandering and scratching the fresh paint.

Before drilling, position the emblem over the masking tape to check the accuracy of each measurement. The mounting studs should align with each marked hole, as shown in photo 2. With the correct-size tube nuts in hand, determine the correct-size drill bit. The tube nut should fit snugly into the drilled hole. Drill the mounting holes through the masking tape, remove the tape, insert the tube nuts, and gently push the emblem into place.

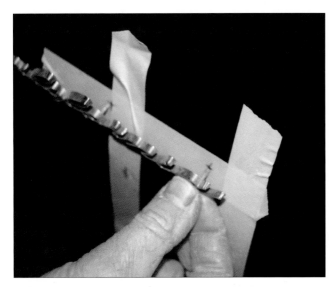

PHOTO 2: Before drilling, the hole locations are checked against the actual emblem to ensure accuracy.

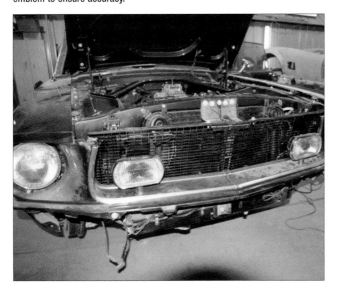

PHOTO 3: Notice the absent "pony" emblem in the center of the grille. The California Special didn't use one.

ASSEMBLE THE GRILLE

The grille for the Mustang needs to be painted before being installed. I start by sanding the grille on both sides using 320-grit sandpaper, then refinish it by first applying a coat of PPG D8085 sealer and three coats of PPG #32930 Charcoal Metallic. This is the same color used to paint the style of steel wheels on the 1965 through 1967 Mustangs and is available in aerosol cans from any of the suppliers mentioned in chapter 1.

While the grille is drying, I have several other pieces of the grille unit that need attention, starting with the right- and left-side grille opening panels. These panels are made of aluminum and are painted the same charcoal color as the grille. I scuff sand both panels using a Norton Bear-Tex Scuff Pad before refinishing them with sealer and paint.

While the grille opening panels are drying, I polish the right and left grille surround moldings as well as the Lucas fog lamps that mount inside the grille assembly. Eastwood's Canton #13057 flannel buff used with Jeweler's white rouge compound does a nice job of bringing back the shine.

The completed grille assembly is shown in photo 3 and follows this order of assembly: mount the right and left opening panels first, followed by the surround moldings, then gently drop the grille into place behind the opening panels, and finish by installing the Lucas fog lamps. Where's the "pony" emblem? The California Special doesn't use one.

The Painless Performance wiring kit I installed earlier didn't include a wiring harness for the Lucas fog lamps, so I have to wire these myself. I use the original fog lamp switch from the old harness and mount it under the dash just below the ignition switch. I add a relay to the circuit to ensure that I have 12 volts going directly to the lamps without subjecting the switch to the same 12 volts. That prolongs the life of the switch and ensures that the lamps get the necessary voltage for proper operation.

MOUNT THE BUMPERS

I could have packed up the old bumpers from the Mustang and sent them out to be chrome plated, but at roughly half the cost, quality reproduction bumpers and brackets were available from California Mustang. I selected a complete rebuild package that contained everything from the bumpers to the brackets to new bumper bolts. The bumper kit shown in photo 4 is for the front. The rear bumper kit, not shown, also contains the same necessary mounting components as the front.

Installation is a matter of mounting the brackets on the bumper, then mounting the completed assembly on the car. Call your buddy; this is a two-person job. Mount the bumper brackets on the frame rails and snug-tighten the bolts. Leaving the brackets a little loose allows you to shift things to gain a good fit. Once the bumper is in good alignment, perfectly level, and spaced out from the body about 1 inch, the bolts can be tightened, starting with the mounting bracket-to-frame bolts and finishing with the bolts on the bumper.

The procedure for installing the rear bumper is the same used for installing the front bumper with the exception of the bracket mounting bolts. Access to these bolts is found inside the trunk.

INSTALL THE FRONT VALANCE PANEL

With the bumpers in place, the front valance panel can be installed. But before I install this panel, a few preliminary details must be attended to. It is much easier to mount the parking lamps with the panel still on the bench, so I'll do that first. While I'm at it, I'll add quick-disconnect plugs to the wiring pigtails. That will allow me to unplug the lamps from the wiring harness should it become necessary to remove the valance panel in the future.

To install the valance panel, I first attach the four center-mounting bolts found under the bumper, and then I attach the panel to each fender, taking care to align the panel with the fenders as I tighten the bolts.

AFFIX THE STRIPE PACKAGE

Depending upon the year model, Mustangs used just about every conceivable style of stripe package. Some years they were wide, other years they were narrow, but all years used some type of stripe down the sides of the car. The 1968 California Special Mustang incorporated the use of a wide stripe down each side of the car with an added GT/CS insignia over the side scoops, located at the leading edge of the quarter panels. To complete the package, the 1968 California Special also used a narrower stripe across the rear of the car. For an exact factory replacement set of decals, I turned to AAPD.

The decal package came as a single large sheet of pre-cut decals, so the first order of business is to refer back to the photographs taken during the disassembly stage of this project to determine where each stripe piece should be placed. As each stripe piece is identified, I mark its location—right fender, forward stripe; right fender, rear stripe; and so on—on the decal sheet.

> **TIP**
>
> *A little masking tape around the ends of the bumper protects the fenders while mounting the bumper.*

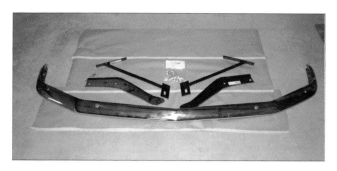

PHOTO 4: Ordering a kit like this ensures that you will get everything needed to install the bumpers.

PHOTO 5: To prevent chipping the paint on the fenders, the ends of the bumper are taped before installation.

Once the locations of the decals have been identified, the next step is to install the decals. Installing the decals is a matter of getting the stripe locations on the car laid out correctly, then getting the stripes themselves laid down without air bubbles or wrinkles. I start the installation process by wiping down both sides of the car with PPG DX 330 degreaser to ensure that the stripes will stick to the car once they are laid in place.

Next, I need to determine where on the sides of the car the stripes will be located. The only given I have is that the side stripes were centered over the side spoilers. To find the center of the spoilers, I measure the width of both spoilers and find them to be 9 inches wide. Dividing that in half gives me 4½ inches. That's the center of the spoiler, so I place a mark at that point. I then measure the width of the stripe, which measures 3 inches, including the pinstripes above and below the primary stripe. Next, I divide the width of the stripe in half, which gives me 1½ inches. I measure 1½ inches above and below the center mark on the side spoiler and mark those locations on the car. That places the stripe perfectly centered on the spoiler. I mark the measurements on a piece of masking tape to make finding the measuring points much easier.

PHOTO 6: Masking tape is used to help locate and mark the center of the side spoiler. This will be the center baseline for laying out the stripes.

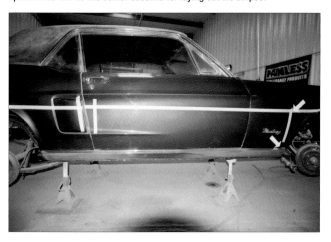

PHOTO 7: Height marks for the stripe are based on the rocker panel molding and marked on the side of the car. After that, a horizontal line of masking tape is stretched along the side of the car to mark the top of the stripe.

PHOTO 8: With the stripe laid in place, the soap and water solution is gently pushed from under the stripe using the squeegee.

To position the stripe along the sides of the car, I use the rocker panel molding as a baseline measuring point. I determine the distance from the rocker panel molding to the top mark on the spoiler to be 14 inches. I then transfer that measurement to the fender and place another mark.

Next, I lay a horizontal strip of masking tape that runs the entire length of the side of the car, using the height marks as a guide. That allows me to remove the vertical height markers and back away from the car for a good look at where my stripe will be located. Once satisfied with the location, I can begin striping the car.

Because I previously marked each stripe on the sheet of decal paper, I locate the stripe for the right door and cut it out of the sheet. This is the first stripe to go on the car.

To install the stripe, I mixed a solution of 1 quart water to 1 tablespoon liquid dishwashing soap and pour that into a spray bottle. I then lay the decal on a clean flat surface and gently peel away the backing, taking care to spray the soap and water solution on the sticky side of the decal. There are some rules to keep in mind when dealing with decals:

Do not touch the sticky side of the decal until it has been thoroughly coated with the soap and water solution.

Never soak decals in water before application. This can cause the stripe to disintegrate.

Once the decals have been applied, do not apply wax or compound to vinyl stripes. Darker stripes can be discolored, and the wax or compound can be forced under the edge of the stripe, compromising its ability to stick to the paint.

Now I am ready to place the decal on the car. This is where the tape line previously laid out on the side of the car proves its worth. It is the only guide I have to ensure that the stripe goes on straight and in the correct position. This isn't as difficult as it may seem. As long as the stripe is dripping wet, it will move freely over the surface of the panel, making positioning the piece extremely easy. Once the stripe is in position, I use the plastic squeegee provided in the stripe kit to gently push the soap and water solution from under the stripe. This is as much a process of feeling as it is of seeing because all of the air bubbles must be removed from under the stripe. I begin near the center of the stripe and work toward the ends.

I continue to place the decals on the car, using the photographs as a reference and measuring when necessary. The only difficult areas to contend with are where the stripes wrap around the ends of the doors and the fenders. The decals can fold over themselves at these points and leave behind wrinkles. To combat this problem, I allow the stripe to dry for at least three hours before gently removing the protective covering, and only then do I wrap the stripes around the door edges.

Where the stripes meet the fender wheel openings, they do not wrap around the opening edges. Instead, they are cut to follow the contour of the fender where it flares into the opening. That means I need to cut each stripe individually where it meets the contour.

To do this, I start by laying a strip of ¾-inch-wide masking tape along the crease of the car's contour where I want to cut the stripe. The masking tape will prevent the razor blade I'll be using to trim the stripe from cutting the paint beneath. Next, I use ¼-inch-wide tape over the ¾-inch-wide tape to more precisely follow the contour of the wheel opening. This allows me to define exactly where I want to cut the stripe. Next, I install the stripe and allow it to cover the masking tape at the wheel opening. I then squeegee out any air bubbles and allow the stripe to dry and adhere to the fender for a few hours.

Once the stripe has sufficiently dried, I am ready to cut around the fender. With the protective covering still on the stripe tape, an easy way to define the cut line is to do a pencil rubbing over the stripe to make the masking tape lines stand out, as shown in photo 10.

I then use a safety razor to cut along the inside edge of the marked ¼-inch tape line. After that, I carefully remove the backing from the stripe. I pick a spot near the middle of the stripe and tear the backing. This allows the backing to be gently pulled away from the stripe without disturbing the stripe itself. Once the backing has been removed from the stripe, I carefully pull away the ¾-inch-wide tape. This separates the trimmed excess end of the stripe from the body of the stripe. After that, the end of the stripe can be pressed into place.

INSTALL THE STEERING COMPONENTS

Moving to the interior of the car, the plan calls for reusing the original steering wheel once it has been restored. This wheel is cracked in several places, and the center trim pad is missing a few of its small round buttons. New buttons were provided by AAPD, and the wheel itself will be repaired using Norton epoxy structural adhesive #6115.

PHOTO 9: Cutting the stripe at the wheel opening starts by masking along the cut line, then overlaying the masking tape with additional tape to define the actual cut line.

PHOTO 10: With the stripe in place, a pencil rubbing is taken over the masking tape. This helps better define the line for cutting.

PHOTO 11: After removing the backing, the masking tape is carefully removed, which allows the stripe to be pressed into place on the fender.

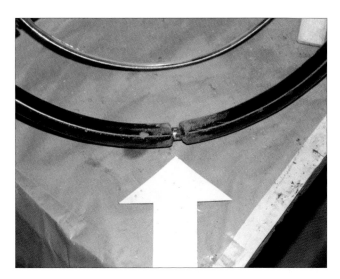

PHOTO 12: The epoxy-based adhesives available today make repairing a crack like this very easy.

PHOTO 13: The floor pan gets a layer of R Blox insulation to make this ride a quiet one.

Cracks like the one shown in photo 12 are easily repaired by first grinding a V-shaped groove deep into the crack using a die grinder with a 3-inch cutoff wheel. The groove is then cleaned with DX 330 degreaser and filled with epoxy adhesive. Once cured, the epoxy is sanded smooth using 180-grit sandpaper. I selected an epoxy-based adhesive because it allows me to fill any minor voids left in the repair with Evercoat Metal Glaze without having to prime over the adhesive first, as would be required if I had elected to repair the wheel using a urethane-based adhesive.

Once repaired, the steering wheel gets three coats of PPG 2K Chromatic Surfacer D8005, blocked smooth using 320-grit sandpaper, a seal coat of PPG D8085, three coats of PPG Deltron 2000 DBI 9600 semigloss black, and two coats of PPG DCU Concept 2002 polyurethane clear.

Why add the clear? The steering wheel was originally shiny black. Adding two coats of clear will gloss up the black and make the steering wheel extremely durable.

Next on the list is the steering column. This item also needs to be cleaned and sanded using the same procedures as those used with the steering wheel, and it needs to be refinished with three coats of PPG Deltron 2000 DBI 9600 semigloss black before installation.

After the steering wheel has dried, I slide the restored column through the opening in the floor pan and connect it to the steering gearbox. Next, I install the six bolts attaching the column to the dash, cover the floor pan opening with the two-piece metal close-out panel, and attach the wires.

To connect the Painless Performance wiring kit to the steering column, the original turn signal pigtail from the old wiring harness must be used. This may look impossible to change over, but it is a simple matter of cutting the pigtail free of the old harness, then using a pair of needle-nose pliers to push one wire at a time through the plastic pigtail. As each wire is removed from the pigtail, I replace it with the same color-coded wire from the Painless Performance wiring harness by pushing the new wire up into the pigtail in the same direction the old wire was pushed out.

To check my work, I connect a 12-volt battery charger to the battery cables and turn on the ignition switch. The turn signals, emergency flashers, and taillamps should work. I test the horns later, after the steering wheel is installed.

INSTALL THE CARPET

Before installing the carpet, I need to cover the floor pan with a layer of R Blox insulation. R Blox gives the car a little extra insulation from sound and heat. It comes in 16-inch-wide rolls and is best installed by cutting 36-inch-long strips and covering small sections of the floor at a time. All I need to do is clean the floor pan, remove the protective backing, and lay each strip in place, as shown in photo 13. Each roll of R Blox comes with a handy roller to press the strips into place for a firm fit.

I turned to The Paddock Parts for a heat-molded and fitted set of carpet halves to install in the Mustang. The front section comes with the heel and toe pads already sewn into place, and both halves come with the insulation pad prebonded to make installation a snap.

Installation begins by positioning the front carpet section in the car, then locating the position for the headlamp dimmer switch because a hole must be cut into the carpet to allow access to this switch. Included with the carpet is a period-correct grommet that surrounds the dimmer switch and prevents the carpet from fraying at the cut edges. Photo 14 shows how the completed dimmer switch installation should look.

The only other trimming that is required is around the floor shifter and where the front bucket seat bolts and seat belt bolts are located. I use an ice pick to punch through the various floor pan mounting holes, then trim the carpet just enough to expose the holes.

ATTACH THE INTERIOR TRIM

The interior trim on this Mustang is basic and includes the kick panels, the inner quarter panel trim panels, the door panel trim, and the scuff plates. The kick panels are made of plastic and require only a good cleaning before installation.

The inner quarter panel trim panels are made of metal and are in need of a fresh coat of paint. They first need a good cleaning and degreasing. Soap and water will get rid of the grime, and PPG DX 330 degreaser will remove any remaining Armor All or other interior cleaners that might affect the paint. These products must first be removed

PHOTO 14: A new grommet for the dimmer switch is provided with the carpet from The Paddock Parts.

because painting over any product that contains silicone will cause the paint to fish-eye during application and will eventually cause the paint to flake off once dried. A good degreasing cleans the panel thoroughly, and a good sanding with a Norton Bear-Tex Scuff Pad etches the panel enough to ensure good paint adhesion. To refinish, I use the same PPG Deltron 2000 DBI 9600 semigloss black used to spray the dash and other interior parts.

Once the trim panels are back in the car, I install the new scuff plates from California Mustang, and this car is ready for a console.

NOTES

_____

_____

_____

_____

_____

_____

_____

_____

CHAPTER 21

INSTALLING
THE CONSOLE AND
RE-COVERING
THE SEATS

Moving ever closer to the completion of this project, I now have the console to rebuild and install and the seats to re-cover and install.

INSTALL THE CONSOLE

Photo 1 shows a collection of old and new parts that constitute the radio surround panel, which mounts at the front of the console and sweeps up into the dash. The arrows point to the void of metal in the original base panel where a CD player replaced the AM radio once mounted there. To the lower right of the base is the original padded cover that would have mounted over the base panel. Like the base panel, the center of this piece has been trimmed away to make room for the CD player. All this trimming and cutting has left the upper console looking like, well, like it has been trimmed and cut to make room for a CD player.

To the lower left in photo 1 is a new metal baseplate that I have cut and shaped to fit over the old base panel. It doesn't look like much now, but once it is padded and attached to the original base panel, it should greatly improve the looks of the upper console as well as replace the missing metal that was cut away for the CD player.

Because of the odd shape of the surround panel, an expert in the upholstery field recommended I use expandable foam to cover my new baseplate. I selected a hobby grade, two-part foam product that I could mix and pour over the panel. It works great for this purpose in that once cured, it is easily sanded and shaped using 80-grit sandpaper to achieve the built-up look I need.

Did it work? Check out photo 3. After shaping the foam, I covered the piece with black vinyl before mounting it to the old base. The CD player housing is partially slid into place to test the fit. Once the console is back in the car, the CD player housing will be pressed into place and permanently seated in the panel.

The console itself needs a little TLC. In this case, TLC means refinishing the hard plastic base with PPG Deltron 2000 9600 semigloss black and giving everything else a thorough cleaning before assembling the console and

PHOTO 1: The old radio surround panel with the center cut out (arrows), along with the old padded trim cover (right) and the new radio surround panel insert (left). These pieces need some help.

PHOTO 2: The new base plate is mounted over the old plate, and everything is covered with expandable foam. The foam will be sanded and shaped to form the new radio surround panel.

PHOTO 3: The new radio surround panel with the CD player housing mounted to verify the fit.

PHOTO 4: The new radio surround installed in the car looks almost as if it were factory made.

installing the components. Did I succeed in curing the console problem? It isn't factory, but it isn't bad either.

RE-COVER AND
INSTALL THE SEATS

The last major hurdle to restoring the interior of this Mustang is to re-cover the seats. To accomplish this, I need to first break down the old seats. Then I can make them look like new by ordering new covers and accessories and rebuilding the seats. Then the seats will be ready for installation.

To be sure that I would move through this process without any problems, I did two things. First, I turned to The Paddock Parts for a complete set of replacement seat covers and hog ring retainers. What are the hog ring retainers used for? The seat covers are held in place on the seat frame with C-shaped metal wires called hog rings. These extremely stiff wires could be thought of as staples on steroids and are what hold the seat cover to the seat frame. The hog ring kit from The Paddock Parts comes with a pair of hog ring pliers to help hold the rings as they are clamped into place. By ordering from The Paddock Parts, I know I'll be getting a set of first-class covers for both front bucket seats and the rear bench seat. The second thing I did was to tap Legendary Auto Interiors for a little seat cover installation information. After all, if you plan to do things the right way, who better to ask than the guys who know it all?

Seat cover replacement begins the same way that I've started every other replacement process on this project: by laying out the new covers for inspection to make certain I have the correct covers. Which cover is correct? That can be a difficult question to answer. If the cover is removed from a bucket-seat frame out of a 1966 Mustang and the frame is placed side by side with a 1968 Mustang seat frame, they will look almost identical. The difference is in the padding and in the way the cover is installed. So if over the course of 40 years someone has changed the seats in your ride, you need to be sure the covers you've just purchased are identical to the covers you have on your car. Covers are not interchangeable from year to year.

Did I mention a sturdy workbench is needed to re-cover the seats? I have a heavy-duty bench with a work surface measuring roughly 3 x 4 feet, ideal for this type of repair. It is large enough to handle even the rear bench seat without a problem.

BREAKING DOWN THE SEATS

I begin working on the seats by breaking down one of the front bucket seats. I separate the back of the seat from the seat base by removing the trim covering the two hinge bolts; removing the hinge bolt retainer clips, one on either side of the seat; then gently prying the hinges outward and off the bolts. For now, the seat base is set aside while I concentrate on replacing the cover on the seat back.

The first item to be removed is the trim panel covering the back of the seat. This cover is held in place with the same type of wire clips used to secure the door trim panels to the doors. A trim removal tool, Eastwood's #52035, works great to pop off the panel.

Once the back is removed, the hog rings attaching the cover to the frame are exposed. A good pair of side cutter pliers makes short work of the old hog rings, and once removed, the back flaps of the cover easily slip off of the seat, exposing the foam pad beneath.

On the front of the seat, the pleated insert is held in place by a wire loop tucked and hog ringed into a channel cut into the foam. The easiest way to gain access to this loop is to fold the outer flaps previously released from the back of the seat over the pleated section of the seat and look for the hog rings attaching the wire loop to the foam. Once the hog rings are cut, the cover comes right off. Hold on to the old cover for now.

Next, I remove the foam pad and any burlap or felt stripping from around the perimeter of the seat frame. What's the burlap and felt used for? They prevent the metal frame from prematurely wearing through the cover. I hold on to the old burlap and felt stripping for now, but later when I'm ready to assemble these seats, I'll replace both with new material purchased from a local upholstery shop.

That leaves the seat stripped down to the bare frame. Although no one will ever see this part of the seat once the new cover is installed, Legendary Auto Interiors suggested the frame be media blasted and refinished. That's a good idea since rust has a way of attacking bare metal, and a lot of the paint on the frame has been rubbed away from years of use. I sent the frame out to be soda blasted, a cleaning process similar to media blasting that removes all of the old paint but doesn't harm the metal.

To refinish the seat frame, I spray it with PPG Omni MTK Acrylic Urethane Gloss Black #9600. MTK is a single-stage urethane finish that can be applied over almost any properly sanded and sealed surface. This is a lower-cost

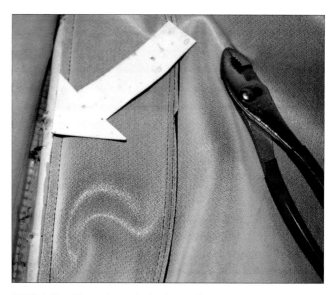

PHOTO 5: The old cover is attached to the seat frame with wire hog rings. I use a good pair of side cutter pliers to remove the rings.

urethane paint product made by PPG, but it is more than adequate for this purpose. MTK mixes at 4:1:1, 4 parts MTK to 1 part MR 186 reducer to 1 part MH 168 hardener. Apply two medium-wet coats using a Binks M1-G spray gun, allowing 10 minutes between each coat. MTK is dust free in about 45 minutes and cures in about 16 hours.

REBUILDING THE SEATS

I start the seat rebuild by installing new burlap and felt around the perimeter of the frame. Recall the old burlap and felt I held on to previously? I use these now as patterns to cut the new pieces for the seat.

Next, the foam pad is laid into place. Your pad is in sad condition? Most of the suppliers mentioned during this restoration carry new foam pads.

Remember that I prompted you to keep the old cover? This is where it comes in. I remove the wire loop from the old cover, and carefully slide the loop into the presewn pocket of the new cover. This will be the first part of the new cover to be attached to the seat frame.

I continue by positioning the new cover over the seat foam padding. Next, I fold the flaps of the new cover over the center section of the seat to expose the loop pocket in the pad. I then use the hog ring pliers and several new hog rings to clamp the wire loop to the seat frame. I space the hog rings about 3 inches apart around the seat. This secures the pleated inner section of the seat to the seat frame and will, in turn, allow me to pull out all the wrinkles from the outer sections of the seat while securing the remainder of the cover to the seat frame.

> ### TIP
>
> *Legendary Auto Interiors suggests steaming the covers to help pull out the wrinkles during installation. Professional steamers are available, but the cost may be prohibitive for installing a single set of seat covers. I suggest trying a steam iron; just be careful to never let the iron come in contact with the new covers. They will melt.*

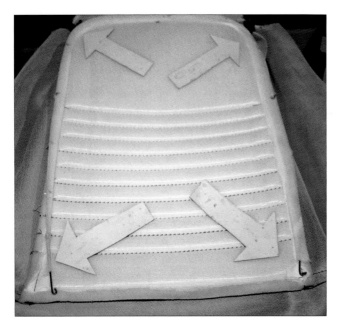

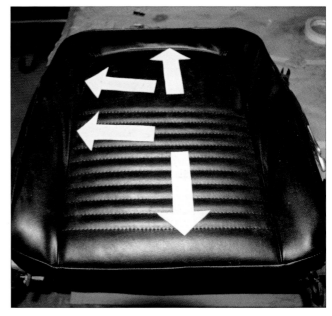

PHOTO 6: This wire loom must be removed from the old cover and installed in the new one before installing the new cover.

PHOTO 7: Pulling on the new cover at each of the points marked by arrows helps me remove the wrinkles.

With the center section of the seat secured, getting the side flaps of the new cover over the seat frame requires a little TLC because the side flaps are stitched to form a box shape and fit snugly over the seat pad once pulled into place. That means the stitching can be easily pulled and loosened if too much pressure is used. I have good luck pulling the flaps over the padding by forcing the padding down into the seat frame while at the same time pulling the seat cover flaps over the scrunched padding.

Once the covers are in place, a quick look at the front of the seat shows me where the bulk of the wrinkles are located. To determine how best to remove those wrinkles, I tug on the new cover in various places to see how the wrinkles react. In photo 7, I've identified some of the areas of the seat where pulling on the flaps removed the wrinkles. What I'm looking for is the magic points at which I can attach the cover to the seat frame with hog rings and remove the wrinkles. It is easier than it sounds, and before long all the wrinkles are out of the seat, and I am left with only a few attachment points that require hog rings.

When installing the hog rings, fold the seat material double everywhere a hog ring will be installed. This increases the holding power of the ring and reduces the chances of the material tearing once the hog rings are in place. Also, when securing the cover to the frame, I place

each hog ring opposite the previous hog ring by moving from one side of the seat to the other or from top to bottom. This helps keep the cover centered on the seat frame and makes removing the wrinkles easier.

How may hog rings does it take to secure one seat cover? The seat frame has a series of elongated holes spaced roughly every 3 inches around the perimeter of the frame. I clamp a hog ring into each hole, and that seems to do the job.

The last step in rebuilding the seats is to cover the exposed back of the bucket seats with an upholstered panel provided in the seat cover kit. I transfer the wire retainer clips from the old back panel to the new panel and snap the panel into place.

INSTALLING THE SEATS

It is necessary to remove the seat tracks from the bottom cushion of the front bucket seats to install the new covers. This is a good time to refinish and then lubricate all four tracks before installing them back on the seats.

If you haven't guessed by now, I elected to go through the process of covering the most difficult seat cushion in the car. Re-covering the remaining seat cushions is a walk in the park compared with this one. I suggest starting the re-covering process with the back seat. It's big but easy to re-cover and will give you some useful on-the-job training for tackling the more difficult front seat covers.

NOTES

CHAPTER 22

REPLACING THE FRAME RAILS

This book began life as a series of articles published in *Auto Restorer* magazine. As the readers became involved with the project, I began to field various questions concerning the restoration of a Mustang, all of which have been answered in one form or another over the course of this book. However, a difficult question to answer concerning frame rail replacement continues to come up. Although this Mustang does not require it, I feel it prudent to try to cover frame rail replacement here.

When replacing any parts, such as frame rails, there are important considerations to keep in mind regarding the structural versus the nonstructural parts. It's also important to learn how to take measurements to properly install the new frame rails. I will provide instructions for building your own tram gauge to take these measurements if you don't own one.

I'll start by explaining how this car was built and why care must be taken when replacing any of the frame rails. This Mustang is a unibody vehicle. For that matter, every Mustang ever built has a unibody construction. What is a unibody? In layperson's terms, it is a reinforced tomato can. That means it has an outer skin made up of panels such as the hood, the fenders, the doors, and the quarter panels with lots and lots of reinforcing members behind those panels all welded together to form a complete unibody package.

That makes this a very strong car, but it also means that if one area of the unibody is impacted during a collision, the entire unibody structure can be affected. But I am not going to move into the abyss of heavy collision repair or delve into collateral damage; I am going to stick with the basic parts, and that is the replacement of noncollision damage-related structural components. If your ride has been crashed and is in need of structural repair, send it to a body shop. Period.

REPLACE THE STRUCTURAL VERSUS THE NONSTRUCTURAL PARTS

When making the decision to replace any rusted area on a given car, the first consideration must be whether the part to be replaced is structural or nonstructural. What is nonstructural on a unibody? Aside from the bolted-on panels, the nonstructural components are considered to be the quarter panels, the floor pans, and the trunk pans. The good news is that nonstructural pieces can be cut, trimmed, sectioned, and welded as much as necessary to complete a rust repair.

When it comes to structural components, it's a different matter altogether. What's structural? The frame rails, the rocker panels, the cowl post, the roof panels, and every boxed attachment member supporting any of the above-mentioned parts. When replacing a structural piece, the Inter-Industry Conference on Auto Collision Repair (I-CAR) recommends installing the entire piece, with no cutting, trimming, or sectioning.

Why is installing the entire piece recommended? Even way back in 1968, when this car was built, the automobile manufacturers understood the need for crush zones. Crush zones are points designed into the frame rails and other structural components of the car in the form of notches, convolutions, dimples, and holes. They are put there to allow the unibody structure of the vehicle to collapse and absorb energy from a collision at a controlled rate. This helps manage the impact in such a way as to allow the damage to flow around the passenger compartment rather than move through it and possibly cause bodily injury.

A good example of a crush zone point is shown in photo 1. This fender apron isn't a major structural component of the car, but it is still a structural component and must collapse in a prescribed manner during a collision. If impacted from the front, this dimple will be the first area to collapse and fold.

So what happens if this fender apron is sectioned and the crush zone point is used as a welding point? The integrity of a very complex safety design built into the car has been compromised by making it rigid and unable to collapse if impacted. That is the primary reason for replacing an entire structural piece: to maintain the integrity of the part as well as retain its ability to absorb an impact.

Is the sectioning of structural parts safe on any part of a vintage Mustang? Let's look at a rear frame rail. This is a structural part of the car that is prone to rust and is often repaired in sections rather than replaced in its entirety. But hold the phone; didn't I just say the recommendation is not to section structural components? Yes, I did. So now it is safe to section frame rails? Yes, but only for rear rails. Photo 2 is a replacement rear frame rail section for a 1966 Mustang. All of the suppliers mentioned in this book carry them, and a lot of vintage Mustangs have been safely repaired using them. How can that be so? This frame rail replacement piece has been designed with the structural integrity of the vehicle in mind. Installing this piece in its entirety using an overlapping weld seam at the joint is quite safe and can be easily accomplished.

Why is it safe to cut a rear frame rail and section in a small piece? It's one of those lesser of two evils things. If you have repaired one of these cars before, you know this short piece in no way constitutes the entire rear frame rail. The complete rail is a long unit that extends from the rear body panel all the way forward to a point just under the rear seat. That's a major piece of the car, and having replaced these rails in the past, I can tell you installing a complete rear frame rail is no picnic. The car literally has to be cut apart to install this rail, and if it's not done correctly, the results could be disastrous for both you and the car. Sectioning in a short piece that is designed to be spliced into an existing rear frame rail all of a sudden makes a lot of sense.

PHOTO 1: The arrow points to a dimpled crush point in this fender apron. If this car is impacted from the front, this will be one of the first areas to collapse.

PHOTO 2: Rear frame rails are often sectioned using an aftermarket piece such as this one.

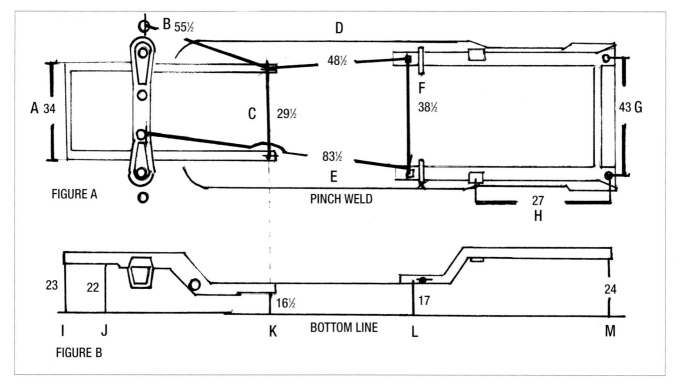

ILLUSTRATION 1: The unibody measurements for a vintage Mustang.

What about sectioning a front frame rail? Check any of the Mustang parts catalogs you can find, and I promise you won't find a short section of this rail that can be spliced into place. I could go into a thousand-word dissertation on why this rail must never be sectioned, but to keep it short, let's say there are too many reinforcements, attachments, bracing members, high stress points, critical fatigue issues, and other factors that make sectioning a front frame rail unsafe at any level. You can purchase an outer front rail, an inner front rail, and even a complete front frame rail assembly in the aftermarket, but you can't purchase front rail sections. I've replaced the outer rail and even the complete rail, but I've never found the advantage to replacing only the inner rail.

So here's the summation on frame rail sectioning on any unibody vehicle. You can safely section a rear frame rail if the piece is available in the aftermarket, but you should never section a front frame rail. Instead, replace this rail in its entirety.

TAKE MEASUREMENTS

So with that out of the way, let's get down to the real world of Mustang restoration and look at a worst-case scenario.

A Mustang project car was purchased from an individual who had previously removed the rusted core support, the right fender apron, and the frame rail. With no core support or fender apron on the car to serve as a guide, determining where to place the new rail might seem impossible. Where do you start?

You start with measurements. Where do you find unibody measurements for a vintage Mustang? To my knowledge, they are no longer readily available, so I have compiled a set of measurements taken from my Mustang project car that provides the necessary information.

The measurements in illustration 1 may look a little perplexing to anyone unfamiliar with repairing unibody structural components but will make complete sense to anyone working in a modern-day body shop. Datum lines and tram measurements are all familiar to those folks, and all they need now is for me to get out of the way so they can go to work. But if you aren't into repairing heavy collision damage, a little more explanation is necessary. Let's start by figuring out what these measurements are, understanding the need for tolerance when taking these measurements, learning how to establish a datum line, and learning how to use a tram to take the measurements.

THE NEED FOR TOLERANCE WHEN MEASURING

Believe it or not, even the vintage Mustang was a precision piece of technology in its day. The car was built under precise guidelines, using an established set of tolerances to ensure that any fender stamped out on a given day would fit any unibody welded together on any other given day. Granted, the tolerances used in 1968 were lax compared with the strict tolerances used to assemble vehicles today, but nevertheless, tolerances were used, and I'll use those tolerances as starting points to work on the old ride today.

On a modern unibody vehicle, the allowed tolerance for replacing structural members is 3 millimeters, or roughly ⅛ inch. That means a part such as a replacement front frame rail can be safely installed up to ⅛ inch shorter or up to ⅛ inch longer than the established dimension used to construct the car in the first place. That's not much when you consider 3 millimeters is the thickness of three dimes, and this tolerance is certainly much stricter when compared with the tolerances of up to ½ inch used for the Mustang in 1968. Be that as it may, if I state a measurement as being 34 inches, I'm assuming a cushion of ⅛ inch that can be added to or subtracted from that measurement to keep the vehicle within tolerance.

ESTABLISHING THE DATUM LINE

Knowing that a frame rail should extend 40½ inches horizontally beyond the firewall doesn't help much if you don't know how the rail should sit vertically. To determine that measurement, the car must be mounted on some type of level platform from which vertical measurements can be taken. To do that, you need a datum line.

The datum line is an imaginary horizontal line beneath the car. This line allows the engineers who designed the car to specify height measurements for various points on the vehicle. In its most basic form, the datum line could be considered the curb height of the vehicle.

Figure B, illustration 1, shows an example of how a datum line works. To determine the vertical location of the leading edge of the front frame rail, you would refer to the datum line. In this case, that measurement is found at point I and is 23 inches. How did I arrive at that measurement? With the car sitting on jack stands, I measured the distance from the bottom of the rail to the floor of the shop. Will this measurement process work for your project? Probably not, unless your jack stands are identical to mine. So how do you establish a datum line for your particular pony?

Looking back at figure B, you will notice additional measurements taken at points K, L, and M. In this case, they measure 16½, 17, and 24 inches, respectively. Now let's assume you place your pony on jack stands and take measurements at these same points and come up with 18, 19½, and 26 inches front to rear, respectively. When

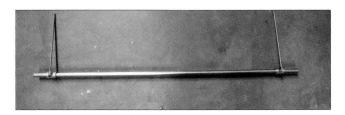

compared with the measurements I took under my Mustang, we have a difference of 2 inches at each point. So what would be the correct height at the leading edge of the front frame rail on your car? It would be 25 inches, as determined by adding 2 inches to the established datum line of my Mustang. Seem too easy? This isn't rocket science, especially when the car hasn't been in a wreck and all you are doing is replacing rusted metal.

USING A TRAM GAUGE TO MEASURE THE CAR

Now for the easy part, measuring the car. Figure A, illustration 1, shows the cross measurements taken at several points along the underside of the car. This is a symmetrical vehicle, so all of these measurements are equal from side to side. That makes determining the dimensions of this car very easy. But there is a wrench to be tossed into the gears. You cannot slide under the car and use a tape measure to check these measurements. Why not? Tape measures must often have to traverse mechanical and structural obstacles to extend from one measuring point to another, and that can affect the reading. To avoid that problem, I use a tram gauge to make sure I get accurate measurements.

So what is a tram gauge and how does it work? A tram gauge, as pictured in photo 3, is a bar with two movable pointers that slide along the length of the bar and is used to take point to point measurements. To use a tram gauge to take dimensional measurements, adjust the two pointers to equal lengths on the bar. Make them long enough so that the bar does not interfere with any mechanical or structural pieces under the car, and then slide one of the pointers to the end of the bar and lock it into place. Next, place the locked pointer at a prescribed measurement point, such as the hole in the frame rail at point C, and adjust the opposite pointer to meet a desired cross-measurement point such as point A. Tighten the pointer to prevent movement on the tram shaft, and then measure the distance between each pointer. In this case, the reading should be 66 inches.

Don't have a tram gauge lying around the shop? I'll tell you how to make one at the end of this chapter.

There are some handy things to know before crawling under the ride with a tram gauge. Unless otherwise specified, all measurements are taken from the center of the bolt or from the edge of a hole. Rarely will a frame rail measurement be taken from the center of a hole unless that hole once contained a bolt. Ball joint measurements are normally taken from the center of the ball joint.

TAKE VERTICAL MEASUREMENTS

So how do you measure to install a missing frame rail? Looking back at illustration 1, the first measurement determined must be the distance from point C to point D, in this case, 48½ inches. This establishes the horizontal placement of the rail beneath the car. Next, measure from point C across the car to the opposite point C. In this case, the reading is 29½ inches. This measurement establishes the correct placement of the rearmost point of the rail. Next, take a cross measurement from point C on the driver's side to point A on the new rail. This verifies the correct length at 66 inches. Next, measure across the car at point A to verify the front of the rail is positioned 34 inches from the front of the opposite rail. Finally, the height is determined using the established datum line at points A and C.

Seems too simple? That's really all there is to it. Measure three or four times and weld once. By the way, secure the rail with sheet metal screws as you go, and if you are replacing parts such as the core support or fender aprons, measure and screw all of these pieces into place as well. To help position the core support and fender aprons, illustration 2 gives the upper body tram gauge measurements taken from my Mustang. When everything is correct and you are ready to begin welding, drill all of the spot weld holes to 5/16 inch to ensure a solid weld, and clean every weld point thoroughly.

A final check before doing any welding is to temporarily install the fenders and hood to be sure they fit. If you have measured everything correctly, they will fit; if not, the misalignment will tell you to bring out the tram gauge once again.

Haven't operated on your pony yet? Good. Because before you do, this is the time to remove all necessary mechanical components and take the existing measurements from the car. In essence, you will be creating your own set of frame measurements, and replacing a rusted frame rail will become a matter of removing the old one, precisely placing the new one, and welding it solid.

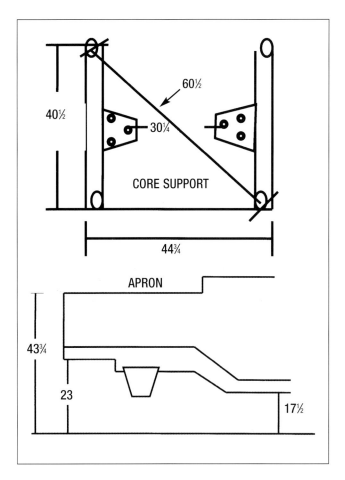

ILLUSTRATION 2: Upper unibody measurements from my Mustang.

BUILD THE TRAM GAUGE

To build your own tram gauge, you will need a wire welder, Vise-Grip pliers, and a trip to the local home improvement store to purchase an 8-foot length of ½-inch metal electrical conduit, two pieces of 5/16-inch all-thread bolt at least 12 inches long, two 5/16-inch threaded collars, two 5/16-inch bolts with nuts 1 inch long, and one 6-inch length of ¾-inch plumbing pipe.

On opposite ends of the ¾-inch plumbing pipe, drill one ⅜-inch hole. Weld the 5/16-inch nuts over the open holes. Turn the pipe exactly 45 degrees, and weld the 5/16-inch threaded collars perpendicular to the welded nuts about an inch away. In effect, when looking through the ¾-inch pipe, the nuts are pointing to the nine o'clock position, and the threaded collars are pointing to the twelve o'clock position. Cut the welded pipe pieces 1½ inches long, thread the all-thread into the collars and the 5/16-inch bolt into the nuts, and slide both pieces over the electrical conduit. You now have a tram gauge with adjustable pointers capable of taking almost any desired measurement on your pony.

CHAPTER 23

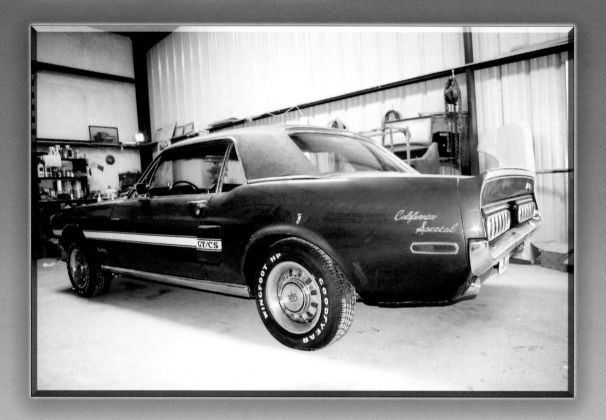

COMPLETING
PROJECT MUSTANG

The paint is on the car, the trim has been installed, and except for a few last minute details, this California Special is ready for the road.

The final steps to complete this Mustang are to replace the decals, add the liquids, and set the engine timing. Then I am finally ready to start the car and take it on a test drive.

REPLACE THE DECALS

I need to replace all of those information decals Ford so thoughtfully posted at strategic locations throughout the car. This pony needs everything, from the emissions decals in the engine compartment to the metal options plate on the left door to the jacking instruction decal for the deck lid. To be sure I have all of the correct decals for this car, I once again turn to Marti Auto Works. It supplied me with a decal kit that contained everything I needed, plus a couple of decals I didn't know I needed.

All of the decals from Marti Auto Works have peel-off backs, so installation is a simple matter of wiping the area on the car clean using a lint-free polishing cloth, peeling off the backing, then carefully positioning the decal. To be sure I place each decal in its proper location, I refer to the photos I took of the car way back at the beginning of this project and position the decals accordingly.

The metal options tag located inside the left door does not have an adhesive back and must be installed using the correct fasteners. Marti Auto Works also provided me with the correct fasteners.

ADD THE LIQUIDS

If you are a fan of any of the popular car rebuilding shows on the tube, you know the climactic point of the entire show is the starting of the engine. This may be a minor detail in the larger scheme of automotive restoration, but it is a detail that gets everyone's attention. People walk around the car, staring at the paint, admiring the interior, and touching the chrome, but when the key is finally turned for the first time, all eyes are on the engine. Will it

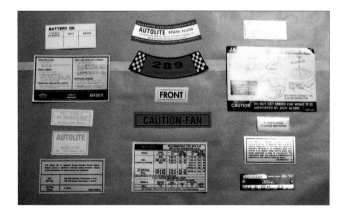

PHOTO 1: A complete set of instructional decals for Project Mustang. These decals are best purchased in kit form to ensure that you get all the necessary decals for a particular year model.

PHOTO 2: A very detailed engine compartment.

start or won't it? It will if all of the other engine details have been taken care of beforehand.

One such detail is adding fluids. The 289 CID engine in this Mustang needs 5 quarts of oil, 2 gallons of antifreeze, 2 quarts of power steering fluid, roughly 2 gallons of automatic transmission fluid, and at least 5 gallons of Texas sweet tea (gas).

PHOTO 3: Marti Auto Works provided me with this metal options tag listing the correct options for this car.

But filling this corralled Mustang with liquids doesn't mean I can start the engine and light up the back tires. I need to be sure those 5 quarts of oil poured into the engine aren't just lying around doing nothing. I need to put them to work, now.

Back in the engine rebuilding phase of this project, I positioned the crankshaft to TDC on the power stroke of number 1 cylinder. In that position, the distributor is set to fire on the number 1 cylinder, and that should guarantee this engine will crank with very little fuss. The problem is that the engine will crank with very little oil coating the major internal parts of the engine. That's not a good thing. Engines don't last long without a good coating of oil. So before starting the engine for the first time, I need to prime the oil pump and circulate oil throughout the engine.

I use an oil pump primer shaft available at most automotive retail parts stores and in most performance parts catalogs for just a few bucks. What is a primer shaft and how does it work? It is a long steel shaft that chucks into any ⅜-inch drill and is designed to slip down through the distributor mounting hole located near the front of the engine block and engage the oil pump driveshaft. Be sure the primer shaft is the correct shaft for the engine being primed and that it is securely seated in the distributor opening and fully engaged with the oil pump driveshaft.

With the primer shaft engaged and ready to spin the oil pump, the ignition key can be turned to the on position to monitor the oil pressure gauge. But this still isn't the time to crank the engine. It wouldn't start anyway, and I would be creating one big headache for myself trying to retime the engine to the distributor.

Got a beer-drinking buddy? These guys are seldom hard to find, so to lure one into the shop, I sit a cold one on the dash, and within moments one usually appears. I invite him to sit behind the wheel with instructions to keep his eyes on the oil pressure gauge and his hands on the beer and on nothing else. This is important. Trust me on this one.

Now it is time to spin the drill. The 289 distributor turns counterclockwise, so a reversible drill set to turn in the reverse position is a must to get the oil pump spinning in the correct direction. As the drill turns, the oil pump will begin to circulate oil throughout the engine, and the oil pressure gauge will begin to read pressure up to about 40 pounds. When your beer-drinking buddy indicates the gauge is reading pressure, the engine is properly oiled, and it is now safe to start. I can turn off the drill and the ignition key, toss the beer-drinking buddy out of the shop, and install the distributor.

SET THE ENGINE TIMING

I know that setting the correct engine timing is going to come up because beer-drinking buddies can't seem to keep their hands off of shiny new keys. If the engine is turned without the distributor in place, it must be retimed. Here's how. All four-stroke engines have a power stroke and an exhaust stroke. All four-stroke engines time on the power stroke. Which stroke is the power stroke? The best way to determine that is to install a compression gauge in the number 1 spark plug hole and watch for the gauge to read compression. That's the power stroke.

As the compression gauge begins to read compression, observe the timing mark on the harmonic damper as it approaches TDC. Carefully turn the engine until the timing mark reads 6 degrees before top dead center (BTDC). Stop and install the distributor so that the rotor is pointed straight back to the carburetor. That is where the number 1 cylinder spark plug wire goes. From there, wire the distributor counterclockwise according to the firing order of the engine. The engine is now timed and ready to start.

> ### TIP
>
> *The oil gauge doesn't register pressure? Replace the sending unit located on the front left side of the block.*

START THE ENGINE

OK, even guys who can build engines in their sleep occasionally screw up. Knowing that makes me feel better about my problem. The Mustang won't start when I turn the key. Unless you have been around and worked on engines all of your life, you may not understand when I say the engine didn't sound right as it turned over. However, I've bent enough pushrods and broken enough timing chains to recognize the sound of an engine that isn't firing right. I immediately begin a check for things that could have gone wrong. I know through photographic evidence that the crankshaft is in perfect time with the camshaft, so that's out. I also know the distributor had been installed and timed correctly to the crankshaft. That leaves one area to check, and sure enough, I find my problem.

During the engine rebuilding phase, I always soak the lifters in clean oil to preload them with oil before installation. If the hydraulic lifters on a vintage 289 Ford engine are installed without first loading them with clean oil, the valves cannot be correctly set prior to starting the engine.

For whatever reason, the lifters did not have sufficient oil, so once oil pressure is created in the engine, the lifters load with oil and force the valves to stay open during the compression stroke. I have to remove the valve covers and adjust the valves for a second time. That's one of those little details that can cause gray hair.

Once this problem is fixed, I start the car again. The moment the engine comes to life, the gauges need to be monitored. The oil pressure gauge should read at least 40 pounds of pressure. As the engine warms, the temperature gauge should begin to climb and top out around 180 degrees F. A quick spike above 180 could signal air trapped inside the engine. If this happens, kill the engine, allow it to cool, and add more antifreeze to the system.

With the engine running smoothly and all gauges reading normal, the engine timing should be set at 6 degrees BTDC using a timing light to monitor the timing mark on the harmonic balancer, and the idle speed at the carburetor should be set at 550 rpm using a dwell meter with a tachometer setting wired to the distributor. The power steering should be turned fully in both directions several times to purge air from the system, and the transmission should be monitored for the correct fluid level. The car is now ready for a test drive.

TEST DRIVE THE CAR

Out on the highway with the radio turned up, someone always asks me about the proper procedures used to break in an engine. Over the years, I've heard just about every engine break-in scenario there is, from wild procedures of driving the car hard for so many seconds, down shifting and revving the engine, pulling over and letting it cool then starting all over, to drive it and forget it until the next oil change. I do something in between. I don't baby the engine, but I don't push it to its limits within the first few hundred miles either. I try to vary the speed and engine load conditions as much as possible for the first 100 miles or so, and then I slowly work the car toward a more normal driving pattern.

This method also gives me plenty of opportunities to make bug checks and take care of all those little annoyances that seem to pop up after a total restoration. For example, in this case, the power steering control valve decided 40 years of good service was enough and it was time for retirement. How did I know the control valve was defective? The power steering worked intermittently, and the car wanted to walk all over the road when driving despite having the front end professionally aligned. The bad news about having to change a defective steering control valve is that once installed, the steering wheel needs to be centered again. That requires the services of a front-end alignment professional.

But despite having to make two trips to the front-end shop, I consider the failure of the control valve a minor glitch and nothing out of the ordinary for a ground-up restoration on such a great car. The Mustang rides nice, handles great, and has all the pep anyone could ask for.

SUMMARY OF PROJECT MUSTANG

So what did it take to bring the car to this point? If you followed this restoration through *Auto Restorer* magazine, you know this project spanned almost two years. That's pretty typical for a ground-up restoration, especially when every step must be documented and photographed. In real time, minus time spent cussing parts that didn't fit or time wasted scratching my head wondering why this or that didn't work the way I wanted it to, I put in just over 500 man hours restoring this California Special and replaced approximately

$12,000.00 worth of parts. Considering the above-average condition of this car when I started this project, the final cost would be considered lower than normal for a ground-up restoration.

A car in worse condition will take longer and cost more. Now that's a detail worth noting. It is also one of the reasons I always do an initial inspection before making the decision to do a ground-up restoration. I want to have a minimum ballpark figure of what it is going to take to restore a car before I ever commit to spending the time or the money required for such an undertaking.

In one of my past lives as a body repair technician, we had a saying about repairing aging automobiles: If you spend $5,000.00 on a $2,000.00 car, you still have a $2,000.00 car. That adage may be true if the proposed restoration project is a 1976 Ford Pinto, but it isn't specif-ically true for a vintage Mustang. It is, however, something to bear in mind when venturing into the world of automotive restoration. It is very easy to spend far more money restoring an old car than the car will ever be worth.

That said, since you have spent the time to follow along on this project, you obviously have a love for old cars and I hope a wish to do your own restoration. So my final words of advice are to find the car of your dreams, spend some time browsing parts catalogs to get an idea of the cost, add 50 percent to that figure, estimate it will take twice as long as it should, then tack a picture of the proposed end result on the garage wall for inspiration. After all, the shell of a car pictured in chapter 9 looks nothing like the car pictured in photo 4, but I can assure you they are one and the same. I just spent a few more dollars and a lot more hours completing the change.

PHOTO 4: Project Mustang.

Appendix

PARTS SUPPLIERS

Aftermarket Automotive Parts Distributing (AAPD)

7810 SW Miller Hill Rd.

3611 Short Oak Dr.

Newberg, OR 97132

http://www.aapd.net

American Designers

8774 South State Rd. 109

Knightstown, IN 46148

800-628-5442

http://www.autobpa.com/~autobpac/members/designers/

The Antioch Mustang Stable

9701 E. McKellips Rd.

Mesa, AZ 85207

480-357-1006

http://www.tankarmor.com

California Mustang

19400 San Jose Ave.

City of Industry, CA 91748

800-775-0101

http://www.cal-mustang.com

The Eastwood Company

263 Shoemaker Rd.

Pottstown, PA 19464

800-345-1178

http://www.eastwood.com

Legendary Auto Interiors

121 West Shore Blvd.

Newark, NY 14513

800-363-8804

http://www.legendaryautointeriors.com

Marti Auto Works

12007 W. Peoria Ave.

El Mirage, AZ 85335

623-935-2558

http://www.martiauto.com

National Parts Depot

900 SW 38th Ave.

Ocala, FL 34474

800-874-7595

http://www.nationalpartsdepot.com

Norton Abrasives

1 New Bond St.

PO Box 15008

Worcester, MA 01615

http://www.nortonabrasives.com

The Paddock Parts

7565 South State Rd. 109

PO Box 30

Knightstown, IN 46148-0030

http://www.paddockparts.com

Painless Performance

2501 Ludelle St.

Fort Worth, TX 76105

817-244-6212

http://www.painlessperformance.com

PPG Industries

One PPG Place

Pittsburg, PA 15272

412-434-3131

http://corporateportal.ppg.com/ppg/

R-Blox Sound Control, Inc.

1530 Enterprise Rd.

Corry, PA 16407

888-747-2569

http://www.r-blox.com

Index

masking paper, 75, 104-5, 112, 118, 152
masking tape, 19
masks, 35, 60, 88-89, 113
master list, 8, 30, 57
measurements
    of engine compartment, 67-68, 69
    frame rail placement, 179-81
    for mounting emblems, 163
    for positioning decals, 166
    top cover seamlines to drip rails, 139
mechanical components of dash, installing, 122-23
media blasting, 95-96, 173
metal glaze, 82, 83, 90-91
metallic finishes, 104
metal nibbler, 18
metal parts, painting, 96
metal working dollies, 17-18
mini dual action sander, 18
mini grinder, 18
molding attachment holes, 83
molding retainer clips, 140
moldings
    disassembly and, 21
    drip rail, 29-30
    with grille, 22, 164
    quarter to roof, 29
    reveal moldings, 27-28
    rocker panel, 158, 166
    roof belt, 29
    sail panel molding, 140
money spent ledger, 8, 185-86

N
name plate attachment holes, 83
National Institute for Occupational Safety and Health (NIOSH), 88-89
National Parts Depot, 11, 49, 133, 187
new parts list, 8, 57
nonstructural components, 178
Norton Abrasives
    about, 187
    adhesives, 45-46, 167-68
    sanding supplies, 19, 35, 42, 46, 57, 59, 73, 89, 98
    scuff pads, 69, 95-96, 98, 134, 151, 155, 164, 169

O
oil, 21, 183-84
oil clearance, 148, 149
oil filter, 21
oil pump primer shaft, 184
organization, value of, 7-8, 41
overhang, 20-21
overspray from factory paint job, 58, 100, 106-7

P
The Paddock Parts, 11, 67, 125, 126, 139, 140, 168-69, 172, 187
Painless Performance, 121-22, 135, 168, 187
paint
    base color, 20, 104, 106-7, 113-15
    choosing a color, 103
    inspecting, 58
    removing, 19, 35-36, 42, 45, 58-60, 132
    removing from fiberglass, 46
    test panel for paint sprayers, 114

    types of, 96, 99, 104, 106-7, 123, 164, 169, 173, 175
paint edges, removing, 83-84, 95
painting
    body and doors, 113-16
    clear coats, 104, 105, 107, 115
    console, 171-72
    dash, 106
    deck lid, 135-36
    doors, 104-7, 111-15
    engine, 151-52
    engine compartment, 99-100
    fender aprons, 99-100
    finish coats, 74-77, 96, 104, 115-16
    grille, 164
    guide coat, 82-83
    the interior, 104-7
    metal parts, 96
    overspray from factory paint job, 58, 100, 106-7
    plastic parts, 96
    preparing for, 104-6
    seat frame, 173
    spray plan, 103-4
    steering wheel, 168
    trunk compartment, 104-5, 107
    the underside, 99-100, 155
    See also spraying
painting rack, 132
panel alignment gauge, 127
panel gap gauge, 17, 111
panel repair kit, no-weld, 66
panel-to-panel alignment, 41-42
panel-to-panel overlap, 76-77
parking lamps, 165
parts
    for engine assembly, 148
    for front suspension assembly, 133
    liquid coating, 133
    new parts list, 8, 57
    painting plastic and metal parts, 96
    powder coating, 132-33
    restoring and refinishing, 96-97, 131, 132-33
    See also exploded view photographs
parts suppliers, 11, 30, 187. *See also* supplies; specific suppliers
patch panels, 65-67
photographs
    referring to, 134, 165, 166
    taking, 7-8, 21, 26, 30, 49, 57-58
    See also exploded view photographs
piston and rod assemblies, 149-50
planishing hammer, 17
plastic body filler
    applying, 80
    for deck lid repair, 46
    fragility of, 97
    lead versus, 35
    repairing poorly filled areas, 74
    sanding, 18-19, 80-83, 84
plastic parts, painting, 96
plasti-gauge, 149, 150
plumber's torch, 35, 60, 98
pneumatic tools, 18
polisher/grinder, 18
polyester glazing compound, 80
polyurethane clear, 19, 104, 107, 115, 168
powder coating, 96-97, 131, 132-33

power steering, 185. *See also* steering components
power steering control valve, 185
PPG Industries
    about, 187
    degreaser, 69-70, 74-75, 92, 95-96, 104, 113, 132, 151, 165, 169
    paints, 96, 99, 104, 106-7, 123, 164, 169, , 173, 175
    product line, 19-20, 74
    refinishing products, 75-76, 79, 87, 107, , 113, 115-16, 133, 152, 155, 168
    static electricity eliminator, 135-36
primer
    about, 19-20, 87
    applying, 87-88, 92
    sanding, 88-92
    for weld spots, 62
    See also epoxy primer
primer blocks, 18-19
priming the oil pump, 184
products for project, 19-20
project summary, 185-86
propane torch, 35, 60, 98
pulleys and belt brackets, 50, 152

Q
quarter glass, 27, 142, 144, 145
quarter glass weather strips, 28-29
quarter panel-deck lid alignment, 43-45
quarter panel extensions, 45-46, 75, 111, 112, 136
quarter panel trim, 27

R
R-12 Freon, 20
radiator, 21, 49-50, 158, 183
radio surround trim panel, 15, 30, 171-72
R-Blox Sound Control, 187
rear axle, 135, 136-37
rear frame rail sectioning, 178
rear of the car, tearing down, 22
rear wiring harness, 122
refinishing components, 96, 131, 133, 167-68
refinishing products, 19-20. *See also specific suppliers*
refinishing strategy, 103-4
reflective coating, 160
regulators, 26-27, 104, 142-44
respirators, 88, 89, 113
reversed door trim tool, 17
rivets for patch panels, 66
rocker panel molding, 158, 166
rocker panel spray, 106
rolling the car, 97, 98-99
roof belt molding, 29
roof panel, 29, 30, 178
rubber gasket-mounted glass, 144-45
rubberized undercoating, 155
run channels, 26, 27, 142, 143-44
rust, 15, 65-67, 67-70
rust dots, 66-67
rust prevention process, 74-77

S
sail panel mechanical fasteners for headliner, 141
sail panel molding, 140